Talk and Interaction in Social Research Methods

Talk and Interaction in Social Research Methods

Edited by
Paul Drew, Geoffrey Raymond and Darin Weinberg

⑤ SAGE Publications
London ● Thousand Oaks ● New Delhi

Editorial arrangement and selection @ Paul Drew, Geoffrey
Raymond and Darin Weinberg 2006

© Sage Publications 2006

First published 2006

 SAGE Publications Ltd
1 Oliver's Yard
55 City Road
London EC1Y 1SP

SAGE Publications Inc
2455 Teller Road
Thousand Oaks, California 91320

SAGE Publications India Pvt Ltd
B-42, Panchsheel Enclave
Post Box 4109
New Delhi 110 017

British Library Cataloguing in Publication data

A catalogue record for this book is available
from the British Library

ISBN 0 7619 5704 9   978 0 7619 5704 1
ISBN 0 7619 5705 7   978 0 7619 5705 8

Library of Congress Control Number 2005929139

Typeset by C&M Digitals (P) Ltd., Chennai, India
Printed on paper from sustainable resources
Printed and bound in Great Britain by Athenaeum Press, Gateshead

Contents

● ● ● ● ● ● ● ●

List of Contributors   vii

Transcription Symbols   x

1   The Language of Social Science: A Brief Introduction   1
    Darin Weinberg

Part I: Talk-in-Interaction in the Context of Research Methodologies   **7**

2   Standardization-in-Interaction: The Survey Interview   9
    Douglas W. Maynard and Nora Cate Schaeffer

3   Interaction in Interviews   28
    Robin Wooffitt and Sue Widdicombe

4   Analysing Interaction in Focus Groups   50
    Sue Wilkinson

5   When Documents 'Speak': Documents, Language and Interaction   63
    Paul Drew

6   Observation, Video and Ethnography: Case Studies in Aids
    Counselling and Greetings   81
    Anssi Peräkylä

7   Language, Dialogue and Ethnographic Objectivity   97
    Darin Weinberg

**Part II: Talk-in-Interaction in the Context of Research in Fields
    of Substantive Sociological Research**   **113**

8   Questions at Work: Yes/No Type Interrogatives in Institutional Contexts   115
    Geoffrey Raymond

••• Contents •••

9 Understanding News Media: The Relevance of Interaction   135
   Steven E. Clayman

10 Talking Sex and Gender   155
   Celia Kitzinger

11 Anomalies and Ambiguities: Finding and Discounting the Relevance
   of Race in Interracial Relationships   171
   Byron Burkhalter

12 Using Talk to Study the Policing of Gangs and its Recordwork   190
   Albert J. Meehan

References   211

Index   228

List of Contributors

•••••••

Byron Burkhalter received his PhD from UCLA in 2002. He is currently an independent scholar and teacher working in San Jose, California. His research focuses on the interactional management of race. His other works have pursued this interest in internet communities, interracial relationships and in racial discrimination lawsuits.

Steven E. Clayman is Professor of Sociology and is affiliated with the Communication Studies Program at UCLA. His research concerns the intersection of talk, interaction and mass communication, with an emphasis on forms of broadcast journalism. He has examined the dynamics of news interviews and presidential press conferences, journalistic gatekeeping processes, and collective audience behaviour in political speeches and debates. His articles have appeared in a range of social science journals, and he is the co-author (with John Heritage) of *The News Interview: Journalists and Public Figures on the Air* (2002).

Paul Drew is Professor of Sociology at the University of York, UK. His research in conversation analysis focuses on communicative practices which underlie ordinary conversational interaction, as well more specialized interactions in the workplace and institutional (especially legal and medical) settings. He is the co-author (with Max Atkinson) of *Order in Court: The Organization of Verbal Interaction in Judicial Settings* (1979) and co-editor (with John Heritage) of *Talk at Work* (1992). He has published in such journals as the *American Sociological Review, Language in Society, Research on Language and Social Interaction* and the *Journal of Pragmatics*. He is currently working on projects concerning affiliation and disaffiliation; and communication between patients and medical professionals.

Celia Kitzinger is Professor of Conversation Analysis, Gender and Sexuality in the Department of Sociology at the University of York. She has published nine books and around 100 articles and book chapters on issues relating to language, genders and sexualities.

Douglas W. Maynard is a Professor in the Department of Sociology, University of Wisconsin, Madison. Recently, he is co-editor (with Hanneke Houtkoop-Steenstra, Nora Cate Schaeffer and Hans van der Zouwen) of *Standardization and Tacit Knowledge: Interaction and Practice in the Survey Interview* (2002), co-editor (with John Heritage) of

Communication in Medical Care: Interaction between Physicians and Patients (in press), and author of a monograph, *Bad News, Good News: Conversational Order in Everyday Talk and Clinical Settings* (2003).

Albert J. Meehan is Professor of Sociology at Oakland University in Rochester, Michigan. He has a long-standing research interest in police recordkeeping practices, the interactional organization of police work, and the impact of information technologies on the police. His work has appeared in *Justice Quarterly*, *Sociological Quarterly*, *Psychiatric Quarterly*, *Symbolic Interaction*, *The British Journal of Criminology* and *Urban Life*.

Anssi Peräkylä is Professor of Sociology at the University of Helsinki. His research interests include conversation analysis, medical interaction, psychotherapeutic interaction and emotional communication. He has published *AIDS Counselling* (1995) and numerous articles in social scientific and medical journals.

Geoffrey Raymond is Assistant Professor of Sociology at the University of California, Santa Barbara. His research interests include the study of talk-in-interaction, the role of talk in the organization of institutions, and qualitative research methods. Recent publications on these issues have appeared in *American Sociological Review*, *Discourse Studies* and *Research on Language and Social Interaction*.

Nora Cate Schaeffer is a Professor of Sociology at the University of Wisconsin, Madison, where she also serves as Faculty Director of the University of Wisconsin Survey Centre. Her research examines issues in survey measurement, including the design of survey questions and instruments, and the interaction between the interviewer and respondent. She is co-editor (with Douglas Maynard, Hanneke Houtkoop-Steenstra and Hans van der Zouwen) of *Standardization and Tacit Knowledge: Interaction and Practice in the Survey Interview* (2002). Maynard and Schaeffer are continuing to collaborate in studying the survey interview. Current research draws on data from the Wisconsin Longitudinal Study and concerns the interactional measurement of cognitive functioning.

Darin Weinberg teaches in the Department of Sociology, University of Cambridge and is a fellow of King's College, Cambridge. The bulk of his research focuses on the practical purposes to which concepts of addiction, mental disorder and learning disability are applied in various historical and contemporary contexts. He is particularly interested in how these concepts figure in state-sponsored campaigns of social welfare and social control, and what their uses reveal about how and why people distinguish the social and natural forces held to govern human behaviour. His recent books include *Of Others Inside: Insanity, Addiction, and Belonging in America* (2005) and (edited) *Qualitative Research Methods* (2002).

Sue Widdicombe is a lecturer in Psychology at the University of Edinburgh, UK. Her research interests include language, interaction and identities, especially religious and Arab identities, constructions of individuality, and critical social psychology.

Sue Wilkinson is Professor of Feminist and Health Studies in the Department of Social Sciences at Loughborough University, UK. She is the founding and current editor of *Feminism & Psychology: An International Journal* and has published widely in the areas of gender, sexuality and health, as well as on feminist and qualitative research methods. Her current research projects are on breast cancer, equal marriage, and the use of 'reaction tokens' in conversation.

Robin Wooffitt is senior lecturer in Sociology at the University of York, UK. His research interests include language and interaction, the relationship between conversation analysis and forms of discourse analysis, and consciousness and anomalous experiences.

Transcription Symbols

● ● ● ● ● ● ● ●

All the chapters in this book show and analyse examples of actual interaction, recorded in a variety of natural settings, whether in news interviews, survey interviews, courtrooms, police–suspect interactions, medical consultations, focus groups, or more ordinary, mundane conversations between family or friends. For the purposes of analysis and publication, these recordings – whether they are audio or video recordings – have to be transcribed. In transcribing what is said, we try to capture not only the words which are spoken, but more precisely *how* and *when* things are said. To do this, authors have used a transcription notation which is widespread not only within conversation analysis, but increasingly among those investigating language use and discourse in any depth and detail, from a range of analytic perspectives.

The most important of these transcription conventions are shown below. We have kept these to a minimum, to avoid unnecessary technical detail. A fuller account of these transcription conventions will be found in Max Atkinson and John Heritage (eds) *Structures of Social Action: Studies in Conversation Analysis* (1984: ix–xvi).

The relative timing of utterances

Intervals either within or between turns, or periods of silence (pauses), are shown thus (0.7) (to the nearest tenth of a second)

A discernible pause which is too short to be timed mechanically is shown as a micro-pause, thus (.)

Overlaps between utterances are indicated by square brackets, the point of overlap onset being marked with a single left-hand bracket

Contiguous utterances, where there is no discernible interval between turns, are linked by an equals sign (=). This is also used to indicate a very rapid move from one unit in a turn to the next

Characteristics of speech delivery

Various aspects of speech delivery are captured by punctuation symbols (which, therefore, are not used to mark conventional grammatical units) and other forms of notation, as follows:

A period (full stop) indicates a falling intonation

A comma indicates a continuing intonation

A question mark indicates a rising inflection (not necessarily a question)

An upside down question mark indicates a rising inflection that is between the intonation indicated by a comma and that of a question mark.

The stretching of a sound is indicated by colons, the number of which correspond to the length of the stretching

.h indicates inhalation, the length of which is indicated by the number of 'h's

h. indicates outbreath, the length of which is indicated by the number of 'h's

(hh) Audible aspirations are indicated in the speech in which they occur (including in laughter)

° ° Degree signs indicate word(s) spoken very softly or quietly

A £ symbol is used to indicate a 'smile voice'.

Sound stress is shown by underlining, those words or parts of a word which are emphasized being underlined

Capital letters are used to indicate a word, or part of a word, that is spoken much louder than surrounding talk

Marked pitch raises are indicated by upward arrows, thus ↑, while marked falls in pitch are shown by downward arrows, as ↓

If what is said is unclear or uncertain, that is placed in parentheses. So either the transcriber can hear that something is said, but cannot make out any particular sounds or words (   ); or the transcriber shows his/her 'best hearing' of what is said, (So I said)

CHAPTER ONE

The Language of Social Science: A Brief Introduction

Darin Weinberg

This book is intended for undergraduate and graduate methods courses in sociology and the social sciences more broadly. In this sense, it is certainly a 'methods text' – that is, a text intended to help students become better practitioners of social scientific research. However, it is a methods text with a difference. Instead of providing standardized statements of social research methods, defending their validity and/or specifying their scope, we actually describe social research methods *in action*. More particularly, we show how in various ways social research methods are inevitably linguistic devices and that their use is always and inevitably responsive to the exigencies of language use. This is not only true of the techniques we employ to gather and interpret data, but is equally true of a vast range of the social phenomena we seek to understand. By describing methods in this way, it is hoped this text will acquaint students with the realities of social research at a level of depth and detail they have seldom, if ever, been able to see.

Perhaps more than any other single social phenomenon, language has always held a place of foundational importance in the social sciences. For many of the earliest social scientists, it was our capacities as language users that distinguished humanity from the animal kingdom and thereby set the primordial boundaries for the subject matter of the social sciences. Around the turn of the twentieth century, social scientists also began to demonstrate that language not only describes but also profoundly and systematically shapes the character of the social world. In doing so they helped establish the independence of the social sciences from biologically determinist visions of the human condition. For if language not only depicts, but shapes, social life, then the users of *different* languages (and the structures that comprise their respective societies) must also be shaped in systematically different sorts of ways. Because our biological characteristics are largely uniform across different human societies they cannot but provide rather blunt theoretical instruments for the study of human historical and cultural variation. Thus claims that language – and more specifically, linguistic diversity – is a fundamental feature of the human condition rose up together with claims for the importance of the social sciences as such.

However, the social scientific celebration of linguistic diversity and a distinctively *sociologically* deterministic vision of the human condition was haunted from its inception by a rather ironic spectre. Just as they touted the reality of linguistic diversity and linguistic determinism in the wider social world, social scientists also clung fast to uniform and standardized conceptions of their 'science' itself (see Mead 1923). The social sciences may study myriad social processes that are themselves shaped by language, but they were held to do so by virtue of a unified and determinate 'Scientific Method' that was completely immune to corruption by any type of social influence, including that of language. This image of 'Scientific Method' was borrowed from the natural sciences and reflected a philosophical commitment to the belief that science is exclusively concerned with producing universally valid statements that correspond with a unified and unchanging natural world. Unlike the flawed belief systems that science was intended to replace, the 'Scientific Method' was thought to fortify scientists against the biases introduced by the social contexts within which their investigations were conducted. Hence, whether social scientists conducted participant observation, surveys, archival investigations, life histories, interviews, or any other manner of social analysis, they were enjoined to adhere to strictly specified procedures with the aim of fortifying themselves against social biases and producing universally valid statements regarding the nature of the social world. The diverse linguistic forces shaping and particularizing social reality beyond the walls of academia were not held to exert any significant influence on the social scientific work conducted within those walls.

This unself-conscious exaltation of a unified 'Scientific Method' and what Hilary Putnam (1987) has called 'seventeenth century objectivism'[1] remains with us in many of the most established branches of the social sciences. However, it has become increasingly obvious that this position endures more by virtue of the intellectual inertia of its adherents than the soundness of the arguments in its favour. Beginning in the 1960s, a growing number of social scientists began paying more serious attention to science, discovering it to consist less in a uniform logic of inquiry than a collection of social institutions, social organizational contexts, and/or particular types of collective action. This movement in the social sciences was greatly inspired by Thomas Kuhn's seminal text *The Structure of Scientific Revolutions* (1962). Building on Kuhn's achievements, David Bloor, Barry Barnes, and several of their colleagues at the University of Edinburgh produced some of the first thoroughly[2] sociological studies of science and established what became known as the strong programme in the sociology of scientific knowledge.

The Edinburgh group took a macro-sociological approach to the study of scientific knowledge, linking the findings of various historically notable scientific projects and the macro-social contexts within which those findings were produced. By and large, their explanations highlighted how powerful social 'interests', rather than adherence to a uniform logic of empirical inquiry, governed the directions taken by scientific progress (see Barnes 1977). Following closely on the heels of the 'Edinburgh school', a micro-sociological approach to the study of scientific knowledge production emerged around Harry Collins and his colleagues at the University of Bath. In place of 'interests', the Bath school tended to highlight the contingently negotiated patterns of social interaction according to which scientific controversies were resolved and credible knowledge produced (Collins 1985). As the decade of the 1970s closed, a handful of new approaches to the sociology of science emerged, many of which utilized discourse analytic and/or ethnographic approaches to highlight the important roles played by various *linguistic* processes in the production of natural scientific knowledge (see Garfinkel et al. 1981; Gilbert and Mulkay 1984; Latour and Woolgar 1979).

I have dwelt for a time on these discoveries in the sociology of the natural sciences for the simple reason that social scientists, particularly those of us interested in scientific methodology, have for many years looked to the natural sciences for our models of what sound scientific practice ought to look like. Very often claims that the social sciences are vulnerable to social influences have been made to distinguish them from the natural sciences and to denigrate their legitimacy as sciences. Whereas natural scientists were held up as dispassionate and value-free practitioners of universally valid methods of empirical inquiry, social scientists have been dismissed as *ad hoc* ideologists, slapdash and irrational advocates of one or another partisan outlook on the proceedings of the social world.

Hence, insofar as social scientists have sought to model their own research methods on those used in the natural sciences, detailed empirical studies of how natural scientists actually go about their research should be profoundly instructive. One of the most recurrent findings these studies have produced is that there is generally a rather considerable divergence between philosophical, programmatic, and/or other *post hoc* accounts of research methods in the natural sciences and the actual achievement of natural scientific research in practice. Whereas philosophical and programmatic generalizations overwhelmingly emphasize unity, formal logic, and the rigorous standardization of natural scientific methods, empirical observation of natural scientific research in practice overwhelmingly tends to reveal a world of contingency, improvisation, and local variation in natural scientific work (see Lynch 1993). As it turns out, there is a good deal more to the actual 'methodology' of natural scientific work (if by this we mean the practical procedures through which good science gets done), than orthodox texts on 'scientific method' have ever told us. Attention to the empirical details of natural science in action has shed light upon a rather vast collection of practical skills and co-ordinated activities that merely formal accounts of natural scientific method have completely overlooked.

While social scientific research on natural scientific practice has grown into a thriving sub-discipline within the social sciences, interest in turning the social scientific gaze back upon the social sciences themselves has been slower to materialize. There are, however, several noteworthy exceptions to this general rule. For example, important socio-historical analyses have been done of the social sciences in general (see Ross 1991), of statistics (see Hacking 1990; Porter 1996), anthropology (see Asad 1973; Kuklick 1991; Pagden 1982; Stocking 1987), economics (see Mirowski 2001), history (see Novick 1988), psychology (see Dansiger 1990; Rose 1989), and others.

With respect to sociology itself, distinguished scholars, including Stephen Turner and Jonathan Turner (Turner and Turner 1990), Jennifer Platt (Platt 1995), Martin Bulmer (Bulmer 1984), Charles Camic (Camic 1989, 1995), Jean-Michel Chapoulie (Chapoulie 1987), and Martyn Hammersley (Hammersley 1989) have produced exemplary socio-historical analyses. Their work has cast new and invaluable light upon the origins and changing institutional characteristics of academic sociology and their respective effects on the substance of sociological knowledge itself. Programmatic calls for a 'reflexive sociology' (see Bourdieu and Wacquant 1992) also indicate an increasingly broad appreciation for the value of doing sociological research on the production of social scientific knowledge.

In addition to research on the social history of the social sciences there is now an important body of sociological research concerning the linguistic performances through which the authority of social scientific research is sustained (see Atkinson 1990; Clifford and Marcus 1986; Pollner 1992; van Maanen 1988; Woolgar 1988). Moreover, a growing number of ethnographers and discourse analysts are also beginning to produce epistemologically self-conscious studies of the mundane practices through which they or other social scientists collect and analyse their data itself (see Bourdieu 1996; DeVault 1999; Emerson et al. 1995; Gubrium and Holstein 1997; Harding 1991; Maynard and Schaeffer 2000; Maynard et al. 2002; Pollner and Emerson 1988; Smith 1989). The present volume builds upon and develops this programme of research into the linguistic and interactional details of social scientific knowledge production. By bringing together essays on the diverse roles played by language and linguistic interaction in the practical accomplishment of research using key social scientific methods and in several key substantive research areas it offers the most in-depth treatment of these issues yet available.

The first section of the book is comprised of essays focusing on how language and linguistic interaction figure in six of the most heavily utilized methods of conducting social research in the world today (i.e. survey research, interviews, ethnography, audio/video analysis, focus groups, and the analysis of documents). In the essays comprising the book's second section, attention is given to the insights and analytic advantages to be had in researching language and linguistic interaction as they figure in five major substantive research areas in the social sciences (i.e. gender and sexual identity, race, crime and deviance, news media, and social institutions). While space constraints do not allow me to summarize the findings of each of the contributions to this volume here, in what follows of the rest of this introduction I will briefly sketch what these chapters have in common and what is unique about the contribution this volume makes as a whole.

In the first place, each of the following essays is premised on the observation that social research methods, as well as a vast range of the substantive topics we consider through the use of those methods, are fundamentally and inescapably linguistic phenomena. This is so in the very obvious sense that formal specifications of social research methods and findings must inevitably take linguistic form and therefore must yield to the constraints that this form exerts upon them. But less obviously, the chapters that make up this volume also demonstrate how in various ways our *practical implementations* of social research methods and the *practical realization* of our phenomena themselves must inevitably bend to the pressures the routine demands of ordinary language use exert upon them. No matter the extent or the ingenuousness of our efforts to standardize the procedures through which our research is conducted, these procedures cannot be made immune to the vicissitudes imposed by linguistic interaction. This is not, however, treated as cause for scientific despair but for vigilant attention to the precise manner in which our research practices and topics might be influenced by their embodiment in linguistic interaction.

In the second place, each of the chapters that make up this volume treats the nature of language in a particular kind of way. In stark opposition to analytic approaches like structural linguistics and speech act theory, each of which construe 'language' as a relatively static system of symbolic structures that is distinguishable from its instantiation in the everyday conduct of social life, contributors to the present volume are aligned in treating language as a form of incarnate social action. According to this approach, it is the social contexts within which linguistic gestures actually occur and the range of activities those contexts are held to warrantably accommodate, that alone provide for the intelligibility that social actors find in linguistic gestures. Hence, the analysis of language must consist in detecting the collaborative activities conducted through actual instances of language use rather than constructing abstract systems from decontextualized bits of symbolic structure. For the contributors to this volume, analysing research methods as linguistic phenomena thus means analysing them as linguistically embodied devices for the conduct of particular types of empirically identifiable social activity.

Implicit in the treatment of language as social action is the view that competent language users possess and routinely employ a catalogue of tacit skills for identifying the practical upshot of linguistic gestures in context. Hence, another set of insights that flow from the contributions to this volume concerns the relationship between these kinds of skills – what ethnomethodologists have often called 'mastery of natural language' or 'ordinary practical reasoning' skills – on the one hand, and the more explicitly acknowledged and narrowly specified skills generally presumed necessary to conduct sound social scientific research on the other. Harold Garfinkel (1991: 16) has famously argued that our ordinary practical reasoning skills, while irremediably unavoidable, are 'specifically uninteresting' to those who possess and rely on them. In many cases this is quite true. However, readers will find that several of our contributors provide specific and compelling arguments for why social scientists *ought* to be interested in the relationship between the ethnomethods at work in social scientific practice itself (and in the social worlds we study) and social science research methods more traditionally construed.

A fourth point of commonality among the contributions to this volume is their orientation to the nature and importance of social context. As was noted above, early social scientists viewed scientific methods largely as techniques with which to fortify themselves against the corruptions introduced by social contextual influences. The project of science was thought to require purification from the particularities of one's social context and production of epistemologically transcendent truths or what Thomas Nagel (1986) has aptly called a 'view from nowhere'. Sociologists have effectively questioned this view and have argued that various features of social context, including, of course, the interactional and linguistic context, are not only unavoidable but are in fact indispensable to science. The contributors to this volume share this view. But in addition to *shaping* how scientific methods are used, contributors to the present volume treat social context as in fact reproduced and altered in and through the course of linguistic practice itself. John Heritage (1984b: 242) makes this point as follows:

> Since every 'current' action will itself form the immediate context for some 'next' action in a sequence, it will inevitably contribute to the framework in terms of which the next action will be understood. In this sense, the context of a next action is repeatedly renewed with every current action. Moreover, each action will, by the same token, function to renew (i.e. maintain, alter, or adjust) any more generally prevailing sense of context which is the object of participants' orientations and actions.

Many of our contributors therefore pay close analytic attention to the conversational sequences within which social research methods are put to use and demonstrate in various ways how the sequence of talk has consequences for the ways in which these methods are operationalized and understood. Once again, these points are not made in a spirit of correction or critique, but only to demonstrate the benefits that may accrue to social scientists by taking these influences into account in the conduct of their research. Taken together, these essays powerfully demonstrate the fundamental place that language and linguistic interaction occupy in social science methodology and hence the importance of analysing language and linguistic interaction to fully grasp those methods. This, in turn, opens up a wide range of novel or hitherto under-appreciated topics, research questions, and research directions for future sociological consideration. The chapters that comprise the second part of the volume go some considerable distance in specifying just what some of these new research questions and agendas are and could become.

Notes

1. By this Putnam means the doctrine that science consists solely in the work of producing theories that correspond with a uniform and constant reality that exists independently of our efforts to understand it.
2. Earlier sociological research concerning the natural sciences (see Mannheim 1936; Merton 1970 [1938]) tended to immunize the putative core of natural scientific research from sociological influence and was, in this sense, less thoroughly sociological than that of Bloor, Barnes, and company, who insisted the influence of sociological forces went all the way to the core.

PART ONE

●●●●●● **Talk-in-Interaction in the Context of Research Methodologies**

CHAPTER TWO Standardization-in-Interaction: The Survey Interview

Douglas W. Maynard and Nora Cate Schaeffer

The survey interview as a form of social scientific research is ubiquitous almost beyond comprehension. Its use spans disciplines (especially psychology, political science, and sociology), national boundaries, government and business organizations, public and private sectors, and so on. In addition to its information-gathering function, it is a tool for administering and governing society – in the USA, for example, officials conduct the national census using a form of the survey interview, and the Current Population Survey, by which the government ascertains employment figures on a monthly basis, is a tool for forging economic policy. Most generally, the survey interview is a means for measuring demographic characteristics and aggregate attitudes and opinions in many societies and sub-societies around the world. Surveys do this in a systematic way: sampling a population and then using standardized measurement in order to estimate various characteristics of it.

Over the years both practitioners and critics of standardized surveys have considered how the fundamentally social nature of the interview affects the data. Critics have presented examples of the awkward, or even bizarre, interactions that sometimes occur in survey interviews as evidence that the resulting data cannot be valid (e.g. see Cicourel 1974; Mishler 1986; Suchman and Jordan 1990). Practitioners (Kahn and Cannell 1957), on the other hand, view such individual incidents as resulting from unusual circumstances or badly designed survey questions; they argue that adherence to rules of standardization improves the overall quality of the data in the aggregate, even if those rules seem to be awkward in some individual situations (Cannell et al. 1975). Indeed, the desire to improve data quality is the justification for the rather rigid-seeming survey instrument in the first place.

Whether one approaches the survey interview as critic or supporter, an intriguing question is how participants organize their interactive relations. This chapter examines what happens in the talk between interviewer and respondent that enables the former to record codified answers from the latter on a computer for later aggregation with other such interactionally generated raw data. From quantities of 'conversations with a purpose' (Bingham and Moore 1925; Schaeffer 1991), in other words, researchers are able to discern patterns and make inferences about the characteristics of whole populations. Our interest is in the 'interactional substrate' (Maynard and Marlaire 1992) – the social organization in talk that makes 'accountable' data gathering possible with whatever degree of standardization the process exhibits.

In this chapter, we first review the justification for standardization in the survey interview: we summarize recent debates, discuss different varieties of standardization, and consider the limits of standardization. By considering these limits, we draw attention to the role of tacit and common-sense knowledge in the conduct of the survey interview. Tacit knowledge is what Polanyi (1958: 20) terms 'an essential personal participation of the scientist even in the most exact operations of science'. Personal or common-sense knowledge 'co-operates' with formal or impersonal (standardized) judgements about how to act, just as tacit understandings combine with explicit rules and procedures and as 'subsidiary' comprehension of how to do some task joins with more 'focal' and instrumental awareness of the task. We subsequently argue for studying interaction in the survey interview using an approach we call analytic alternation. Because of the tension between the procedures for social measurement and the practices of ordinary talk, interviewers alternate between following the rules of standardization and using the tacit knowledge available to competent social actors who must solve problems that arise as their work tasks unfold. Analytic alternation means following the situated oscillations between formal rule-following and the practices that interviewers enact in concert with survey respondents to make standardized measurement happen even when it seems most threatened. In particular, we examine both (a) the interviewing sequences by which survey instruments are administered, and (b) instances of what we call post-sequence elaborations, when respondents, having provided a recordable answer to an interviewer, make some comment that retrospectively changes the quality of that answer. In some cases, these elaborations re-open interviewing sequences that appeared to have been closed. We trace the consequences of elaborations both for the interaction and for standardization and social measurement.

Why standardization in the survey interview?

The varied practices that researchers refer to as 'standardization' evolved in response to early studies that demonstrated how the behaviour of interviewers affects error in survey estimates (Groves 1989: 380–1; Hyman et al. 1975 [1954]: 257). Interviewers were found to be highly variable in ratings they themselves made and in the number of responses obtained to open questions. Possible sources for such variability could be the expectations of interviewers – for example that respondents have consistent attitudes or that their attitudes would be associated with particular social characteristics (as when an interviewer expects that poor respondents would favour government programmes to aid those with low incomes). Practices for expressing these expectations would include 'probing', the action whereby interviewers query respondents who have not provided an adequate answer to some interview question. When interviewers vary in the way that they ask questions or probe, this is known as *error*. If, however, interviewers share certain expectations and consistently ask questions or probe in ways that express them, this is known as constant error, or bias. Summarizing the effects of the interviewer on the distribution of answers, Hyman, Feldman and Stember (1975 [1954]: 271) say, '… the only reasonable answer seems to be that absolutely anything can happen'. So, the rules of standardization attempt to control the behaviour of the interviewer. The goal is to reduce variable error by having interviewers behave in the same way and to reduce bias by restricting opportunities for the interviewer's expectations or opinions to intrude on the process by which the respondent's answer is generated, interpreted, or recorded.

Standardization works mainly to reduce interviewer variability. However, it does not *eliminate* the effect of interviewers on respondents. An interviewer who follows the rules of standardization might react to a respondent's ambiguous answer by repeating all the response categories, for example. From the point of view of standardization, this would be preferable to alternative behaviours, such as using beliefs about the respondent's likely answer to choose which response categories to repeat. Accordingly, standardized repetition of response categories does influence how respondents express their answers and, over the course of the interview, probably has the desirable outcome of training respondents to choose a category from among those offered rather than answering in other terms. This is clearly an effect of the interviewer on the individual respondent. Nevertheless, if standardization were comprehensive and perfectly implemented, we could say that the interviewer did not affect responses – in the very specific sense that the influence of any interviewer would be the same as that of any other interviewer. That is, in the best world of survey administration, interviewers are interchangeable.

Concerns about standardization

Standardizing the survey interview involves rules or principles that Fowler, Mangione and Mangione (1990: 35) codified in their well-known book on this topic. These principles are comprehensive and refined through many years of practice and observation:

1 *Read questions as written.*
2 *Probe inadequate answers nondirectively.*
3 *Record answers without discretion.*
4 *Be interpersonally nonjudgmental regarding the substance of answers.*

These principles are widely accepted by survey researchers, although specific practices derived from them can vary substantially, as researchers and staff charged with supervising field operations have derived their own specifications for training interviewers (Viterna and Maynard 2002).

Standardization is focused on reducing interviewer variability and thus on improving reliability, so that different interviewers act according to interviewing rules and obtain the same answers from similar respondents. However, standardization may neglect issues of validity (Hyman et al. 1975 [1954]: 20–1). Critics like Cicourel (1963), Briggs (1986), Mishler (1986), and Suchman and Jordan (1990) argue that the rigidities of standardization lead to awkward interactions and inaccurate answering. For this reason, they propose allowing more natural or 'recipient-designed' questions and more expression of respondents' lay understandings with respect to survey topics.

Despite the concerns from inside and outside the survey enterprise about reliability and validity, very little is known about how interviewers actually behave, how their behaviour affects the answers given by respondents in the immediacy of the interaction, or how conversational practices from other sorts of talk (including what is often called 'ordinary conversation') are used in standardized interviewing. This means that the survey interview is ripe for investigation and understanding as a form of talk-in-interaction. Consider Schegloff's remark about the survey interview as a measuring instrument:

> *Although an interview cannot in any case be like a thermometer ... reliable exploitation even of a thermometer requires knowing the properties of mercury, the glass in which it is encased, and so on, and incorporating these properties in the extraction of the desired information from the measurement device. It is by no means clear that we have such elementary understanding of the constitutive components of the survey interview ... a more general inquiry into the features of the survey interview as an organized occasion of talk-in-interaction may help us think through in a thoroughly informed way how exactly to understand the methodological, epistemological, and theoretical features and status of the interview as a tool of inquiry. (Schegloff, 2002: 156)*

Given the survey as an organized occasion of talk-in-interaction, *standardization-in-interaction* points to understanding and analysing surveys as they are enacted through the tacit knowledge of both participants to the interview, performing in concert with one another, alternating between what is scripted for them to do and – when contingencies of asking or answering arise that the script does not cover – what their common-sense tells them to do. Historically, as Schaeffer (1991: 367) observes, the survey interview has been called a 'conversation with a purpose', which recognizes that, although the interview depends upon conversational skills, it is not an 'ordinary' conversation. As a form of talk-in-interaction that attempts to regulate both what the participants say and how they say it, the aim is to maintain a uniformity in asking and answering questions that aids in social measurement by minimizing error and bias. The degree of uniformity that participants achieve, however, is contingent upon the vicissitudes and contingencies of their actions and reactions to one another in and through talk. By the phrase 'standardization-in-interaction', we mean to capture the real but organized flow of such talk, including the speech practices and non-vocal behaviours of interviewer and respondent. Studying standardization-in-interaction contributes both to understanding the organization of interaction in the interview and improving the quality of data it produces.

Alternation to the tacit realm

At any Computer-Aided Telephone Interviewing (CATI) Survey Research Centre, it is possible to observe interviewers reading verbatim from the screen in front of them to their respondents, listening to respondents' answers, and entering into the computer the resultant codes or categories. The interviewers can appear to be operating in a strictly standardized or routine fashion, enacting what the survey instrument on their computer screen tells them to do as they talk, listen and type. However, survey practitioners explicitly or implicitly recognize that interviewers inevitably must alternate between the rules of standardization and supplementing those rules with common-sense practices. At any unpredictable moment, interviewers will glance away from the screen, move their hands from the keyboard and gesture more or less expansively, producing talk that is neither scripted nor otherwise pre-designed, in order to handle some departure from the routine, with the aim of being able to return to that routine. For example, the interviewer may find it necessary to gesture while explaining something learned during training about the survey to a respondent. Although the gesturing is not something that the respondent sees, it might help the interviewer in articulating a point, or in emphasizing a significant piece of talk, or co-ordinating some other aspect of the verbal presentation. When done with the articulation, or emphasis, or co-ordination, the interviewer returns gaze and hands back to the computer and keyboard. For example, an interviewer calling back and trying to recruit or 'convert' a call recipient who recently refused a request to participate may employ unwritten but familiar rhetorical devices and gesture in a way that enhances words or phrases by emphasizing certain speech particles (Maynard and Schaeffer 2002a). After obtaining the respondent's co-operation, it is possible for the interviewer to return to what is scripted on the computer screen, reading and speaking in a more standardized way. In short, interviewers momentarily alternate from standardized, formal practice to the tacit realm and engage practices designed to provide for alternation again back to the formal realm. Analytic alternation is an inevitable aspect of standardization-in-interaction.

It may be that survey researchers, understandably emphasizing standardization so as to improve measurement and the quality of data, have neglected the essential pairing that occurs between the formal and the tacit, or between instructions and the alternate 'lived work' and courses of action involved in implementing instructions (Garfinkel 1988, 2002; Lynch 2002). Early on, Garfinkel (1967a: 97–8) demonstrated how rules for coding require a variety of *ad hoc* procedures to make them work, and other ethnomethodologists have expanded the point (Lynch 1991; Zimmerman 1970). Most recently, sociologists have more fully appreciated that tacit and common-sense understandings are situated within 'communities of work', embodying commitments of trust and mutual orientation (Collins 1985; Lave and Wenger 1991; Shapin 1994; Suchman 1987). In addition, studies of technology and social action are shedding light on, as Heath and Luff (2000: 4) put it, '… the ways in which individuals, both alone and in concert with each other, use tools and technologies in the practical accomplishment of their daily work'. Along these lines, Hak (2002) provides an enlightening study demonstrating the importance of *ad hoc*ing, tacit knowledge, and practical interpretation in the coding of CATI survey responses.

The interviewing sequence

Some time ago, Schuman (1982: 22) observed: 'Surveys start from two of our most natural intellectual inclinations'. Those two inclinations are to ask questions in order to obtain information and to sample in such a way as to have this information generally reflect a larger universe. As an example, consider how, at professional meetings, one participant might ask another whether there is a good restaurant nearby (Schuman 1982: 22). Extending this example, we can imagine how the restaurant seeker might decide that information from just one person would not be good enough, and that it would be better, therefore, to ask a few haphazardly if not entirely randomly chosen people. Therein lies the basis for the more systematic and analytic way of doing social measurement. In everyday life, participants have tacit knowledge enabling them to obtain information about worldly matters and to do so in relatively methodical ways that enhance the quality of this information.

One form in which tacit knowledge about how to gather information is exhibited in interaction is through the use of a generic 'interviewing sequence' which unfolds in three turns: (1) question, (2) answer, and (3) acknowledgement.[1] To continue with Schuman's (1982: 22) illustration, the turns might be: (1) 'Do you know of a good restaurant?'; (2) 'Yes, try the Grille just two blocks down on the right side'; (3) 'Okay, thanks!' (which contains a gratuity in addition to the acknowledgement). And we can observe this generic interviewing sequence at the very start of a formal survey interview. The parts of two interviewing sequences are indicated with arrows (number signs, as at line 6, denote keystrokes), while the interviewer is indicated with 'IV' and respondent with 'R':

```
(1)   AW01:A
 1    IV:    1-->   Oh kay: (.) a::nd >now we'll get started?< .hhh first
 2                  (.) how many persons live in your househo:ld counting
 3                  all adults and children and including yourself.
 4    R:     2-->   four
 5    IV:    3-->   .hhhh okay(gh): a::[::nd? now we have some questions=
 6                                     [##
 7    IV:           =about government agencies. .hhh as you know:? every ten
 8                  years there is a census of the population of the
 9           1-->   United States. .hhh how confident are you: (.) that the
10                  census bureau protects the privacy of personal information
```

```
11                    about individuals and does not share it with other
12                    government agencies. .hhh very confident (0.4) somewhat
13                    confident (0.5) not too confident? (0.2) or not at all
14                    confident.
15                              (1.0)
16    R:              Share it with what other governments?
17    IV:             (tch) .hh well the question doesn't specify: but (0.3) it
18                    just says other government agen[cie]s
19    R:                                             [oh]
20    R:    2-->      Probably very confident
21                              (0.5)
22    IV:   3-->      °Oh kay.° People have different ideas about what the census
23                    is used for ...
```

Not all survey questions appear in this three-part format, with an 'okay' or other object in the third position. Often, a two-part question-answer sequence, which omits the third position, appears. For example, in extract (2), when the interviewer has a block of questions to ask about a single topic, she withholds the acknowledgement:

```
(2)   AW01:B
1     IV:   1 -->     Okay our next questions have to do with government?
2                     .hhh on a scale of one to ten (.) where one means very
3                     ↑poo:r and ten means excellent °.hhh° >how would you
4                     rate the< job the president is doing.
5                               (1.4)
6     R:    2 -->     Uh:::m::: (0.9) six
7     IV:   1 -->     .hhh and on the same one to ten scale? where one means
8                     very ↑poo:r and ten means excellent °'hh° >how would
9                     you rate< the job the congress is doing.
10                              (1.0)
11    R:    2 -->     Uh::: (0.5) four
12    IV:   1 -->     .hhh on the same one to ten scale where one means very
13                    ↑poor and ten means excellent (.) >how would you rate
14                    the job< the supreme court is doing?
15                              (0.8)
16    R:    2 -->     Uh:m five
17    IV:   1 -->     .hhh on the same one to ten scale where one means very
18                    poor and ten means excellent (.) >how would you rate the<
19                    job the military is doing?
20                              (0.9)
21    R:    2 -->     Uh::m:: (1.3) eight(h)
22    IV:   3 -->     Eight ↑okay please tell me whether you agree: or disagree:
23                    with each of the following statements? .hhh the first
24                    statement is (0.4) people like me don't have any say about
25                    what the government does.
```

Notice that at line 22, when the interviewer is done with the questions that ask the respondent to rate the president, Congress, and Supreme Court, she repeats the respondent's answer ('eight'), and then produces the third-turn acknowledgement, an 'okay' that is dual in character – marking the end of one activity and the start of another (Beach 1993). Here, it is accompanied by a polite request form ('please tell me') that also may project a forthcoming next question distinct from the previous series. It could be said that interviewers have ways of signifying the boundaries of related questions, withholding third-turn acknowledgement when a subsequent question links to the topic of its predecessor, and producing such an acknowledgement when the next question does not. Thus, even when they read a script more or less verbatim, survey interviewers, in interaction with respondents, are engaged in performances that improvise on the script.

The survey interviewing sequence: questions and answers

Questions and answers – the first two turns in an interviewing sequence – have interactional facets, only some of which have been investigated. That is, interaction-based research on the survey interview and the sequences it comprises is still in its infancy. The limited research that has been done is suggestive, however. For example, Schaeffer (1991: 386–7), drawing on conversation analysis (CA) research about the projectable completion of turns at talk (Sacks et al. 1974), observes that many survey questions are vulnerable to interruption because they can be heard to implicate a response from the respondent before the scripted question or its response options have been completely read. A typical example is when interviewers ask respondents for their political party affiliation:

```
(3)   AW01:364
1     IV:    Generally speak↑ing do you usually  think of yourself as a
2            re↑publican (0.4) demo[crat        ] independent? Or=
3     R:                           [republican ]
4     IV:    =something else[:? re[publican?   ]
5     R:                    [     [republi    ]can
6     IV:                   [#    [#
```

According to how this item was written, the interviewer is required to read the entire list of response options ('republican, democrat, or something else') before the respondent answers. However, in this instance, in overlap with the interviewer completing the list (line 2), the respondent produces an answer (line 3), thereby intersecting the full reading. Nevertheless, IV continues with the list (lines 2, 4), and then asks if R said 'republican' (line 4), thereby retrieving that item from the overlap for confirmation, which R provides in line 5. Although the verification produced by IV would be judged directive by the strictest versions of standardization, it could have been awkward had the interviewer ignored the content of the respondent's interruption and attempted a re-reading of the list of choices. Often, in fact, when respondents answer prematurely, interviewers do modify their reading of questions or response options. Again, interviewing establishments may vary in how they implement standardization; and within establishments, interviewers may vary in how standardized they are. In circumstances where respondents can project completion of questioning turns, it appears that Dutch survey interviewers become more 'conversational' while US interviewers are stricter in following rules of standardization (Houtkoop-Steenstra 2000: Chapter 5).

Whereas respondents can interrupt standardized question-asking, their answering is also vulnerable to interactional effects. Particularly when they display 'uncertainty' (Maynard and Schaeffer 2002b: 24–7), respondents may provide 'occasions for intervention' (Schaeffer and Maynard 2002) on the part of interviewers. One such occasion occurs when, instead of using survey categories for their answers, respondents engage in 'reporting', whereby they detail an activity without making the upshot explicit (Drew 1984). In excerpt (4), the respondent, when asked if he owns his own business or farm, does not produce an answer that is formatted in the proper response categories. Instead he begins with a particle 'Weahh' (line 2) that sounds like a combination of 'Well' and 'Yeah'. This particle suggests a mitigated agreement or acceptance of the presumption of the question. There is then a full 'Well' and a report that he is in business with his sister.

```
(4)   008c0301, version C: 11
1     IV:    Do you have your own business or farm?
2     R:     Weahh, well I'm (.) in partnership with my sister in the shoe
3            repair business?
4                  (1.5)
5     IV:    O:kay so that would (.) uh qualify as your own business?
6     R:     I guess so=
7     IV:    =uh huh
8                  (6.0)
9     IV:    Now I'm going to ask a few questions about …
```

The particle 'well' is known to preface disagreements or to provide for sequentially weak agreement or acceptance (Pomerantz 1984). Moreover, the answer at lines 2–3 follows a yes–no interrogative and, as a nonconforming answer, takes issue with premises of the prior turn (Raymond 2003). After a delay (line 4), the interviewer responds in the form of a probe that draws the upshot for the respondent to confirm (line 5). The respondent's reply (line 6) confirms the probe in a hedged way by saying it would be a 'guess', and thereby it displays uncertainty; nevertheless, the interviewer acknowledges this answer (line 7), which completes the interviewing sequence. She also records the answer (line 8), and moves to the next set of questions (line 9).

In the survey interview, the use of a report implies that it is the interviewer's job to gather the upshot and map the report on to the proper response category (Moore 2004; Schaeffer and Maynard 1996, 2002). In most versions of standardization, however, survey interviewers are required to avoid making even obvious inferences and resubmit answer categories to respondents (Schaeffer and Maynard 2002: 272). When interviewers do propose an upshot, as in excerpt (4), it is often a directive probe that violates protocol. On the part of respondents and interviewers both, the proclivity to use ordinary conversational devices during the survey interview can intrude on standardization.

The survey interviewing sequence: third-turn acknowledgements or 'feedback'

Survey methodologists refer to the third turns of the interviewing sequence as 'feedback'. Depending on how it is produced, this turn has the potential to convey interviewers' evaluations or expectations rather than something more neutral. Acknowledgements or feedback include subtle forms of interviewer behaviour as well as the more formal tokens that interviewers use after a respondent has produced an answer to a survey question.

In environments other than surveys, third turns perform various kinds of interactional work. For instance, following information-seeking question-answer sequences in conversational contexts, third turns register that the information is informative to the questioner. Turns in the excerpt below are labelled:

```
(5)  Heritage (1984b: 285-6)
S:      1-->    .hh When do you get out. Christmas week or the week before
                Christmas.
                    (0.3)
G:      2-->    Uh::m two or three days before Ch[ristmas.]
S:      3-->                                    [Oh:,    ]
```

The 'Oh' in turn 3 indicates a 'change of state' in the answer recipient's knowledge (Heritage 1984a). In educational settings, 'instructional' sequences involve teachers asking 'known information' questions, and providing evaluative feedback in the third turn:

```
(6)  Mehan (1979: 52-3)
T:      1-->    ((Holding up card)) This is the long word. Who knows what
                It says?
S:      2-->    Cafeteria.
T:      3-->    Cafeteria, Audrey, good for you!
```

In contrast with conversational and educational settings, there are other institutional settings in which questioners withhold third-turn responses of either variety (indicating a change of knowledge state or evaluation of an answer). Prominent are courtrooms (Atkinson and Drew 1979), job interviews (Button 1987), and news interviews (Clayman 1988; Heritage and Greatbatch 1991). These venues have in common that interviewers (attorneys or employers or newscasters, as the case may be) are soliciting answers for an overhearing or what we might call a lurking audience of some kind who may do their evaluations of interviewees and their answers at some distance from the interview itself.[2] By refraining from post-answer commentary, interviewers exhibit themselves as conduits for those answers to flow to those audiences – who are then in the position of supplying that commentary in another social context, such as a jury room, a recruitment committee, or a political meeting. For an obvious example, it is during their later deliberations that jurors, having observed attorneys interview witnesses in the courtroom, may discuss and evaluate witnesses' answers to the attorneys' questions. With survey interviews, it is the researchers who later evaluate answers as they incorporate the codified results of the survey into an aggregate analysis using the tools of statistical inference.

Still, important differences exist in the ways that potential third turns are fashioned for lurking evaluators. An informal or formal rule that forbids third-turn responses, as in news or courtroom environments, may be relatively easy to follow. More difficult are protocols under which the interviewers are permitted or even encouraged to produce third-turn acknowledgements but are to refrain from evaluating the content of the answers they acknowledge. This creates a dilemma of being permitted to respond to second-turn answers but in restricted ways, and it characterizes not only the survey interview, but also educational testing interviews. Indeed, the protocols for tests such as the Woodcock–Johnson Psychoeducational Battery may warn administrators: 'Be careful that your pattern of [third-turn] comments does not indicate whether answers are correct or incorrect' (Mehan et al. 1986: 96–7). Administrators may produce 'neutral' acknowledgements ('okay', 'thank you', and the like) after a child has answered a test item. Despite these protocols, research demonstrates that administrators sometimes alter their third-turn responses systematically – using 'good' when an answer is correct, and 'okay' when it is incorrect; they may also give encouraging non-vocal signals by smiling or nodding when a child's answer is right, and appearing more taciturn when it is wrong (Maynard and Marlaire 1992). Although such acknowledgements do not necessarily affect an individual answer, they may have a cumulative influence on the child's performance and at some point alter subsequent responses.

Extrapolating from research on educational testing, the concern that most survey centres have over third-turn 'feedback' is no doubt well placed, and in fact survey researchers have long recognized that fine gradations in these responses potentially influence the answers of a respondent (Marquis et al. 1972). When survey practitioners first documented how interviewers follow respondents' answers with feedback, the impulse of survey researchers was to standardize that feedback. Controlled feedback (e.g. 'thank you', 'that information is helpful') is intended to reinforce thoughtful respondent behaviour positively without appraising the answer. Although this is not a uniform finding (Miller and Cannell 1982), some experiments with controlled feedback suggest that it may improve the accuracy of reports (Cannell et al. 1981), possibly because it teaches respondents what kinds of effort and answer the interviewer wants. However, survey centres are not in full agreement about what 'controlled' feedback is exactly (Viterna and Maynard 2002). That is, practitioners agree on the principle that feedback should not evaluate the content of the answer, but differ in specifying the purpose of feedback – whether it should be used to provide reassurance, sustain motivation, praise the respondent's level of effort, or notice that the respondent's answer meets task requirements, etc. Survey centres differ, as well, in defining the proper content of feedback and enumerating how frequently interviewers should provide it.

Elaborations occurring after a possibly complete answer[3]

Having examined the interviewing sequence and its elementary interactional features, we now turn our attention to a phenomenon that can create interactional and procedural difficulties during the interview. On occasion, after providing a codable answer or after an interviewing sequence is completed, respondents may produced more information or commentary. In effect, they are keeping the answering activity going after the point when it has, at least for the interviewer, been brought to a conclusion for the purposes of the interviewing task at hand. We refer to post-answer or post-sequence turns of talk that are relevant to the previous question as 'elaborations'. These elaborations are like what Schegloff (1995) calls 'post-expansion' items. Actually, the third turn of the interviewing sequence is one minimal type of post-expansion, meaning that it is delivered after the completion of the question–answer pair of turns and has closure of the sequence as its task. The kind of post-expansion that elaborations constitute, in Schegloff's (1995) terms, 'post-completion musings' or 'post-mortems'. They somehow comment on the prior sequence in an 'out-loud' fashion. In our data, some elaborations are unproblematic and not consequential for the interaction of the recorded survey answer. Others, however, can create troubles for the interactional trajectory of the interview. The prior sequence may be 're-opened' to deal with the trouble that the elaboration poses. Indeed, if the later talk conflicts with an already-chosen response, it also implicates problems of measurement.

The data on which this analysis is based are from two audiotaped collections of random-digit-dial telephone interviews: labour force participation questions in pretests for the redesign of the Current Population Survey (CPS) conducted by the US Bureau of the Census, and interviews of public opinion conducted by the Letters and Science Survey Center (LSSC) at the University of Wisconsin. In the CPS interviews, the interviewer asks the respondent the same set of labour force questions about each adult member of the household. The LSSC interviews are divided into a number of different topics (taxes, government, economic expectations, etc.), and within each topic a particular question form is repeated for several items. Our purpose here is to illustrate in more detail what we mean by analytic alternation, and the variable effects that elaborations may have on recorded answers and quality of data.

Unproblematic case of an elaborated answer: achieving rapport

---

Our first instance is one in which the respondent, after answering a question, invites and obtains laughter from the interviewer. R and IV then 'laugh together' (Jefferson et al. 1987) in a prototypical exhibit of achieving momentary rapport within the interview (Lavin and Maynard 2001).

```
(7)   112L02030
1     IV:    O:kay ##    hh an: how would you rate the job the military
2            is doing
```

```
3                (2.8)
4    R:     Oh I think the military is doing very well hh probably:: (.) well
5           let's go with an eight
6    IV:    Oka:y=
7    R:     =There's always room for improvement right?=
8    IV:    =Yeah ehh heh [heh .hh hh YEAH heh .hh O:kay .hh]=
9    R:                   [heh heh ehh heh heh heh  .bh]=
10   IV:    =generally speaking do you usually think of yourself as:
11          a republican? a democrat an independent or: what.
```

R's answer to the survey question (lines 1–2) is an extended one, accounting for her forthcoming answer (line 4) before it arrives (line 5). Immediately after IV acknowledges this answer in line 6 with 'Okay', R produces an idiomatic evaluation of her answer by commenting about 'room for improvement' (line 7). With the tag-question 'right?', she also asks for affirmation. At line 8, IV provides an affirmative response and begins to laugh. Subsequently, R (line 9) joins the laughter and the two participants laugh together for several particles. In the midst of this, IV at line 8 produces another agreement token, and then bids to end the laughter and initiate the next question with an 'O:kay' token; R's laughter stops after the 'Okay' appears, as both parties draw inbreaths. Subsequently, IV issues the next interview item (lines 10–11), but the way that IV and R track each other during the laughter shows how the resolution of these elaborations is an interactional matter involving both inter-viewer and respondent contributions.

The respondent in excerpt (7) elaborates on her response in a way that both par-ties treat as humorous. Although some survey centres, in the interests of standard-ization, work to prohibit interviewer laughter, not all do (Lavin and Maynard 2001; Viterna and Maynard 2002), and this instance, at this survey centre, is not problem-atic interactionally or for the proper conduct of the interview.

Unproblematic case of an elaborated answer: talk beyond keyboard entry

Other kinds of elaboration also may be inconsequential, although interviewers may record answers so quickly during an elaboration that it may not yet be clear to the interviewer whether the elaboration is relevant to that coding operation. This is because, at the first point where a respondent's turn of talk contains evidence of a recordable answer, interviewers may key a code into the computer. Excerpt (8) shows how an interviewer treats an in-process answer:

```
(8)  211LI306
1    IV:    (U-) ((tch)) okay and do you think that during the next twelve
2           months it will be larger or smaller than during the past
3           twelve months:? or about the same.
4    R:     Oh bout the s::[ame] I guess
5    IV:                   [ # ]
6    IV:    Okay hh an: what about interest rates: (.) uh do you think that
7           during the next twelve months interest rates will: go up? (.)
```

```
8              come down or: stay about the same as [they are now]
9     R:                                            [.hhhhh      ]hhhhh hhhhh
10             °well: let's see, they've gone down° they'll probly stay[: ]=
11    IV:                                                                [#]
12    R:       ='bout what they are now
13    IV:      Okay (0.2) ((tch)) .hh and in what state do you live . . .
```

As soon as R produces, in line 4, an utterance that is recognizably matched to one of the answer categories (i.e. just after IV hears 'bout the s::.'), she appears to enter a code for 'about the same' on the keyboard (line 5). IV waits until R completes the utterance with 'I guess' before providing the third-turn 'Okay' receipt (line 6) and reading the next question, but the answer has been mechanically recorded well before that.

Such 'recognition-point' (Jefferson 1973) data entry also occurs at the end of R's next answering turn (lines 9–10). Near the completion of IV's question (lines 6–8), R begins her answer. Then, as soon as R says something that is hearable as one of the offered answers (i.e. when R has completed 'they'll probly stay' in line 10), IV makes a keyboard entry (line 11). Given the capacity for turn projection, then, interviewers can and do treat the speech material following a codable answer as so much chaff. Stated differently, as soon as an answer can be recorded using the material in a respondent's turn-so-far, it often is. The interview progresses according to the CATI instrument without any obstacles. However, not everything that follows a codable answer in a respondent's turn is chaff, or is treated as such by the interviewer.

A problematic case: sequential implications of an elaborated answer

Some post-answer elaborations are very interactionally consequential in that they can affect the subsequent course of the interview. In a variety of ways, they can implicate alternation away from the instrument as an interviewer engages in tacit forms of handling the emergent material. Consider this:

```
(9)   OI5C0403
1     IV:      Did you do work at all last week not counting work around the
2              house?
3                   (0.4)
4     R:       No: I run back and forth to the hospital
5     IV:      h Alright (.) then is it correct that you did not have a job or
6              business from which you were temp'raly absent or layoff last
7              week?
```

After IV's question (lines 1–2), R begins his turn in line 4 with a 'No:', which provides an initial properly formatted survey response. If that were all of R's answer, it would be what Raymond (2003) calls a type-conforming one – grammatically fitted to the yes/no interrogative it follows. However, R's continuation beyond the 'No:' develops a nonconforming response, which exhibits the inadequacy of and resists presuppositions in the question. This R proposes that a simple 'no' to the question could allow for assumptions about his status 'last week' as one who did not 'do work'. His nonconforming response provides an account for not working that possibly depicts himself as responsibly occupied nevertheless.

Of further significance in this excerpt, and consistent with Raymond's (2003: 951–4) observations, the nonconforming response has sequential implications for the ensuing talk. These implications, in turn, are significant for the proper conduct of the survey. After receiving the R's nonconforming response, IV alters the wording of the next question. The scripted question is 'Did you have a job or business from which…?'. However, she changes the question, forming it, in survey terms, as a 'verification' question that incorporates an interpretation of the respondent's 'no' answer, and asks for confirmation of a statement that R did not have a job (lines 5–7). In conversation analytic terms, the question *prefers* a confirming answer (Sacks 1987). For the survey, this means that the question she produces presents an inference based on R's previous answer and thus violates some versions of standardization. Nevertheless, this interviewer is showing conversational competence, in that producers of yes/no interrogatives (survey questions here) who receive nonconforming responses regularly work to deal with the resistance these responses display.

Another problematic case: correcting the interview's trajectory

In our previous cases, a respondent's continuation past the production of a codable answer occurs within the same turn as the answer that the interviewer recorded. In excerpt (10) the pattern is slightly different. R, in line 4, provides a survey-formatted, type-conforming answer, which is complete and perfectly recordable for the interview. A silence follows (line 5), and when the interviewer resumes talking at line 6, she starts to ask the next question. However, at line 7, R interjects an elaboration to his previous answer, offering an account for the 'nope' at line 4. This effectively deletes IV's initiation of the next question, connecting the line 4 and line 7 utterances and assembling a nonconforming answer.

```
(10)    022C0505
 1      IV:     Last week (0.4) did you do any work at all include work for pay
 2              or other types of compensation
 3                      (0.4)
 4      R:      Nope
 5                      (1.8)
 6      IV:     Last week=
 7      R:      =I'm on full disability for [Sosh] Security disability=
 8      IV:                                 [uhh ]
 9      R:      =[cause] I've got asbestos in my lungs
10      IV:      [uh-  ]
11      IV:     Okay last week you're (a d-) okay you are disabled
12      R:      [Yes]
13      IV:     [Oka]:y hbh and (0.3) will your disability prevent you from
14              accepting …
```

This nonconforming answer turns out to be very interactionally and instrumentally significant. On the CATI screen, there are answer categories besides 'Yes' and 'No' for the question produced at lines 1–2. One of these, 'No, disabled', is a blind category, which the interviewer does not use unless the respondent volunteers the relevant information. When it is used, and a 'No, disabled' answer is entered in the computer, the CATI program skips to a different set of questions from those that appear after a simple entry of 'No'.

As R produces his announcement of the disability (line 7), IV acknowledges this additional information with 'uhh' (line 8), and produces another 'uh' (line 10) as R completes his announcement (line 9). IV also backs up in the CATI program to change the previous answer to 'No, disabled', asking for confirmation (line 11) and then, according to the program, initiating a different next question about whether R would be prevented from accepting a job (lines 13–14). In this case, unlike the previous example, the interviewer corrects the trajectory of the interview in a way that fits the protocols for standardization. Rather than altering the wording of the following question on her own, as IV did in excerpt (9), that is, this IV uses the R's elaboration to record the R's situation more accurately and to obtain computer-guided further questions.

Final problematic case: ambiguous answering

The next instance of elaboration is built into a single turn of talk. The construction of this turn is such that its ending appears to contradict what appears (to the interviewer) to be a codable answer in the beginning of the turn. The CATI screen for the question read at lines 1–3 in excerpt (11) offers the answer categories 'go up', 'go down', and 'stay where they are now' (lines 2–3).

```
(11)   182L1004
  1    IV:    Mkay .hh .hh and then during the next twelve months do you think
  2           prices in general will go up? go down? or stay where they are
  3           now?
  4                  (2.1)
  5    R:     They'll hold their: s:pot but they .hh they should be going down.
  6                  (0.4)
  7    IV:    Nkay?
  8                  (0.6)
  9    IV:    So:: do you wanta say they'll stay the same then:?
 10                  (0.6)
 11    IV:    What you're saying?=
 12    R:     n::Well they'll  [stay    the     same-         ]
 13    IV:                     [Or do you think they'll be going ] down
 14                  (0.6)
 15    IV:    Okay # .hhhh and then how bout interest rates...
```

After a silence (line 4), R starts his turn with a component ('hold their: sp:ot', line 5) that could be taken as the equivalent to the 'stay where they are' category. However, after a token of contrast ('but'), he continues with another component ('... should be going down') that has similarities to a different category. This implies an ambiguity: does R's 'should be going down' indicate his opinion of what will happen or what ought to happen?

The interviewer's hesitations and actions indicate that *he* regards the R's turn as ambiguous. He lets a 0.4 second silence pass, then responds with a question-intoned marker of receipt ('Nkay?', line 7), which is itself 'lax' and indefinite as to whether it is neutral and accepting of the prior turn, or possibly a complaining rejection of that turn (Jefferson 1978). Another pause follows (line 8), and then IV begins a candidate reformulation or paraphrasing (line 9) that retrieves the initial part of line 5 for confirmation. This paraphrasing of a respondent's talk is a directive probe and is (as we have observed before) incorrect under most rules for standardized interviewing procedures. However, in conversation, repeating a portion of a prior turn for confirmation is a common device by which speakers ask for clarification.

Despite the probe, R still does not speak (line 10). IV probes again, in a more neutral manner this time (line 11), and as he reaches the end of his utterance and the tone goes up, R immediately initiates a turn of talk (line 12) that eventuates in an unambiguous answer ('stay the same'). Before R can speak the disambiguating part of his turn, IV continues his own prior turn and produces, in overlap, an alternative candidate answer (line 13). (This is not the original wording of the question, but the wording that the respondent offered in line 5.) Having received no apparent response to his suggestion of 'stay the same', IV turns to the other interpretation of R's initial elaborated answer. After the overlap and completion of his own utterance, and a silence, IV produces a clear acknowledgement token and makes a keyboard entry (line 15). If we assume that IV has heard R's line 12 utterance, IV would register his answer as the 'stay the same' response option. In this extract, then, a respondent's elaboration results in an ambiguity to which the interviewer is attuned. In an effort to disambiguate the elaborated answer and register a code properly in the computer, and in a manner similar to that of the interviewer in excerpt (9), he acts as a competent practitioner conversationally even when violating protocols of standardization.

Elaborations and their consequences

Elaborations on answers to survey questions, we noted, expand the question answer and interviewing sequences they follow (Schegloff 1995). At times, interviewers treat talk after an already-produced answer as irrelevant to collecting and recording data in an interview. This may happen because at the first moment when interviewers hear a codable item in the respondents answering turn of talk, they may perform a keystroke to enter the item in the computer. At other times, elaborations of an answer significantly affect the course of the talk and what the interviewer does to register a code in the computer. As the talk develops to handle an elaboration, it may be done in a way that stays within protocols of standardization. However, because elaborations often mean that a previous answer is now incorrect or ambiguous, interviewers, as they alternate away from the CATI script, may be prompted to invoke their conversational competence – their generic knowledge of how to handle interactional mistakes – and break protocol inadvertently.

In practical terms, interviewers do manage to record answers to each item, and do so even when the answer is complicated by elaborations. Without further study of a quantitative and distributional kind, for example by coding to examine the relation of interactional variables to outcomes such as accuracy, it is not possible to determine whether post-answer elaborations affect the reliability and validity of the data collected. In their study of the accuracy of reports about legal custody, Schaeffer and Dykema (2004) found that elaborations occurred in approximately 1 to 14 per cent of cases (across six items presented in two different orders). Although elaborations lowered the odds of reporting accurately, the effect was not statistically significant in predicting the accuracy of answers, except for lagged analyses wherein elaborations are associated with significantly lower odds of reporting accurately for joint legal custody and reports about dates of marriage. A study by Dijkstra and Ongena (2004) shows that elaborations[4] are a fairly regular occurrence after initially adequate answers but it is difficult to determine how they affect the overall validity and quality of the data. More research needs to be done to answer definitely whether and how much post-answer elaborations affect the quality of data.

Conclusion

The section of this chapter on elaborative talk demonstrates that respondents are not what Garfinkel (1967: 67) called 'judgemental dopes'. Much as a survey can prescribe what and how they should reply to items on an instrument, respondents exercise and display forms of reasoning to accompany what can appear to be just-now codable answers for the survey instrument. However, whereas from an interviewer's perspective, respondents may initially have offered a codable answer, interaction is temporally organized in a manner to allow for talk to emerge that clarifies the significance of the already-said (Garfinkel 1967: 41). Thus, sometimes despite the efforts of interviewers to mark a respondent's turn or turn-so-far in a way that will conclude an interviewing sequence, respondents may elaborate their answer and defy what turns out to be premature codification.

If respondents are not judgemental dopes, neither are interviewers. That is, their handling of elaborations is also a skilful endeavour not fully encompassed by protocols for standardization. Sometimes, an interviewer's recording of an answer at a point of recognition in its production may make an elaboration irrelevant or redundant to the coding of an answer. At other times, elaborative talk appears to seduce interviewers into alternating away from CATI scripts so as to handle competently what the elaboration exhibits in relation to the original answer on which it is parasitic. Interviewers' alternation involves an invocation of tacit knowledge by which they may accomplish actions that diverge from the interviewing task *per se*, but that build rapport or record answers efficiently. And when an elaboration contradicts its preceding answer, interviewers necessarily perform a correction and may have to alter the course of the interview altogether. That they may violate protocol in doing so is testament not to the inadequacies of survey interviewing but to interviewers' conversational and interactional skill as they work with respondents to accomplish the rather challenging tasks of social measurement the research instrument puts before them.

Standardization in survey research or any other realm is not guaranteed by its rules and procedures. Standardization has to be achieved according to the variegated circumstances that impinge on any attempt to follow those rules and procedures (Maynard and Schaeffer 2000). Because of this, at least for the survey interview, it is best to investigate attempts to enact the uniform asking and answering of questions as standardization-in-interaction. Such investigation means paying attention to turn-taking (i.e. the interviewing sequence) and the variety of practical ways that this sequence is implemented to accommodate the vagaries of tapping the social entities a survey measures. It also necessitates analysis of the interactional details by which interviewers and respondents fit the instrument, with its codified questions and answers, to the respondents' circumstances. Studying talk-in-interaction in the survey interview, in other words, is an invaluable way to do research on standardization-in-interaction, a phenomenon that is endemic to many organizational settings. The interactional structures by which participants accomplish their tasks during the survey, attempting to facilitate good social measurement, are the site of actions whose pattern and organization are of immense importance for ethnomethodology and conversation analysis, survey design, data collection, and a variety of other theoretical, methodological, and empirical endeavours in the social sciences.

Notes

1. For a discussion of the generic interviewing sequence, see Maynard and Schaeffer (2002b: 15–16).
2. See Houtkoop-Steenstra's (2000) consideration of 'participant roles' and 'footing' (Goffman 1981b) in the survey interview. The interview implicates more than just an 'interviewer' and 'respondent', as interviewers exhibit themselves as 'animators' or 'relayers' of text that is designed by others, the 'authors' or 'formulators'.
3. We are very grateful to Robert Cradock for collecting and helping in the preliminary analysis of post-answer elaborations, and this section draws upon an earlier collaborative paper (Cradock et al. 1993).
4. Their term for elaboration is 'consideration'.

CHAPTER THREE **Interaction in Interviews**
●●●●●●●●●

Robin Wooffitt and Sue Widdicombe

Our aim in this chapter is to highlight the way that talk-in-interaction is fundamental in conducting and analysing interviews, and to argue that it is important to consider interviews as instances of social interaction. To substantiate this argument, we re-examine interview data using an appropriate analytic method, namely conversation analysis (CA). This analysis reveals three potential problems with failing to take account of the interactional character of interviews. We then reflect on more general methodological implications of our observations regarding the use of interviews as tools in social research.

―――――――――――― **Interviews as social research tools** ――――――――――――

Interviews are widely used throughout the social sciences. To go further, it is probably accurate to claim that the majority of qualitative research conducted in the social sciences has to some degree drawn upon data generated through interviews between researchers and members of the public. There is a vast amount of research which relies exclusively upon verbal reports of experiences and opinions offered by respondents in face-to-face interviews. Interview data may also play a part in research projects which use other kinds of qualitative material. For example, interviews may be employed as part of a broader ethnographic study, or to supplement the findings from the study of texts, such as the print media. The use of interviews in these kinds of study has been facilitated by advances in audio recording technology which have made the research interview an even more attractive method of data collection. Cheap and discreet tape recorders can record the respondent's words with greater accuracy than can be achieved through obtrusive and disruptive on-the-spot note taking, and relieves the researcher from any subsequent attempt to reconstruct what the respondent had said. Finally, the research interview can play a part in the collection of quantitative data (see Chapter 2 in this volume). Many large-scale national surveys are administered by researchers in interviews with respondents, in which answers are recorded in such a way that they are suitable for subsequent statistical analysis.

Of course, the research interview may take different forms, depending at least in part on the purposes for which they are to be used. Four main types of interview have been distinguished (Fielding 2001). These vary according to the degree to which the interviewer's and respondent's contributions are constrained through the structure of the interview. Thus, there are structured, semi-structured and unstructured individual or group interviews. We will consider briefly the features of these different types of interview. This will provide a point of reference for our subsequent argument that although the format differs, interviews share a common basis in interaction. We shall confine our remarks about the potential consequences of ignoring this fact mainly to structured and semi-structured interviews. However, our observations can be applied to some degree to all types of interview.

The standardized or structured interview is associated with questionnaire research and statistical analysis. The interviewer simply administers a questionnaire or survey to the respondent. This is the most formal kind of interview setting: the interviewer follows the survey or questionnaire much like a script, and records the respondent's answers on the questionnaire. The wording and order of questions is constant, which ensures continuity across all the interviews with all the respondents. This in turn allows statistical analysis of the data thereby collected. Questions are designed so that the respondents' participation is constrained and minimized, thus ensuring that their answers can be easily coded. Many of these features are illustrated in extract (1), which comes from Suchman and Jordon's (1990) study of interaction between respondents and researchers completing a Social Survey and a Health Survey in the USA. (1) (In this and all subsequent extracts, 'I' is the interviewer, 'R' is the respondent.)

I: During those two weeks, did anyone in the family receive health care at
        home or go to a doctor's office, clinic, hospital or some other place. Include
        care from a nurse or anyone working with or for a medical doctor. Do not
        count times while an overnight patient in hospital.
R: (pause) No::
(Suchman and Jordan 1990: 233)

Compared with the structured interview, which is designed to obtain factual information, the semi-structured interview is often constructed to elicit views or accounts in relation to quite specific questions. Moreover, in contrast to the structured interview, in a semi-structured interview, the sequence of questions can be varied, as can the wording of questions. The researcher has some scope to pursue themes which may emerge during the interview. In some studies this facilitates the possibility of later quantitative analysis while preserving the researcher's option to develop particular topics, although semi-structured interviewing is also more commonly used in purely qualitative research. There is more respondent participation, and this is not directly constrained by the interviewer's questions. To illustrate, consider extracts (2) to (4) overleaf. These come from interviews with members of youth subcultures.

They were conducted as part of a project on social identity. The interviews were started with a question which invited the respondents to describe themselves. Extract (2) provides an example.

```
(2)      ((Tape starts))
1        I:    CAn you tell me something about your sty:le
2              and (.) °y'know°
3              (.)
4        R:    [°uhm°
5        I:    [the way you're dressed
(Widdicombe and Wooffitt 1995: 78)
```

However, this question was not stated in exactly the same way on each occasion. In extract (3), a tape problem meant that the first part of the interviewer's question is lost, but it is clear from what remains that it is phrased differently from the version in extract (2). Extract (4) illustrates another variation on the wording of the interviewer's first turn.

```
(3)      ((Tape starts))
1        I:    ... about your sty:le
2              (.3)
3        I:    and who you are
4              (.4)
5        I:    how would you describe yourselves
6        R1:   huhh huhh hhagh punk rockers
7        R2:   punk rockers yeah huhh huhh
8        I:    How long have you been punk rockers,
9        R2:   three:- ah've been three years
10       R1:   yeah three
(Widdicombe and Wooffitt 1995: 78)
```

```
(4)      ((Tape starts: respondents talking to each other about Princess Anne for approximately 12
          seconds.))
1        I:    can you tell me something about your style and the way
2              you look,
3              (0.7)
4        I:    how would you descri:be yourselves
5              (0.7)
6        R1:   °huhh°
              (.7)
8        R1:   I dunno >I hate those sorts of quest[ions uhm
9        R2:                                        [yeah horrible
10             isn't it
(Widdicombe and Wooffitt 1995: 96–7)
```

In standardized or structured interviews, the respondents' answers are constrained: the questions are worded to ensure that they require yes/no answers, or a simple factual statement (e.g. the number of visits to a doctor in the past month). But in semi-structured interviews, respondents' replies can take various forms. In extract (3), for example, respondents address the interviewer's first turn by identifying themselves in terms of a subcultural label (punk rockers), but in extract (4) the respondents adopt a more hostile stance, declaring their dislike for this type of question.

The third type of interviews is known by a variety of terms: the non-standardized, unstructured, or focused interview. This type of interview is used more to explore issues or themes which are relevant to the researcher's interests, and of which the respondent is likely to have some direct experience or thoughts. The interview structure is loosely organized: instead of a series of specific questions, the interviewer may simply have a list of issues she wishes to raise with the respondent. It therefore differs from both structured and semi-structured interviews in that the interviewer does not follow predefined guidelines. Moreover, the interaction is relatively unconstrained, in that the researcher may depart from an interview guide to pursue novel topics which are introduced by the respondent. The respondent's participation is not constrained and may be extensive: they may offer lengthy accounts, narratives, anecdotes and stories to illustrate experiences or opinions. It is assumed that by encouraging respondents to reflect on and relate their experiences at length, the researcher is more likely to obtain rich data which will yield greater insight into the personal experiences of the respondents. Extract (5) illustrates the start of a focused interview. This comes from Wooffitt's (1992) study of accounts of paranormal experiences.

```
(5)    ((Tape starts))
 1   I    well then (.) if you'd care tuh (.) tell me
 2        what happened
 3        (0.6)
 4   S    well all I know is:: >I< well I'm not sure o' me a:ge
 6        when I (.) i(t)- happened because >ah<* all I know is
 7        I w- (0.2) was at school so it musta bin after
 8        five years of age 'cos we didn't start 'fore five
 9        an' I was losin' a lo(t) of time at school cz I 'ad this: pneumonia, (1)
10        an uh (0.5) a- according to mother I became seriously-at first of all
11        with just (.) normal (0.5) er plain pneumonia an' in those days to
12        treat pneumonia all they °hhh knew about treating' pneumonia in
13        those days was to put hot kaolin poultices on yer °hh chest tuh keep
14        the fluid (1) anyway it didn't do much good an' it got worse un I got
15        into the situation what they call double pneumonia where both
16        lungs become infected °hhhh an just got worse and worse and I was
17        in bed of ooh: eight or nine weeks I s'pose I don't know exactly the
18        number of weeks but I was there a long time in bed (1) an apparently
19        or so my mother told me afterwards when I got better (0.5) that one
20        day the doctors comes 'e says well there's no more I can do he:'s:
21        y'know (0.5) you must prepare yourself for the worse 'e's not gonna
22        make it through the night in my opinion 'e says c'z people become at
23        their lowest ebb (0.5) during the early hours of the morning I don't
24        think he'll make it he says so you (0.5) y'know, all you can do is
25        hope so:: anyway (0.5) when you're in bed that length o' time you
26        don't sleep regular hours like (0.3) when you normally go to bed at
```

```
27       night yu' know if you've been up all day you go to bed you go to
28       sleep (.) hhhh an' you wake up in the morning (.) an' ah musta bin
29       do:zin' there or somethin' un u(h)r: suddenly this: light a very
30       small light (.) must've started playing s:i:lly devils
         ((continues))
```

In this extract the interviewer's first turn simply invites the respondent to report his apparitional experience. In this section of the interview, the interviewer does not intervene, and takes the role of a passive recipient of the respondent's lengthy account of his health problems at the time of his experience. However, the focused interview can be collaborative, with the researcher taking a more participatory role. Consequently, it is often said that the focused interview can come to resemble a conversation, with both participants exploring a range of mutually interesting issues.

Finally, in focus group interviews, a number of people can be brought together to engage in joint discussion facilitated by the researcher, often prompted by consideration of stimulus materials, such as videos, newspaper articles or magazine adverts. This is an extremely efficient method of data collection, as one session might allow the researcher to record reports of opinions and experiences of ten or more people at one time. Moreover, it is possible that the presence of others with similar life experiences may encourage greater participation and disclosure of personal or intimate details, although the presence of others can also inhibit full and frank participation. A more detailed discussion of focus groups is provided in Chapter 4 of this volume.

We noted above that the interview is fundamental to the social sciences, because so much of what we know about the social world comes from analysis of data generated through some form of interview. It is no surprise, then, that sociologists have been keen to explore the ways that interviews may shape the data gathered through them. Attention has focused mainly on two issues. One concerns the factors that can lead to the collection of distorted, biased or irrelevant data. A second concern is with those variables that can inhibit the interview as a data-gathering procedure, for example, by interfering with the smooth execution of an interview. So, in methods textbooks, we can find descriptions of possible questioning techniques including advice on how to ask straightforward, clear questions, exhortations not to ask leading questions, and advice on how to probe for more information or prompt hesitant respondents. We also find discussion of various interpersonal issues. For example, the benefits and dangers of developing rapport with the respondent; general warnings about the ways in which respondents may unwittingly impede the unfettered flow of information; and the effect of social category membership and social status on responses. That is, we are encouraged to ask: is the respondent too keen to please the researcher because of her (perceived) higher status? Does the interviewer's class or gender affect the nature of the respondent's answers?

Nevertheless there is something quite curious about such discussions of interview techniques and methods. In particular, researchers have overlooked the fact that the research interview is a period of social interaction. This lack of interest in the interactional dimensions of social research interviews reflects the broader tendency in the social sciences to treat language either as a passive medium for the transmission of information, or as a canvas which merely reflects the influence of sociological variables such as the participants' relationship, class, gender, status, and so on. However, in the past three decades there has been a sustained criticism of this dominant position, and this critique encourages us to look at interviews in a new light.

Language use as social action

Drawing from the later philosophy of Wittgenstein and the sociological writings of Garfinkel and Sacks, scholars in a range of social science disciplines now treat verbal communication as social action. This is best exemplified in the approach of conversation analysis (CA). Over the past 30 years, CA has emerged as one of the primary methodologies in the analysis of naturally occurring verbal interaction. Some key assumptions inform conversation analysis. The first is that language use is a site for social action: people do things to each other when they talk. Second, the way in which utterances are designed will be informed by the speakers' communicative competencies: procedures, methods, maxims and practices for producing mutually intelligible interaction which are available to them by virtue of their membership of a natural language-speaking community. But utterances are not examined as isolated actions. Conversation analysis is centrally concerned to discover and explicate sequences of utterances – highly patterned ways of talking together in which participants engage in interactional and inferential activities. Part of the work of analysing sequences in interaction requires showing how they are interactionally produced. In other words, CA is interested in showing how participants' orientation to the requirements of that sequence inform their activities, and in so doing 'bring off' or realize that sequence collaboratively. The ways in which utterances are designed, then, will embody the participants' tacit understanding of the normative properties of sequential organization – that certain activities are appropriately placed in specific positions. (For introductions to CA and its methodological orientation, see Drew 1994, 2003; Heritage 1984b; Hutchby and Wooffitt 1998; ten Have 1999.)

Although it is known as conversation analysis, CA's methodological procedures can be applied to any form of naturally occurring talk-in-interaction (Drew and Heritage 1992b). So, in addition to hundreds of studies of mundane interaction, there has been considerable research on interaction in work or institutional settings, such as courtooms, doctors' surgeries and television news interviews (Boden and Zimmerman 1991; Drew and Heritage 1992a). In these formal or semi-formal contexts, the participants' conduct can be investigated to show how their discourse attends to requirements of the setting. For example, in doctor–patient consultations we may examine how the turn-taking system common to everyday interaction may be temporarily suspended to facilitate the doctor's diagnostic work (Heath 1986, 1992). And in televised news interviews, we can examine turn design to reveal how the participants orient to each other's setting-relevant identities: interviewer or interviewee (Heritage and Greatbatch 1991).

Conversation analytic research has produced a cumulative and detailed account of the organization of talk as action. This has important implications for the way we understand what happens between interviewer and respondent in the research interview, and how we view the data which are subsequently produced. In the rest of this chapter, we will explore three (interrelated) issues raised by a CA approach to interaction in the research interview, focusing, as noted above, on structured and semi-structured interviews. First, CA shows that the requirements of the standardized interview may conflict with the expectations associated with everyday interaction. This may make interaction in interviews awkward and uncomfortable. The next two issues apply to the analysis rather than the collection of data and they are therefore potentially relevant to the analysis of all types of qualitative interview data. The second issue is that the analysis of interview data often overlooks the interactional basis of data production and this has implications for the interpretation of that data. Third, analysts may ignore the way that an utterance functions as an action in the interview interaction, interpreting it instead as exemplifying an underlying theme. This may distort the findings or limit the analyst's understanding of what is going on in the interview. We will discuss and illustrate each issue in turn.

Breaching normative expectations

Talk-in-interaction relies upon a shared set of communicative practices which inform our interpretations of and inferences about each other's conduct. However, the conduct of interviewer and respondent may depart from these expectations because of the requirements of the research interview. We will examine what may occur when these normative expectations are breached.

In a structured interview, the interviewer administers a survey to a respondent. The questions are written to require either yes/no answers, or a selection from a range of possible options. The respondent's answers are then coded or recorded in terms of a number of pre-set categories. These formally coded data provide the social scientist with the basis for statistical analysis.

Standardized data are necessary for statistical analysis. Therefore, it is important that the interviewer asks the respondents the same questions in the same way in the same order every time. However, the need to produce standardized answers entails the suppression of some essential characteristics of everyday interaction. Suchman and Jordan (1990) show that this has some very important consequences for the nature of the information actually being recorded. They conducted an analysis of recordings of interviews in which researchers were administering either the General Social Survey or the National Health Survey to members of the public. They noted several ways in which the requirements of the interview constrained everyday communicative competencies. For example, in conversational interaction, utterances are designed for particular recipients: there is an elegance and economy about the ways in which turns can be built to show their relevance to their intended recipients. But in a structured interview, each question must be presented to different respondents in the same way. Therefore, questions have to be written to accommodate a wide range of respondents and their possible circumstances. This means that questions can become awkward and clumsy, as extract (6) illustrates:

(6)
I: During those two weeks, did anyone in the family receive health care at
        home or go to a doctor's office, clinic, hospital or some other place. Include
        care from a nurse or anyone working with or for a medical doctor. Do not
        count times while an overnight patient in hospital.
R: (pause) No::
(Suchman and Jordan 1990: 233)

In everyday conversation, turn exchange is managed with precision: there are few silences between turns, and periods when more than one person is talking at once are shortlived. One of the reasons for this is that we share a tacit understanding of the procedures for turn management, and a sensitivity to where in interaction it is appropriate to initiate turn transfer (Sacks et al., 1974). One such location is at the end of stretches of talk which could be heard as the grammatical end of a sentence. However, because standardized interview questions have to anticipate a range of respondent circumstances, they may contain many clauses, and the end of each of these could be heard as an appropriate place for a respondent to start talking, that is, to provide an answer.

Suchman and Jordon noted that it is not unusual for a respondent to answer a question after an initial clause. However, because of the requirement to ask questions in the same way on each occasion, the interviewer has to continue with the rest of the question even after the respondent has answered it.

(7)
I: Was the total combined family income during the past twelve
        months, that is yours, your wife's Judith's and Jerry's more or less
        than twenty thousand dollars.
R: More
I: Include money from jobs, social security, retirement income,
        unemployment payments, public assistance and so forth. Also include
        income from interest dividends, net income from business or rent, and
        any other income received.
R: More. it was more income.
(Suchman and Jordan 1990: 234)

This is interactionally clumsy. The respondent has answered 'more' at the end of the first part of the interviewer's utterance, and the logic of the question means that his answer will not be altered by his consideration of the instructions which follow his answer. Yet the interviewer is obliged to ask each question in its entirety, in exactly the same way, for each respondent. Thus we have the unsatisfactory situation in which the interviewer has to read out now-irrelevant information, while the respondent waits to repeat his answer.

In everyday interaction, contributions to a conversation can be designed to take account of prior interactional events, or previously disclosed information. This is a valuable resource by which we can avoid repetition, redundancy, and so on. In standardized interviews, however, interviewers have to ignore precisely this kind of contextual knowledge: they are not allowed to incorporate inferences available from prior turns into the design of subsequent questions. This, again, can led to interactional dysfluencies (see Chapter 8 in this volume).

Suchman and Jordan cite an instance concerning the respondent's health. The interviewer establishes that the respondent has a form of skin complaint brought on by playing the violin. The respondent is then asked 'When did you last see or talk to a doctor or assistant about the dermatitis under the neck?' (Suchman and Jordan 1990: 233). However, the respondent's answer reveals that she did not see a doctor about this condition. On the basis of this information, we might draw the following inference: that if a medical condition was not serious enough to warrant a visit to a doctor, it is unlikely to be serious enough to merit hospitalization. Some turns later, however, the interviewer is obliged to ask the following question.

(8)
I: Were you ever hospitali[zed::for
R: [No
(Suchman and Jordon 1990: 233)

Because of the requirement that all questions have to be asked in every interview, interviewers can find themselves having to pose questions to which they already know the answer, to respondents who have already answered.

These features of standardized interviews may be irritating to the respondent ('couldn't she figure that out?'), and embarrassing for the interviewer. But the requirement to depart from everyday conversational practices may have more damaging implications.

During a standardized interview, it is not only the questions which are pre-determined: so too are the kinds of answer respondents can give. This is because answers have to be recorded in terms of the categories or coding schemes built into the survey which is being administered. This means that interviewers are constrained either to ignore the respondent's answer if it deviates from the required format, or to force it into one of the available categories. In the following extract, the respondent is being asked to assess the appropriateness of the amount of money being spent on problems in big cities.

(9)
I: ... solving the problem of big cities
R: Ahm:: (long pause) Some questions seem to be (little laugh)
       hard to answer because it's not a matter of how much money, it's-

I: Alright, you can just say whether you think it's too much, too little or
      about the right amount, or if you feel you don't know you can:: say that of course.
R: Ah from the various talk shows and programs on TV and in
      the newspapers, ah it could be viewed that they're
      spending maybe the right amount of money. but it isn't
      so much the money that they're spending it's the other
      things that-
I: Well do you think we're spending too much too little, or about the right amount.
R: Ahm, I'll answer I don't know on that one.
(Suchman and Jordan 1990: 234–5)

In this extract it appears that the respondent is taking issue with the premise of the question: she queries whether the important issue is the amount of money being spent, and suggests that what matters is how it is allocated. But this does not fit the kinds of category of answer the interviewer can accept, and she urges the respondent to provide an answer which does. Eventually the respondent offers a 'don't know' answer. While this can be coded in terms of the available categories, it is technically untrue. It implies the respondent has no knowledge of or position on this topic, when in fact it is transparently the case that she has a sophisticated and critical appreciation of the issues. The respondent's actual opinion, which she tried to volunteer, was lost.

Standardized interviews require the respondents to offer short, factual answers. Often, though, respondents will provide a longer narrative or anecdote as a way of illustrating an answer. Due to the requirement to furnish standardized answers, the interviewer must ignore these stories. It is possible, however, that these stories may actually contradict the answer which has been given. This problem is illustrated by extract (10) below.

(10)
I: When you think about other doctors in general, how would you compare
      yourself to them. Are you very similar or different?
(Suchman and Jordan 1990: 236)

In this standardized interview, as in many others, respondents are presented with a statement and asked to select from a limited range of possible responses. Here, the respondent has two options: 'very similar' or 'different'.

In mundane interaction, it is noticeable that speakers can appear to agree with a prior statement, but then go on to tell a story or an anecdote which indicates some measure of disagreement. Pomerantz calls this the 'yes but' phenomenon (Pomerantz 1984). A similar phenomenon occurs in the respondent's treatment of the question in extract (10).

(10 continued)
I: When you think about other doctors in general, how would you compare
      yourself to them. Are you very similar or different?
R: I think I'm pretty similar to most doctors.
      Except that a lot of doctors try to stay right in the mainstream of medicine.
      They don't like to be out, away from the drug-oriented type of medical

treatment.In other words, you have a problem. you have drug for it. And
that'll take care of it. Or surgery or something. Cut it off. and you'll be fine
(laughs) And most doctors have that attitude. Then there's a small group
that believe in the reason that you have doctors in the first place. And that
is that we're more holistic. So we can use a more natural approach. The
hippocratic approach. So I think I'm more like that group

(Suchman and Jordan 1990: 236)

The respondent initially states his similarity to most doctors. Then he demonstrates his difference by providing a lengthy account in which he details how he
favours the more holistic approach to medicine advocated by a minority ('a small
group') of medical practitioners. Thus the interviewer is faced with two contradictory
answers. On the one hand, if the interviewer accepts the first answer, she will be
attributing to the respondent an opinion with which he clearly disagrees. On the
other, if she takes account of his subsequent explanation, she will not only have
transgressed the rule that interviewers should disattend to respondent's anecdotal
remarks, but she will also have an uncodifiable answer: 'similar' and 'different'. What
is eventually coded as an answer is not going to be a direct reflection of the respondent's utterances, but the outcome of the interviewer's interpretation of the relationship between what was said and the nature of the permitted responses, an
outcome that the rules governing interviews are ostensibly designed to avoid.

The requirements of standardized interviews collide with the practices of everyday
talk-in-interaction, with significant consequences. First, there may be periods of
interactional dysfluency, and from these may spring embarrassment, irritation, and
so on, thus making the interview a generally uncomfortable encounter for both parties. Second, and more seriously, the nature of the interaction may affect the information recorded during the interview. Suchman and Jordan's analysis shows how
restrictions on everyday conversational practices required by the structured interview
can impact upon the interviewer's decision as to what information the respondent is
actually offering by way of answer. In short, data collected in structured interviews
may be difficult to disentangle from the organization of the talk through which the
interview was conducted.

The (missing) interactional basis of research interviews

Conversation analytic research has shown that turns at talk are built to perform an
activity which 'fits' with, or is relevant to, the producer's tacit understanding of its
context, usually the activity performed by the prior turn. So, if we interpret a prior
turn as doing 'questioning', we infer that 'answering' is a relevant next activity; if we
interpret a prior turn as performing an invitation, we produce an acceptance (or
rejection), and so on. This is a valuable resource by which to ensure intersubjective
understanding: our assessment of the activity performed by a next speaker will allow
us to infer how our prior turn had been understood. Participants' understanding of
their interaction with others thus develops over a turn-by-turn basis.

The research interview is also conducted through a series of turns which alternate between the researcher and respondent. Consider the semi-structured interview: here the researcher may have a set of questions to work through, but there is flexibility in how these may be ordered and worded, and the repondents' utterances are not restricted to yes/no or factual answers. Admittedly, this kind of interaction is more formal and constrained than everyday conversation: there may be a restricted range of activities undertaken by participants, and in many kinds of interview one participant sets the agenda as to what is talked about. But this is a form of interaction, nonetheless. This means that the way utterances are produced will in some way reflect the producer's understanding of the prior turn: it will exhibit design features which show how it is connected to the ongoing stream of interaction.

However, it is noticeable that the majority of research which draws upon data from semi-structured research interviews tends to focus on the respondents' turns as if they were discrete speech events isolated from the stream of social interaction in which – and for which – they were produced.

To illustrate, we will consider Smith and Osborn's (2003) introduction to the methodology of Interpretative Phenomenological Analysis (IPA). IPA is a qualitative method which seeks 'to explore in detail how participants are making sense of their personal and social world' (Smith and Osborn 2003: 51). The data for IPA mainly comes from semi-structured interviews. Analysis proceeds by identifying themes in the respondents' discourse, and then ordering these themes to reveal higher-level systems of meaning which provide insight to the respondents' understanding of their lives. To illustrate this analytic method, Smith and Osborn show the kinds of theme which may be derived from examination of interview data. A section of their illustrative example (from a study of the impact of pain on self-concept) is reproduced overleaf. The data, shown in the left-hand column, comes from an interview with a woman who is suffering from a chronic benign pain; the analyst's thematic notations are reproduced on the right, next to the relevant sections of the data.

Before we proceed, it is important to be clear that we have not selected Smith and Osborn's account as the basis of our discussion because their analytic procedure is unusual. Their general approach to interview data reflects some common methodological practices in a range of social science perspectives; for example, there are similarities between their social psychological approach and the way interview data are analysed in sociological research informed by grounded theory (Charmaz 2003; Glaser and Strauss 1967), and poststructuralist analysts' efforts to identify discourses (e.g. Gavey 1989). Nor have we selected their paper because we think their analytic claims are weak or unsatisfactory. On the contrary, the analysis of their interview data is sophisticated, and shows a sensitivity to the participant's circumstances and the way she is dealing with her condition. Their paper has been chosen because it is an admirably clear account of a way of dealing with interview data which is more or less common to the social sciences. It is this clarity and generality which allows us, first, to indicate how a CA approach differs from more conventional analytic treatments, and second, to establish the wider relevance of the observations which follow.

M. Since it started getting bad, I was always snappy with it but not like this, it's not who I am it's just who I am if you know what I mean, it's not really me, I get like that and I know like, you're being mean now but I can't help it. It's the pain, it's me, but it is me, me doing it but not me do you understand what I'm saying, if I was to describe myself like you said, I'm a nice person, but then I'm not am I, and there's other stuff, stuff I haven't told you, if you knew you'd be disgusted I just get so hateful	*Anger and pain* *Struggle to accept self and* *identity – unwanted self* *Lack of control over self* *Responsibility, self vs pain* *Shameful self – struggle with* *unwanted self* *Fear of judgement*
Int. When you talk about you and then sometimes not you, what do you mean?	
M. I'm not me these days, I am sometimes, I am all right, but then I get this mean bit, the hateful bit, that's not me.	*Unwanted self rejected as true* *self*
Int. What's that bit?	
M. I dunno, that's the pain bit, I know you're gonna say it's all me, but I can't help it even though I don't like it. It's the mean me, my mean head all sour and horrible, I can't cope with that bit, I cope with the pain better.	*Attribution of unwanted self to* *the pain* *Defense of original self* *Ranking duress, self vs pain*

(Smith and Osborn 2003: 68–9)

A first point to note about Smith and Osborn's analytic notations is that they indicate themes which summarize or capture some aspect of the deeper cognitive meanings of the respondent's talk. We will talk more about the focus on themes in respondents' discourse in the next section. More relevant to our present concern is that these notations reflect an exclusive concern with the respondent's talk; there are no similar characterizations of the interviewer's questions. Analytic attention is thus focused squarely on the respondent's turns. This may seem a reasonable procedure; after all, it is the respondent's experiences the analysis seeks to explore. But conversation analytic research repeatedly shows that turns at talk are invariably connected in significant ways to prior turns. Turns in interaction are designed with respect to the activities performed by prior turns. This is true of talk in semi-structured interviews as it is of everyday interaction.

Focusing solely on the respondent's turns, as if they were produced in a social vacuum, divorced from and immune to interactional contingencies, can limit our appreciation of the nature of those materials which constitute the data for empirical research. To flesh out this claim, we will consider some sections of the Smith and

Osborn data. In extract (11) below, the speaker, M. is describing how her pain effects her behaviour. (Smith and Osborn's analytic notations have been deleted.)

(11)
M. Since it started getting bad, I was always snappy with it but not
like this, it's not who I am it's just who I am if you know what I
mean, it's not really me, I get like that and I know like, you're being
mean now but I can't help it. It's the pain, it's me, but it is me, me
doing it but not me do you understand what I'm saying, if I was to
describe myself like you said, I'm a nice person, but then I'm not am
I, and there's other stuff, stuff I haven't told you, if you knew you'd
be disgusted I just get so hateful
Int. When you talk about you and then sometimes not you, what do you mean?

The speaker's turn covers a lot of topics: the onset of her short temper, her feeling that the pain changes her, her inability to control these changes, her reflections on the kind of person the pain makes her become, the tension between that person and her 'true' self, references to other events or behaviours which she is reluctant to disclose, and so on.

The interviewer's next question is 'When you talk about you and then sometimes not you, what do you mean?'. This is clearly 'touched off' by the speaker's prior turn: the question is prefaced with a direct reference to the prior turn ('When you talk about ...') and goes on to develop one aspect raised by the speaker. But the speaker raised many issues which the interviewer could have topicalized, but did not. Some form of selection has occurred.

This kind of selectivity is similar to a phenomenon identified by Heritage and Watson (1979). They explored the ways in which news interviewers formulate the gist, upshot or relevance of the interviewee's utterances in subsequent questions. For example, the following extract is taken from a face-to-face interview with a winner of a 'Slimmer of the Year' competition, which was broadcast on the radio.

(12) (IE = interviewee; IR = interviewer.)
  1   IE: You have a shell that for so long
  2   protects you but sometimes
  3   things creep through the shell
  4   and then you become really aware
  5   of how awful you feel. I never
  6   ever felt my age or looked my age
  7   I was always older – people took me
  8   for older. And when I was at college
  9   I think I looked a matronly fifty.
 10   And I was completely alone one weekend
 11   and I got to this stage where I
 12   almost jumped in the river.
 13   I just felt life wasn't worth it any
 14   more – it hadn't anything to offer
 15   and if this was living
 16   I'd had enough.
 17   IR: You really were prepared to commit

```
18        suicide because you were
19        a big fatty
20    I   Yes because I – I just didn't
21        see anything in life that I had
22        to look forward to ...
```
(Heritage and Watson 1979: 132)

The interviewer's phrase 'a big fatty' preserves the essential aspects of the interviewee's prior utterances – her weight problem. But it also transforms that topic: the phrase 'a big fatty' trivializes the speaker's obesity. This in turn establishes an inauspicious sequential context for the speaker: she can either try to redress the trivialization accomplished by 'a big fatty' (as she does here), and risk appearing pedantic or self-important, or she can expand upon her suicidal feelings knowing that they may now be heard by the radio audience as an unwarranted response to what is a trivial problem. And in this sense, the interviewer's question and the speaker's response are interactionally generated objects.

In extract (13), the interviewer's question 'When you talk about you and then sometimes not you, what do you mean?' performs three operations on M's prior talk (Heritage and Watson 1979): it deletes a range of issues from the prior turn; it preserves one topic of the prior turn; and finally, it transforms that topic – the distinction between 'you and not you' is not offered in terms of unpleasant behaviour caused by constant pain, but is portrayed as an intrapersonal tension independent of such sensitive issues. This in turn establishes a particular kind of sequential context for the respondent's next utterance.

(13)   Int. When you talk about you and then sometimes not you, what do you mean?

M. I'm not me these days, I am sometimes, I am all right, but then I get this mean bit, the hateful bit, that's not me.

The design of the speaker's response seems to be shaped by the design of the prior question. She again raises the intrapsychic tensions and personality changes, but these are not depicted in relation to constant pain. The speaker has preserved the orientation of the prior question, which in turn was built to delete references to pain as a causal agent. Recall that M's turn in extract (13) was identified as exhibiting the following theme 'Unwanted self rejected as true self'. We do not wish to question the validity of this categorization, but we do want to indicate that the utterance so categorized is not an unfettered representation of the speaker's worldview. Rather, is an interactional object, the properties of which are demonstrably shaped by its location in a particular sequence of turns.

The interactional basis for utterance construction is also evident in this sequence.

(14)
M. I'm not me these days, I am sometimes, I am all right, but then I get this mean bit, the hateful bit, that's not me.

Int. What's that bit?

M. I dunno, that's the pain bit, I know you're gonna say it's all me,

but I can't help it even though I don't like it. It's the mean me, my
mean head all sour and horrible, I can't cope with that bit, I cope with
the pain better.

The interviewer's question 'What's that bit?' refers to the speaker's 'I get this mean bit, the hateful bit'. While it preserves a focus on the speaker's self-concept, it is exquisitely designed to neutralize the more explicitly negative features of the previous self-characterization, that is, as only 'a bit', while at the same time maintaing the interviewer's interest in the interviewee's troubles.

What we have tried to demonstrate in this section is that it is important to consider the interviewer's contribution to the interaction which ultimately generates the data for qualitative analysis. In the extract from Smith and Osborn's paper, the analytic focus was on the respondent's utterances. But there was no account of how these utterances were shaped by the interviewer's questions, and there was no investigation of how those questions built on the speaker's previous answers. Yet it is clear that her contributions – the data for subsequent analysis – are not 'stand alone' reports which can be mined to expose deeper meanings or perceptions. This is not to say that Smith and Osborn's analytic categorizations of the themes in the respondent's discourse are inappropriate or unwarranted. But it does suggest that the utterances they are categorizing are, in a significant sense, products of the interaction.

The analysis of themes versus the analysis of actions

Social scientists tend to treat respondents' discourse in research interviews as a medium for the transmission of information, or as a mere reflection of either overarching sociological variables or underlying frameworks of meaning. In these traditions, the kinds of respondents' discourse which is generated in research interviews – descriptions, accounts, narratives, and so on – are basically regarded as discursive moments which passively convey meaning. The analyst's task is to identify this meaning and incorporate it into a broader social scientific story. However, there is a substantial body of research which indicates that utterances are not simply inert vehicles for the exchange of meaningful information. Turns at talk – including turns in interview talk – are designed to perform specific kinds of action to achieve particular interactional ends, and are designed for the specific recipient or audience they target. If we ignore the action-orientation of utterances, analytic claims may be premised on an incomplete or partial understanding of the data. To illustrate these issues, it is useful to compare two different treatments of the same linguistic practice.

In Smith and Osborn's data, there is the following question–answer sequence:

Int. What's that bit?
M. I dunno, that's the pain bit,

The speaker's answer turn begins with 'I dunno', which appears to be a verbalized 'shrug of the shoulders', a simple claim that she lacks knowledge to speak on this matter. Despite this, she does then go on to answer the question, expanding on what 'that bit' means.

Smith and Osborn offer an analytic categorization of this section of M's turn: 'Attribution of unwanted self to the pain'. This illustrates a common feature of social science approaches to interview data: to overlook the details of utterances (in this case, 'I dunno') in favour of trying to identify more general properties of the subtle and fluid ways in which people make sense of their lives. This description is intended to capture an aspect of the speaker's cognition which is taken to be reflected in her utterance. For conversation analysts, on the other hand, such details are functionally or interactionally significant and therefore worthy of analytic consideration. Let us consider, for example, a CA approach to 'I dunno' self-reports.

Edwards (1995) and Potter (1997) have argued that 'I dunno' formulations do not simply represent the status of the speaker's knowledge. Drawing from CA's focus on the actions performed by utterances, Potter (1997) has argued that these are used by speakers to display their lack of interest in, or distance from, claims, opinions or descriptions which are in some way sensitive, or which may be taken as the basis for sceptical or negative assessment. Potter (1997) illustrates some of the work being done by 'I dunno' formulations by examining instances from a now famous interview between a television journalist, Martin Bashir and Diana, Princess of Wales, shown on British television. Some years earlier Diana's husband, Prince Charles, had given a television interview in which he admitted infidelity, and it was widely believed that relations between the couple were frosty. Subsequently, a biography of Diana, written by Andrew Morton, portrayed Diana in a sympathetic light. This book, and Diana's complicity in its writing, was regarded as a way of getting back at Prince Charles.

During the interview, Bashir raises Diana's motivation for her involvement in the writing of Morton's book.

(15)
Bashir:	Did you (.) allow your ↑friends, >your close friends,<
	to speak to Andrew °Morton°
Diana:	Yes I did. Y[es I did
Bashir:	[°Why°?
Diana:	I was (.) at the end of my tether (.)
	I was (.) desperate (.)
	>I think I was so fed up with being< (.)
	seen as someone who was a ba:sket case (.)
	because I am a very strong person (.)
	and I know (.) that causes complications (.)
	in the system (.) that I live in.
	(1) ((Diana smiles and purses lips))
Bashir:	How would a book change that.
Diana:	I↑dunno. ((raises eyebrows, looks away))
	Maybe people have a better understanding (.)
	maybe there's a lot of women out there
	who suffer (.) on the same level

but in a different environment (.)
who are unable to: (.) stand up for themselves (.)
because (.) their self esteem is (.) cut in two.
I dunno ((shakes head))
(Potter 1997: 151)

Bashir is questioning Diana's motives for her implicit consent for the book. She acknowledges that she was unhappy with how she felt she had been portrayed. She also suggests that the expectations about how members of the Royal Family should conduct themselves, as defined by the monarchy, clashed with her personality. Bashir then asks her 'How would a book change that.'

At this point, Diana's involvement in the book is a sensitive matter. Its credibility as an accurate account of her mistreatment by the Royal Family would be at issue if it were to become apparent that it was motivated by revenge or spite. Her answer is prefaced by 'I dunno': this portrays Diana's lack of interest or concern for the possible impact of the book on her own domestic situation. She then goes on to suggest that the book may help other women who are burdened by expectations and responsibilities, thus portraying altruistic motives for the book. Finally she closes her account with another 'I dunno'.

These 'I dunno' formulations open and close a turn in which Diana has to address her own involvement in the production of Morton's book and its anticipated consequences. Potter argues that they allow her to manage a range of potentially unsympathetic inferences: that she was motivated to cause embarrassment for her husband and the Royal Family; that she was driven by revenge, and so on. 'I dunno', then, does a specific kind of work in talk-in-interaction. It is not a simple representation of knowledge, uncertainty, or any other cognitive state.

'I dunno' formulations also occurred in the semi-structured interview data we collected as part of our study of youth subcultures (Widdicombe and Wooffitt 1995). The initial question in the interview was designed as an indirect attempt to get the respondents to identify themselves in terms of particular subcultural group categories: punk, goth and so on. (This was because the interviews were initially undertaken as part of a more traditional social psychology project in which it was necessary to establish the respondents' subcultural affiliations without explicitly presenting them with relevant category terms.) However, it soon became apparent that some of our respondents demurred from offering a subcultural self-identification. It was striking that 'I dunno' formulations were a component feature of the different ways in which this resistance could be managed.

To illustrate, consider extract (16), below.

(16) ((Tape starts: respondents talking to each other about Princess Anne for approximately 12 seconds.))
1   I: can you tell me something about your style and the way
2   you look,
3   (0.7)
4   I: how would you descri:be yourselves

```
5            (0.7)
6     R1:    °hhhh°
             (.7)
8     R1:    I dunno >I hate those sorts of quest[ions uhm
9     R2:                                        [yeah horrible
10           isn't it
```
(Widdicombe and Woofitt 1995: 96–97)

In this extract, the 'I dunno' formulation is a preface to the respondent's statement 'I hate those sorts of questions', which in turn constitutes a complaint about having to provide a characterization of herself. This is a clear resistance to the (tacit) invitation to provide a self-categorization in that it topicalizes the respondent's objections to precisely that kind of self-report.

The respondents in extract (16) were not the only ones who seemed unwilling to categorize themselves in terms of a subcultural label. In extract (17) (which comes from the same corpus of interviews), the second respondent (R2) provides an 'I dunno' formulation on behalf of him and his friend, and then uses another one to preface his claim that his distinctive appearance reflects his own personal taste, rather than a recognizable subcultural style.

(17)
```
8     I:     How would you descri:be the way you look,
             ((some lines omitted))
14    R1:    a*h huh [h
15    R2:            [Er::m:: (.3) we dunn[o
16    R1:                                 [>a good question<
17           (1.3)
18    R2:    ah dunno=ah jus'
19           (.4)
20    R2:    ah jus dress how I feel like dressin'
```
(Woofitt 2005: 123)

In the following extract (again from the same corpus) the respondent eventually acknowledges the relevance of a subcultural identification. However, this is managed very carefully. He does not endorse or provide a self-categorization; rather, he merely acknowledges that there is a consensus that his appearance would be described in terms of a particular subcultural identification. And, again, we find the turn in which this resistance is accomplished is prefaced by an 'I dunno' formulation.

(18)
```
1     I:     OKAy: can you tell me something about
2            yourself your style and that,
3     R:     er::m
4            (1.2)
5     R:     what sort've thing,
6            (.4)
7     I:     WEll how would you descri:be it.
```

```
 8   R:   erh:
 9        (1)
10   R:   ah dunno
11        (.7)
12   R:   most people describe it as punk ah suppose
```
(Wooffitt 2005: 123–124)

These extracts illustrate three methods by which respondents can avoid self-identification in terms of a subcultural category. First, respondents may complain:

'I dunno >I hate those sorts of questions'

Second, they may assert that their (subculturally implicative) dress and appearance is a reflection of personal preference:

'ah dunno=ah jus'(.4) ah jus' dress how I feel like dressin'

Third, the relevant subcultural label may be portrayed as someone else's description:

'ah dunno (.7) most people describe it as punk ah suppose'

These 'I dunno' formulations address a delicate issue in that they are designed to address what could be perceived as a challenge formulated by the question to which they respond. The interview respondents had a distinctive appearance (indeed, this was the basis upon which they were selected for interview). Thus the question about how they described themselves may be heard as a challenge: either the interviewer has failed to recognize the relevant subcultural identity implied by their appearance (thus suggesting that they were not appropriately or sufficiently dressed to establish their affiliation), or the interviewer is implicitly questioning their subcultural affiliation. So the very posing of the question implies a (mildly) confrontational stance and establishes an unpropitous context for asserting subcultural membership. The 'I dunno' formulations acknowledge this challenge in that they suggest that the self-identification which follows is provisional, or is perspectival, in that it reflects only the speaker's views. In this, these formulations display the speaker's recognition that the position he/she is taking may be disputed by the recipient he/she is currently addressing. As such, they have defensive orientation. (We are very grateful to Geoff Raymond for these observations.)

These observations suggest that 'I dunno' formulations and the turns they preface should not be overlooked or automatically be treated as a thematic reflection of the speaker's underlying perceptions, but should be examined as activities. They do not reflect mental states; they perform social actions. They are a resource through which speakers can handle a range of inferentially delicate issues. Moreover, what comes after 'I dunno' may be an attempt to manage what is taken to be the position (or inner state) of the recipient.

Summary and conclusion

In this chapter, we have noted that interviews are central in social science research. They have therefore received much attention in methodology textbooks. In general, however, there is a failure to appreciate that interviews are interactional occasions conducted through language, and that certain features of talk-in-interaction have consequences both for the interview itself and for the nature of the data thereby collected. Using a CA approach, which draws explicit attention to these features, we have shown that interviews, like conversations, proceed via particular conventional expectations. We have also shown that the products of an interview (the data that constitute the basis for any subsequent findings) are interactionally or jointly produced within the turn-by-turn flow of the interview. Finally, we have shown that the details of interview utterances can be analysed as actions.

Nevertheless, these features of talk-in-interviews are overlooked to varying degrees by researchers using different interview formats. The standardizing requirements of structured or survey interviews, for example, breach normative expectations and their interactional and action-oriented aspects are not represented in the quantitative or statistical treatment of the data. Semi-structured interviews may fare better. Their conduct may adhere more closely (never completely of course) to normative conventions of conversation, but the subsequent analysis may ignore their basis in interaction. Thus, accounts generated in interviews may be regarded merely as a reflection of inner experiences or states, not jointly and functionally produced. Similar comments could be levelled at instances of unstructured, focused individual or group interviews.

To conclude, we summarize below some implications and draw out benefits that may be accrued by applying CA to interviews.

- In this chapter, we have begun to use CA to examine extracts from interview data in order to show that interviews are interaction. Nevertheless, the properties of interaction in research interviews need to be understood more fully. Until then, we have an incomplete appreciation of perhaps the most significant method of qualitative data collection in the social sciences. Further conversation analyses of interview data could therefore be undertaken.
- Data from social research interviews – whether in the form of factual statements recorded on a pre-written questionnaire, or accounts and narratives generated in semi-structured or unstructured encounters – are products of social interaction. For example, take the semi-structured interview. We have argued that the respondents' utterances are shaped by, and oriented to, the interactional context. This in turn invites us to give serious consideration to the ways in which the interviewer's participation is significantly implicated in what the respondents ends up saying, and how they say it. Moreover, it suggests that it is important to include the interviewer's turns when using data from interviews in research papers. Offering only the respondent's utterances, which is the conventional practice in most social science articles, means that readers are not permitted to inspect those interactional contingencies which informed the character of those data they are being asked to consider.

- Talk-in-interaction is social action. An appreciation of the interactionally grounded, action-orientation of an utterance may act as a safeguard against hasty or premature interpretation of its relevance in terms of wider sociological categories, or its reflection of underlying psychological mechanisms. Utterances may exhibit particular properties not because they convey some form of meaningful information which the analyst can identify and interpret, but because they have been designed to perform sequentially relevant actions.

- Our argument, that utterances need to be understood in the first instance as activities, might be taken to imply that we reject other analytic perspectives on qualitative interview data, such as those which seek to develop a more thematic analysis. This is not the case. We do think it is important for analysts of all methodological persuasions to be aware of the interactional nature of their data. Equally, however, we think it would be fruitful to see how a CA focus on activities in talk could be harnessed to methodologies which seek to explore more meaningful dimensions of human experience. In some of the data we have examined in this chapter it is apparent that issues to do with self and identity, responsibility and agency, how others may interpret our actions and the inferences they may subsequently draw about us, are all matters which are handled in the turn-by-turn production of activities in interaction. Engagement with the wider meaningful dimensions of human experience is thus embedded in the very fabric of interaction and its products. In this sense, attempts to understand the deeper significance of dimensions of human experience can be enriched by attention to the interactional organization of communication.

CHAPTER FOUR

Analysing Interaction in Focus Groups

Sue Wilkinson

Since the early 1990s, focus groups have gained steadily in popularity as a social science research method, and they are now also thoroughly familiar to the general public in the contexts of political polling and market research. First invented in the 1920s by Emory Bogardus (to test his 'social distance' scale), and subsequently developed in the 1940s by Robert Merton and colleagues to study audience response to radio programmes, focus groups are now used across a wide range of social science disciplines, particularly sociology, social psychology, education, communication and media studies, and health research (see Morgan 1996; Wilkinson 1998a, 1998b for reviews). One researcher describes them as having captured 'the sociological imagination' (Johnson 1996). I have used focus groups extensively in my own research on breast cancer (e.g. Wilkinson 2000, 2005), upon which I will draw in the second half of this chapter.

A brief introduction to focus groups

Focus groups may take many forms but essentially the technique involves engaging a small number of people (usually 4–8) in an informal group discussion 'focused' around a particular topic or set of issues. Typically, the 'focus' of the group discussion relates to the interests or experiences of the group members: for example, young women talking about sexual negotiation, residents of an inner-city housing estate talking about local crime, or diabetes sufferers talking about managing eating regimes. The discussion is usually based on a series of questions (the focus group 'schedule') and the researcher generally acts as a 'moderator' for the group: posing the questions, facilitating the discussion, and keeping it broadly on track. The focus group discussion is usually recorded, the data transcribed, and then analysed using conventional techniques for qualitative data – most commonly content or thematic analysis. Focus groups are distinctive, then, for the method of data *collection* entailed (i.e. informal group discussion), rather than the method of data *analysis*.

There are many variations on this basic data collection procedure (see Kitzinger 1990; Krueger 1994) – indeed, the flexibility of the method is one of its strengths. For example, a focus group project may involve a single group of participants or many groups, and they may meet once or on a number of occasions. The participants may already know each other (e.g. as friends, co-workers or family members), or they may be brought together specifically for the research, perhaps as representatives of particular populations (e.g. rural or urban dwellers, parents of young children, or recipients of different kinds of medical treatment). In addition to, or instead of, discussing particular questions, participants may be given written or visual materials to examine, or they may be asked to complete a task, such as a card-sorting or rating exercise. The moderator may be relatively directive or non-directive, and may participate in the discussion or remain detached from it; groups may even be run without a moderator present, or without co-present members (so-called 'virtual focus groups': see Bloor et al. 2001: Chapter 5). The proceedings may be audio- or video-recorded, with or without accompanying field-notes; and subsequent data transcription may be more or less detailed (or occasionally not undertaken at all). A good way to get a sense of the range of different ways in which the method has been used in social science is to look through one of the many edited collections of focus group research (e.g. Barbour and Kitzinger 1999; Morgan 1993).

There is plenty of advice available on the practical aspects of conducting focus groups, including a number of comprehensive 'handbooks', which deal with everything from the recruitment of participants, through planning and preparation, to running the focus group itself (e.g. Fern 2001; Morgan 1997; Morgan and Krueger 1998). Particular emphasis is placed on effective moderation techniques, including what one researcher calls 'pest control' (Wells 1974), that is, dealing with participants who are considered to present particular 'challenges' for the moderator, such as those who talk 'off topic', 'too much' or 'too little':

> Shy and reflective participants often have great insights, but it takes extra effort to get them to elaborate their views. If possible, the moderator should place shy respondents directly across the table to maximize eye contact. Eye contact often provides sufficient encouragement to speak, and if all else fails, the moderator can call on them by name. 'Tom, I don't want to leave you out of the conversation. What do you think?' (Krueger and Casey 2000: 111–12).

Another researcher offers 'tips on controlling focus group cross talk', suggesting that the moderator deals with occasions 'when more than one respondent speaks at a time, or when respondents interrupt each other' by saying things like 'Shhh! Shhh! One at a time, please' or 'Sally, can you hold onto your thought until Jane finishes' (Tudor 1995: 106). In this chapter, rather than offering still more 'how to' recommendations based on my own experience of focus group research (see Wilkinson 2003a, 2003b for this), my main concern will be the *analysis* of focus group data, which is relatively under-discussed in the (now voluminous) focus group literature, apart from techniques of 'data management' (such as coding and indexing through programs such as NUD.IST or THE ETHNOGRAPH).

The neglect of interaction

Focus groups are *not* simply group interviews, in the sense that the moderator does not ask questions of each participant in turn, but, rather, seeks to facilitate group discussion, actively encouraging group members to interact with *each other*. The dynamic quality of group interaction, as participants discuss, debate, and (sometimes) disagree about key issues, is generally a striking feature of focus groups, which, at times, may have 'the feel of rap sessions with friends' (Jarrett 1993: 194). Although interaction between focus group participants is sometimes viewed as a 'problem', either for the moderator (hence the kind of 'people management' advice quoted above) or for the analyst (insofar as individual responses are taken to be 'contaminated' by what is termed 'the group effect': see Carey and Smith 1994), more commonly it is seen as a distinctive strength of the method. Group interaction has been described as the 'hallmark' of focus groups (Morgan 1997: 2), and focus group researchers often describe it as the major advantage of the technique over one-to-one interviews and ethnographic observation (e.g. Kissling 1996; Stewart and Shamdasani 1990). In particular, they stress the potential of group interaction for generating unexpected insights:

> ... this is one place where focus groups shine. Through group interaction, we learn that something we hadn't noticed before is a significant issue. ... From the way the group takes up the topic, it is clear that something significant is going on, something significant to them. (Agar and MacDonald 1995: 80)

Given the emphasis on interaction, it is astonishing to find that, when it comes to *analysis*, it is largely absent. A 1994 review of more than 40 published reports of focus group studies 'could not find a single one concentrating on the conversation between participants and very few that even included any quotations from more than one participant at a time' (J. Kitzinger 1994: 104). A few years later, my own reviews of the literature (Wilkinson, 1998b, 1999) of well over 200 studies produced substantially the same result, (although there are a few, more recent, exceptions: see below). Focus group data are most commonly presented as if they were one-to-one interview data, with interactions between group participants rarely reported, let alone analysed. Indeed, in projects which use both one-to-one interviews and focus groups, there is often no indication of which quoted extracts are derived from which source (e.g. Espin 1995; Press 1991). Where interactions between focus group participants *are* quoted, they are typically either not analysed at all, or analysed solely at the level of *content*, rather than in terms of their *interactional* features.

The most common way of analysing focus group data is through content and/or thematic analysis (e.g. see Wilkinson 2003a, 2003b). The two are not clearly differentiable, (although content analysis may sometimes include quantification, and thematic analysis may involve more extensive quotation of the data. Essentially, this kind of approach entails coding focus group participants' talk (more or less systematically) into categories in order to summarize its content. The unit of analysis to be coded may be small and clearly specified, such as 'mentions' of risk factors related to heart attacks (Morgan and Spanish 1984) or 'beliefs' about the sources of AIDS (Flaskerud and Rush 1989), or it may be a broader, less defined 'theme', such as 'quality of life issues' for breast cancer survivors (Wyatt et al. 1993) or 'social service concerns' among women infected with HIV (Seals et al. 1995). Although the majority of focus group studies using content or thematic analysis present direct – and often extensive – quotations from participants to illustrate their analytic categories/themes, virtually *all* of the data quoted comes from *individuals* and very little of it is interactional in nature. The argument I will be making here is not only that an analytic opportunity (to make a great deal more of their data than they typically do) is being missed by the many focus group researchers who do not focus on interaction, but that *not* to focus on the interaction is to risk a misleading analysis. This has (sometimes) been recognized in the 'advice' literature. For example, Carey and Smith (1994: 125) warn that focus group researchers who 'do not attend to the impact of the group setting will incompletely or inappropriately analyze their data'. However, it does not appear more generally to have informed analytic practice.

Beginning to analyse interaction

Of course, there are exceptions. Some focus group researchers *do* quote interactions, although they do not always analyse them. When analysis *is* undertaken, this most commonly looks – in a fairly 'broad-brush' way – at agreement and/or disagreement between participants. For example, analysts focus on how the interaction reveals participants' 'shared perception' (J. Kitzinger 1994: 108), 'similar circumstances' (Lyons and Meade 1993: 34) or 'things known in common' (Agar and MacDonald 1995: 83). The following interaction from a focus group of African-American parents – in which, according to the authors, participants 'recognize' their 'shared experiences' – is used to illustrate 'the translation of common knowledge displayed by individuals into shared knowledge elaborated consensually' (Hughes and DuMont 1993: 794–5):

M: Have you ever experienced racism or prejudice at your workplace?
R1:   No, not in the workplace. I have experienced it elsewhere though.
M: Where else? Where at?
R1:   I was stopped ... I went into the service at 19 and by 21 I had me
    a car that was fairly brand new, about a year old. I was always
    pulled over by the cops. I was young, I was black, and I was in
    a poor neighbourhood, South Bronx, with a car. And I guess they
    pulled me over – I know they pulled me over – cause they know I
    didn't make this by earning it, you know. Why they pulled me
    over was: 'this guy dealing drugs or he know somebody but he
    stole this car.'
R2:   [If you're white] You're allowed to have a car. They pulled over
    Branford Marsalis with his BMW.

R3:   Right!
R4:   I was riding with a girl who was white and the cop stopped me. I
        had a new car. He wanted the registration and insurance and
        everything else. I said, 'Well, what's the problem? Why did you
        stop me?'
R3:   [Me], my father and a white kid one time going down town. The
        cops pull us over. Spread eagle ... the whole nines. He [father]
        said, like, 'What's this all about?' [The police said] 'Uh, we
        got a report. Two black guys and a white guy robbed.'
R5:   I was frisked up. I was in the car with my mom before and they
        like, you know, I just had problems.
R6:   Yeah, I've experienced that. Now what's the problem officer?
        'We just got a report ...'
R3:   Yeah!
R1:   That's part of being a black man in NYC.
R4:   Right!

Focus group researchers have also commented on the role of explicit challenge and disagreement in provoking the development and elaboration of accounts. In the AIDS Media Research project, which ran focus groups based on pre-existing social groups (e.g. colleagues, friends), participants often challenged each other on contradictions between what they *claimed* to believe and how they actually behaved: for example, 'How about that time you didn't use a glove while taking blood from a patient?', 'What about the other night when you went off with that boy at the disco?' (J. Kitzinger, 1994: 105). Challenges like these, in forcing people to defend or justify their actions or beliefs, often lead to the production of more elaborated accounts. This process can be seen in another AIDS-related study, with Australian schoolchildren (Houghton et al. 1995). In the following extract, three 14-year-olds are discussing the likelihood of contracting AIDS through being tattooed (although the authors themselves do not analyse this interaction):

Child 1:   Unlikely to get AIDS
Child 2:   AIDS is possible if you share needles
Child 1:   Yes, but you would have to share the needles very
            quickly 'cause AIDS virus is volatile and dies
            within seconds when it gets out of the body
Child 2:   Yes, but still possible
Child 3:   Yes, but you wouldn't just tattoo someone and then
            just switch over very quickly. The only thing
            possible, not in any professional tattooing studios,
            but in any amateur or backyard tattoo and they are
            doing friends or something like that, there would be
            a chance – they just use compasses.
(Houghton et al. 1995: 977)

In these examples – and the more extended ones from my own data which follow – the researchers' interest is primarily in the contribution an interactional analysis can make to an understanding of the topic under study (African-American parents' 'norms, values and experiences'; schoolchildren's awareness of the risks of tattooing; women's experience of breast cancer) – how they talk about it and how it affects their lives. However, in each of these projects, the researchers do not assume that focus group participants simply bring along a set of ready-made views to a focus group discussion, and put them on the table. Rather, in presenting interactional data, they show that 'values', 'beliefs', 'attitudes' or 'opinions' are not (as traditional opinion polls assume) inside individuals' heads, but, instead are actively *constructed* in interactions with others. 'Interactions', say Waterton and Wynne (1999: 136), 'are not just a neutral medium through which intrinsic preferences and values are expressed, but are themselves a substantive part of the *formation* of values and attitudes' (their emphasis). Similarly, in telling about an experience we have had, we do not simply recount one definitive account of that experience, over and over, but we 'fit' the account to the particular context and particular recipients of the telling. 'Last night at the pub' becomes a very different event when described to a regular drinking companion who wasn't there or to parents the morning after, for example. Looked at this way, an analysis of interaction extends the researchers' understanding of the topic they are investigating – although it also changes the nature of that understanding, making it contextually-dependent and much more specific.

There is also an emerging tradition of interactionally focused research which, rather than using focus group methodology to study some topic of interest to the researcher (like AIDS risk perceptions), instead takes the focus group *itself* as the topic and asks what makes it work *as a focus group*. This approach entails analysing focus group interaction for what it can tell us about the specific processes of 'doing being a focus group moderator' (e.g. 'asking elaborate questions', Puchta and Potter 1999) or 'doing being a focus group participant' (e.g. 'displaying opinions', Myers, 1998). It is part of a tradition of social science research that 'treats opinions and attitudes rhetorically, as utterances produced in specific situations, rather than as attributes of subjects' (Myers and Macnaghten 1999: 185); and it involves applying work done in discursive psychology (e.g. Edwards and Potter 1992) and conversation analysis (e.g. Atkinson and Heritage 1984; Drew and Heritage 1992a) to provide an analysis of interaction that is much more 'fined-grained' than any I have outlined so far. Macnaghten and Myers (2004) provide a useful account of the contrast between this approach and the more traditional one described above.

Action-orientation and sequential context

I want to show how we can use conversation analysis (CA) to develop understandings of substantive areas of social life – understandings that go beyond the 'content' of a focus group discussion, and also beyond the 'mechanics' of focus group interaction *per se*. The key to this is the conversation analytic focus on talk (a) as a form of *action*, and (b) as dependent on its *sequential context* (see, for example, Heritage

1984b: Chapter 8). Here's what I mean by that. When we take part in any social interaction (including a focus group), we do not simply drop words at random into a vacuum. We produce talk in order to *do* something: to corroborate, to challenge, to boast, to tease, to emphasize our suffering (or to downplay it), and so on. More specifically, our contributions to a conversation are 'occasioned' by what has gone before – especially just before – as this provides the sequential context for our talk. Typically, we either *respond* to someone else's prior action (e.g. by *answering* a question that they have posed), or we *initiate* a sequence of action of our own (e.g. by *asking* them a question). By looking at what kinds of *action* turns at talk are designed to accomplish, and at how they are 'fitted' to their sequential context (i.e. what kinds of action they initiate or are responsive to), conversation analysis helps us understand why someone may have said that particular thing, in that particular way, at that particular point in the interaction ('Why that now?', see Schegloff and Sacks 1973).

We can begin to think in this way in relation to the interactional data I have already quoted – the extracts from the group of African-American parents (Hughes and DuMont 1993: 794–5); and the Australian schoolchildren discussing the AIDS risk posed by tattooing (Houghton et al, 1995: 977) – in each case taking the analysis beyond that offered by the authors.

For example, in the African-American parents' focus group, we can see how participant R1 tells a story in response to the moderator's initial question (having first checked out that it is acceptable to frame an answer in relation to a context other than the one specified, and having received a 'go ahead'). This is exactly the kind of story that might have been elicited in a one-to-one interview, and which might subsequently have led either to a 'follow-up' question from the interviewer, or to a 'next question' from the interview schedule. Here, however, in a focus group context, this elicited 'first story', in turn, touches off a series of 'second stories' from participants R2, R3, R4, R5 and R6 (all demonstrably related to the first one by their inclusion of being in a car stopped by the police, and/or being interrogated by the police). The interactional effect of these stories, piled up one upon another, is to build a strong sense of consensus – on the basis of reportedly shared and demonstrated-to-be-similar experiences. These interactants are collaborating in producing a series of corroborative stories,[1] providing a powerful, consensual display of the 'racism or prejudice' (in the moderator's words) they have experienced. R1's assertion 'That's part of being a black man in NYC' serves both to aggregate the individual tellings and to propose that (collectively) they typify the experience of anyone with this particular configuration of demographic characteristics. It also implies under-statement of the case, in claiming such experiences as just 'part' of being a black male New Yorker.

Looking similarly at the Australian children's focus group data, we can see how Child 1 initially offers the kind of risk assessment ('unlikely') that could have been recorded via a rating scale or in a structured interview – and this is probably all the information the researcher would have got. However, here, in a focus group context, it prompts a challenge from Child 2 (who suggests a circumstance in which contracting AIDS through tattooing is more likely). This challenge prompts the first speaker to defend her original assertion, and in so doing she offers additional information about her understanding of the AIDS virus. Child 2's subsequent defence of *her* position (as 'still possible') enables Child 3 to enter the discussion, developing the argument in terms of different risks in different contexts. Interactionally, her turn is a nifty one: she constructs it so as not directly to contradict either of the previous speakers. She aligns with Child 2 in her assessment that contracting AIDS is 'possible', but limits this assessment to the context of 'backyard' tattooing with compasses; and she aligns with Child 1 in dismissing the possibility of needle-sharing in professional tattooing studios, as unlikely to be 'very quick'. Child 3 is both managing disagreement and displaying her own knowledge of tattooing practices, as a warrant for her own stated assessment of the risks associated with tattooing.

Talking breast cancer: action-oriented, sequential analysis

For further examples of action-oriented, sequential analysis of talk, I turn now to my own current research: focus group discussions between women who have received a breast cancer diagnosis. These women were individually recruited through a symptomatic breast clinic at a general hospital in a city in the north of England, and attended a focus group, held in a university setting, on one occasion only. I ran 13 focus groups with a total of 77 women, aged 33–84, most within five years of diagnosis. Although they reported a wide variety of experiences during the course of their breast cancer 'careers', most had had surgery, often followed by a course of radiotherapy. The focus groups, which typically lasted for around two hours, were relatively unstructured; I used a topic guide, which included feelings when cancer was first suspected and/or first diagnosed, coping and support, effects on lives and relationships, and ideas about the causes of breast cancer (see Wilkinson 2000, 2005 for more details of the project). Here, I will concentrate on the women's talk about causes, focusing, in particular, on what an action-oriented, sequential analysis of talk can tell us that a content (or thematic) analysis would not.

Data extract (1) (below) involves three focus group participants : 'Freda', 'Doreen' and 'Gertie'. It opens with the question about causes that I (as moderator–SW) pose to the group and continues with Freda and Gertie's responses to this question:

(1)	BCP12: 30 (Tomatoes and plums)[2]	
1	SW:	D'you have any idea what <u>cau</u>sed your breast cancer.
2		((pause))
3		any of you.
4	Fre:	No– What <u>does</u> cause breast cancer do you think.
5		((pause))
6	SW:	What do you think it <u>might</u> be.
7	Ger:	((overlaps)) There's a lot of <u>stor</u>ies going about.
8		=I was once told that if you use them aluminium
9		pans that cause cancer. .hh I was also told
10		that if you– if you eat tomatoes and plums at

11		the same meal ((pause)) that–
12	Dor:	((laughs))
13	Ger:	((to Doreen)) Have you heard all these those things.
14	Dor:	((laughs)) No
15	Ger:	Now that's what I heard and–
16	Dor:	((laughs)) Mm
17	Ger:	Oh there's several things that if you listen to
18		people ((pause)) we::ll–
19	Dor:	Mm
20	SW:	((to Gertie, laughingly)) What else have they told you?
21	Ger:	Pardon?
22	SW:	((to Gertie, laughingly)) What else have they told you?
23	D/SW:	((laughter))
24	Ger:	I can't think off hand I knew a– I knew a lot that
25		I've heard over the years from people who've passed
26		on 'Oh yeah well that causes cancer'.
27	Dor:	Mm
28	Ger:	But I don't know but–
29	Dor:	((cuts in)) I mean uhm–
30	Ger:	Now I've no views on this ((To Doreen)) have you?
31	Dor:	No:- .hh The only thing is, I mean from my point of view
32		I-I don't know they say that ((pause)) they say that breast
33		feeding is supposed to ((pause)) uh:m tch give you some
34		protection.

A content analysis of the first part of this extract might code these women's responses according to the types of 'cause' they mention: perhaps putting Gertie's mention of 'aluminium pans' into a category labelled 'environmental factors', and her mention of 'eating tomatoes and plums at the same meal' into a category labelled 'dietary factors'. Freda's initial response (line 4) might well be coded into a 'don't know' category. However, an action-oriented, sequential analysis considers these responses to my initial question very differently, examining the local interactional context within which they occur. Talk about causes can be interactionally tricky, particularly when a presumed 'expert' is asking questions, or in settings in which potentially equally knowledgeable others might have different or even conflicting opinions. Conversation analysts (e.g. Sacks 1992: 340–7) have noted the asymmetry between being the first to express an opinion and being second – going first means you have to put your opinion on the line, whereas going second offers an opportunity either for agreement or for potential challenge. Consequently, speakers often try to avoid first position, and this is precisely what Freda does in response to the moderator's question: she declines to gives an opinion, and bounces the question right back to the moderator, as a 'counter' (Schegloff 1995: 7–10). It is not simply then, as a content analysis might suggest, that Freda 'doesn't know' what causes breast cancer: she is not here reporting a state of mind, but is engaged in a piece of local interactional business. Simply to code Freda's response within a 'don't know' category, without taking into account the sequential context within which it occurs, would be a clear example of 'incompletely or inappropriately' analysing focus group data through not attending to 'the impact of the group setting' (Carey and Smith 1994: 125).

As moderator, I avoid answering Freda's direct question: instead I reformulate it (in the manner typically recommended for interviewers and focus group moderators), making clear I am interested in what the participants themselves 'think it *might* be' (line 6), rather than in any purported 'actual' (i.e. scientific) causes of breast cancer. It is with this reassurance that Gertie offers some 'stories' (i.e. folk wisdom, labelled as such), thereby putting herself in the vulnerable first speaking position, and attracting just the kind of second speaker disagreement that Freda's counter enabled her to avoid: Doreen, the third member of the group, *laughs* at Gertie's response. Within a typical content analytic framework, Gertie's references to 'stories', and to what she has 'heard over the years', would be taken as transparent reports of the *source* of her ideas about cause: that is as indicating a reliance on folk knowledge[3]. Within a conversation analytic framework, emphasizing the sequential position of Gertie's response, this attribution of ideas about cause to folk knowledge is seen as an *interactional device* seeking to protect the speaker from challenge (although, here, it fails to avert ridicule).

Gertie's candidate causes, then, are presented as 'stories'. However, only moments later, even these 'stories' are retracted. By the end of Doreen and Gertie's subsequent exchange (at line 30), Gertie, like Freda before her, is claiming to have 'no views' on the causes of breast cancer. Again (within this framework), this is not simply a straightforward report of a cognitive state: it arises out of the interactional sequence within which it is embedded, in the course of which both Doreen and the moderator have implied, through their laughter, that Gertie's candidate causes are rather implausible. Indeed, the moderator's probe (line 20) can be heard as 'positioning' (Wilkinson and Kitzinger 2003) Gertie as the sort of gullible person who believes anything she is told. Gertie responds first by reminding everyone that she is not reporting her own views, but those of others, and then she flatly refuses to offer further candidate answers, explicitly handing the floor to Doreen (at line 30) – and it is some time before she re-enters the conversation.

Note the care with which Doreen begins to craft her subsequent entry into the discussion. She also denies having 'views' on the causes of cancer ('No', line 31), then replaces what was on the way to a statement of her own 'point of view' with the generalized attribution 'they say'. Her referent is (deliberately) unclear: 'they' could be people in general, or 'experts' such as members of the medical profession. Either way, she clearly labels the views she is about to present as not her own. This kind of distancing is common across my focus groups. For example, a little later in this focus group Freda says 'sometimes I've heard that knocks can bring one on', and Doreen responds 'I'd heard that from somebody else'. In another group, one woman responds to another's description of 'catching' her breast while 'putting a big tray in the steamer' with the (hearably sceptical) 'they always say that a knock starts it off don't they'.

When Gertie does re-enter the conversation we have been looking at, it is to suggest a different candidate cause for cancer: the idea that cancer is 'dormant' until woken. Remember that her earlier suggestions were laughed at; now she attends to the risk of this happening again by painstakingly constructing the 'dormant cancer' theory as the opinion of a specified medical expert[4] – a doctor at the hospital where most of these women will have received treatment. She distances herself from this opinion still further by having the events reported happen 20 years before (if necessary, she could, of course, claim that medical opinion might well have changed) and by positioning someone else – her sister – as the original recipient of his theory (if necessary, she could, of course, cast doubts on the accuracy of her sister's reporting):

```
(2)   SW: BCP12: 31 (Dormant cancer)
  1    Ger:   My sister was a nurse ((pause)) wa:y back in the
  2             1920s she ((indistinct)). A:nd she–she was at what
  3             is Springfield General now.=She did her training
  4             there and there was a doctor Patterson at the time
  5             .hh who used to lecture to the nurses. .hh And
  6             he told them nurses in his lectures that .hh
  7             everybody ((pause)) has a cancer.
  8             ((pause))
  9             .hh and ((pause)) it's a case of whether it
 10             lays dormant
```

Again, within this kind of interactional framework, the attribution of views to others does not offer a 'transparent' window on to what Gertie 'believes', nor does it indicate that the 'source' of her information is the medical profession. Gertie is not simply repeating what her sister may or may not have told her Dr Patterson had said. Rather, her attribution of the 'dormant cancer' theory to a medical 'expert' is a conversational resource for managing the delicate interactional business of presenting an opinion without attracting scepticism or – still worse – ridicule.

Through the use of an action-oriented, sequential analysis, then, we can see how the purported views of medical professionals are invoked, in the face of (actual or potential) scepticism, as in Gertie's presentation of the 'dormant cancer' theory above, or as a defence in the face of outright challenge, as in the following exchange between 'Marina' and 'Bella' (two participants in another focus group). Again (as moderator), I ask the group about the possible causes of breast cancer (although here, one participant has already presented her views):

```
(3)   SW: BCP1: 22 (Stress)
  1    SW:    Has anyone else got any ideas as to what may
  2             have– ((pause)) have cau:sed it.
  3             ((pause))
  4    ():    I don't kno:w.
  5    Mar:   Stress:.
  6    ():    ((overlaps)) (don't know.)
  7             ((1.2 sec pause))
  8    Mar:   Stress caused cancer.
  9             ((1.0 sec pause))
 10    Mar:   Stress caused diabetes. My husband caused
 11             my diabetes
```

12		((pause))
13	Mar:	because he was thr– str<u>ess</u> (.) through stress.
14		((0.8 sec pause))
15	Mar:	So I think that uh:m ((pause))
16	Bel:	That's what <u>you</u> blame.
17	Mar:	<u>Yes</u>:.=Well not only <u>me</u>: the doctors as well.

Here, Marina's assertion that stress caused her cancer is in trouble right from the outset: it is met with silence from the other focus group participants (line 7). Silence very often signals upcoming disagreement (Pomerantz 1984; Sacks, 1973) – and here we have a very unusual degree of silence (one second is the normal maximum in conversation), and one which re-occurs after each of Marina's next three turns (i.e. at lines 9, 12 and 14). It is also unusual that no one else elects to speak across so many turns (Sacks et al. 1974). When Bella eventually comes in, it is with a direct challenge to Marina (note the heavy stress on '*you*'), and Marina is quick to enlist medical opinion ('the doctors') in defence of her views.

Through using the techniques of CA to analyse these stretches of interaction, then, we have seen how, in interactionally tricky situations (such as talking about causes), speakers may decline to give an opinion, or distance themselves from an opinion by using a generalized attribution such as 'they say' or 'I've heard'. We have also seen how the purported views of medical professionals may be invoked in the face of potential scepticism (as in Gertie's presentation of the 'dormant cancer' theory), or as a defence in the face of outright challenge (as in Marina's assertion that 'the doctors' also believe her cancer was caused by stress). In each of these examples, an action-oriented, sequential analysis has shown us why the speaker said *that* particular thing, in *that* particular way, at *that* particular point in the interaction ('Why that now?').

Conclusion

In this chapter, my discussion of focus groups has highlighted their quintessentially *interactional* nature. Devotees of this method commonly note that the potential of focus groups lies in 'the explicit use of group interaction to produce data and insights that would be less accessible without the interaction found in the group' (Morgan 1997: 2). Yet the methods of analysis they typically use do not seem suited to realizing this potential. Interactions between focus group participants are too frequently reported, and generally rather sketchily analysed (if at all). The (over)use of content and thematic analysis has, at best, often produced impoverished analyses and, at worst, sometimes generated misleading analyses.

I have advocated a much more serious and sustained analytic focus on interaction in focus groups than has hitherto been the case, based on the theoretical position that 'cognitions' and 'experiences' are constructed by and through talk, and that talk is designed for specific recipients, within specific local interactional contexts. In particular, I have argued that the techniques of conversation analysis – as an approach which considers talk as a form of action, dependent on its sequential context – can offer major insights into substantive areas of social life, insights which are simply not accessible through other analytic techniques. I have attempted to support this claim through the brief examples of analysis I have presented here. In my view, conversation analysis offers a method *par excellence* for analysing interaction in focus groups and deserves to be much more widely used in this methodological context.

Notes

1. Much more could, of course, be made of the design of the individual tellings, and of the way in which each is built off the prior, and off the series so far. For example, note that R6 uses the term 'officer' to refer to the police, whereas R1, R4 and R3 have used 'cop'. Jefferson (1974) comments on the interactional work that may be done by the selection of one or other of these reference terms.
2. A note on transcription: You will see that transcription of the data extracts presented in this chapter is more or less detailed, depending on the source from which they are drawn and the purpose for which they were (originally) transcribed. A good general rule is that the level of detail presented in data extracts should be appropriate to the level of analysis which follows. Extracts from my breast cancer data are transcribed using a simplified version of the notation favoured by conversation analysts, which was originally developed by Gail Jefferson (see Atkinson and Heritage 1984: Appendix).
3. For example, one influential study (Blaxter 1983: 68) claims that women's ideas about the causes of disease are derived from three key sources: health professionals, 'the common stick of knowledge in the community', and the media. The 'evidence' provided for the importance of 'folk knowledge' is that women quote 'the sorts of things that people say' (such as 'over the years you hear people saying, rheumatic fever? Oh it leaves you with a murmur in your heart...').
4. This is a different kind of 'footing' (Goffman 1981b) from her earlier use of 'folk wisdom'. The term 'footing' refers to the range of relationships between speakers and what they say. It enables distinctions to be made between people making claims on their own behalf and those reporting the claims of others.

CHAPTER FIVE **When Documents**
●●●●●●●● **'Speak': Documents,**
Language and Interaction

Paul Drew

Documents of one kind or another have long been an important source of data in sociological research. Although interviewing, questionnaires, survey research and direct observation might seem to offer more direct access to social attitudes and other social 'realities', and are probably more familiar sociological methodologies, a moment's reflection should be enough to convince you that documents have been and remain a vital source of social data in almost any area of sociological research. Cases in point are Durkheim's use of records and statistics relating to suicide (Durkheim 1952 [1897]); official statistics in criminological and deviance research (such statistics being, of course, the documentary products of official agencies, for example see Atkinson and Coffey 1997); life histories (including diaries, etc.) in studies of sexuality (Plummer 1981); the use of diaries in sociological research of health and illness; the use of diaries, letters and other personal memoirs in Chicago sociology, especially in studies of deviance, and in the classic study of the life of immigrants, Thomas and Znaniecki's *The Polish Peasant in Europe and America* (1958) (see also Cohen and Taylor's 1972 study of long-term imprisonment using prisoners' essays and stories); the widespread use of documents of many kinds in ethnographic research (Hammersley and Atkinson 1983); and Shapin's account of the emergence of the concept of scientific truth in seventeenth-century England, based upon an enormous range of biographical and autobiographical materials, letters, tracts, papers (including scholarly papers, such as those circulated by the Royal Society) and other documentary material (Shapin 1994). These examples begin to illustrate how documents and documentary evidence – statistics, public records, reports by official agencies, company reports, court records, medical records, newspaper articles and media products more generally, pictures and other visual arti-facts, diaries and letters, popular writing, advertisements (Goffman 1979) – provide just as significant a record of certain social realities as do the data generated by other more familiar methodologies.

However, it might seem odd to include a chapter on documents in a collection which focuses on talk-in-interaction in research methodologies. It's easy to see, now it's been pointed out to you, that interaction is quite central for instance to mass survey research – an approach which after all is essentially a quantitative methodology. As soon as one considers that the information recorded in surveys is elicited through questions and answers in telephone interaction (see Chapter 2 on survey research and Chapter 8 on questions and answers, both in this volume), it becomes clear that it's vital to understand how the interaction between interviewer and respondent has consequences for the information which emerges from survey interviews. But documents? They might seem very far removed from spoken language. I hope to demonstrate in this chapter both that close analysis of the language used in texts – language which derives from and intersects with spoken language – can generate original and illuminating findings and that documents may play a significant and systematic role in spoken interaction.

The approach I take here to documents contrasts with the positivist, objectivist tradition in sociological research. From Durkheim's study of suicide in the late nineteenth century through to current research, documents have been viewed as sources of factual information about some form of social activity or aspect of the social world, either in the past or in contemporary society. In the traditional orthodoxy, documents record facts about society and people's social lives; for this reason, researchers have been concerned primarily with what might broadly be regarded as the *authenticity* and *accuracy* of documents and the information they contain. 'Accuracy' here refers to all aspects of a document's veracity and validity, including the correctness, completeness, truth, selectivity, and the possibility of distortion and error in the information which it contains. These issues associated with the reliability and validity of documents have been so well and thoroughly discussed (for an excellent overview see Macdonald 2001) that there is no need to rehearse them here. The key point is that in the orthodox view, documents have been treated as resources for accessing information about the social world; the value of that information is judged largely in terms of its accuracy.

But there is an alternative to this orthodoxy, in which documents are regarded not so much as resources for gathering social data, but rather are analysed as *topics* in their own right.[1] I can illustrate this most easily through my own research experience when I was studying the conflict in Northern Ireland (commonly referred to there as the 'Troubles') which began with the demonstrations and marches in support of civil rights for the Catholic population in 1968, and escalated into the armed conflict of the subsequent quarter of a century or more. My aim was to trace the emergence and escalating trajectory of the Troubles, through an analysis of the developing incidence, intensity and magnitude of conflict events (demonstrations, marches, bombings, shootings and other forms of attacks directed at one or the other ethnic/religious group in Northern Ireland, or the security forces).[2] In order to gather the statistical information I needed, I reviewed newspaper reports for each day during the period 1968–1971. Newspapers in Northern Ireland are strongly partisan in their affiliation with either the Catholic or Protestant communities, which posed the problem of the reliability and accuracy of the statistical information I was to collect about the (ethnic/religious) identity of participants (including 'attackers' and 'attacked'), the numbers of people involved, the location of the event (bearing in mind the 'religious geography' of cities in Northern Ireland: Drew 1978), the event's duration, the extent of shooting, the number of bombs involved, and so on. I decided that the answer to this problem was to review the reports in three daily newspapers covering the political/religious spectrum: one associated with and read by the Catholic population, the *Irish News*; one associated with the Protestant population, the *News Letter*; and a third, putatively more neutral paper, *The Belfast Telegraph*. For each incident reported in the press, I collected information about numbers involved, location, the 'form' of conflict involved (e.g. whether shooting was involved) and so on from each of these newspapers. They differed greatly in the details they reported about what had happened; one paper might report that a 'mob' of 150 people came down a particular street, while another paper might describe the same group of people as a 'crowd' of only 50 residents. To resolve these discrepancies for the purposes of statistical coding, I simply 'averaged' the details for each incident. I hoped thereby to even out the exaggerations and inaccuracies of each of these politically 'biased' sources, and arrive at (reasonably) accurate information about each incident. I was working within the orthodox framework, believing that the information I gathered from the content of these newspaper reports would reflect the reality of what actually happened.

But as I read these reports, and compared the accounts given in the different papers, I was struck by the ways in which the differences in the 'factual' information reported were related to – indeed were part of – the *moral* work of the report, particularly regarding who was to blame for the incident. So a *mob of 150 people coming down a street* implies to the reader that they were attacking, that they were to blame; whereas to describe the same group as a *crowd of 50 residents* implies something quite different, that they had a legitimate reason to be there and were themselves being attacked by others from outside that street and, by further implication, from the other religion. Don't imagine that I am exaggerating these differences and discrepancies; think, for instance, of the different versions given in the news media of incidents in Iraq at present, or in the Israeli/Palestinian conflict. These differences are all about blaming the other side; so that the account in the *Irish News* was written in such a way as to imply that the Protestants were to blame, were attacking innocent Catholics, and vice versa. Not satisfied that my pragmatic device of averaging the information in the different reports necessarily gave an accurate picture of what really happened, I came instead to focus on how the reports were written to imply that the other side was to blame for what happened. In contrast to using the reports as a resource of factual information about conflict events, I took them to be topics of inquiry, texts which represented the perspectives, definitions and versions of reality held by each side in the conflict. I began, therefore, to examine these reports as texts in which the meaning an event had for each side, particularly the matter of who was to blame for an incident, was constructed through the use of language, including the description of 'factual' information about what happened. 'Blame' was the accountable product of the ways these reports were written. I abandoned any concern with the 'truth' or accuracy of reports, and focused instead on the (political and religious) cultural meanings of particular conflict events, and the values embodied in those meanings, which were to be found through an analysis of newspaper reports as texts. What came to interest me was the language through which these texts were written (constructed) in such a way as to do the moral work of blaming the other side for what took place.

That summarizes in a nutshell the difference between two major analytic stances towards texts. My starting point was the orthodox position that reliable information was to be found through an analysis of the content of newspaper reports about what 'really' happened in a given incident, so long as these reports were accurate. What I came to realize was that these reports reflected and embodied the perspectives of each of the religious groups involved in the conflict. Whether or not the newspaper reports were accurate, complete, comprehensive etc., they were written in such a way that they had a certain accountable, moral meaning. I had come to a position consistent with the *interpretative* tradition which was then emerging (Jupp and Norris 1993). In contrast to orthodox content analysis, interpretative analysis of documentary texts aims to examine *how* the texts are written, how people and events are described, and how, through use of language, accounts are constructed which produce meanings such as that the other side were the attackers and are to blame.

Texts and people's perspectives on their experience

The interpretative tradition is concerned with the *perceptions of reality* which are embodied in documents. Instead of surveying the content of documents for the supposedly factual information they contain, research in this alternative tradition focuses on the perspectives through which people make sense of and give meaning to their experience. According to this analytic viewpoint, documents are valuable sources of information, not about 'facts', but about 'subjective' experience, the ways in which people attribute meanings to their experiences, and the perspectives they develop in ordering and seeing patterns in their experiences. People act, of course, not on the basis of fact, but on the basis of their *perceptions* of fact.[3] Thus studies of people's perceptions and perspectives are vital to our understanding of social action. You can find an extended and really excellent discussion of these issues, across a broad range of sociology, in Plummer's *Documents of Life* (1990), but a couple of examples may help to illustrate this alternative to the orthodox use of documents.

Two exemplary studies which analyse documents from an interpretative perspective are those by Jack Douglas (1967) and Jack Katz (1988). Douglas argued that the kinds of theory of suicide offered by Durkheim (and others in that epidemiological mould) did not properly explain suicide at an individual level. Douglas reasoned that we need to know about the meanings which people who contemplate and commit suicide give to their lives, and specifically what meaning they attribute to the act of suicide itself; how do they see suicide as the right thing to do (as a rational action) (two chapters are particularly worth reading for his account of suicide as 'meaningful' conduct: Douglas 1967: Chapters 16 and 17). The source of Douglas's information about these meanings and perspectives was a variety of documents, notably diaries, psychiatric case reports and newspaper articles. His analysis of these documents reveals, in a richly nuanced account, how persons contemplating suicide understand their lives (and what they regard as wrong with their lives), and the meanings through which the act of suicide comes to be an 'answer'.

Katz also challenged epidemiological explanations, in his case of murder, on the grounds not that the variables often associated with murder (that murderers are typically male, working-class, known or related to the victim, etc.) are not relevant, but that these variables do not really account for how murderers come to kill. Katz argues that we need to understand 'What is the killer trying to do in a typical homicide? How does he understand himself, his victim, and the scene at the fateful moment? With what sense and in what sensuality is he compelled to act?' (Katz 1988: 12). His account of the phenomenology of murder, of how the killer perceives and understands the situation and the conduct of his victim, is assembled through an analysis of newspaper reports, witness statements in police and court records, and 'life history' accounts in popular and scholarly books about murder and murderers. He shows that these materials support a three-part explanation for what he terms 'righteous slaughter', an explanation which in effect describes a process which ends in killing. Just as Douglas showed that what seemed in one view as an irrational attempt to escape was rational from a perspective in which death involved the transformation of the self (Douglas 1967: 286), so too Katz offers a more nuanced account of the role of rage in murder.

Analysing the *language* of texts: a suicide note

These studies by Douglas and Katz are fascinating examples of the kinds of sociological insight we get by adopting this alternative methodological and analytic approach in which documents are examined for what they tell us about the perspectives of certain kinds of people (here suicides and killers) and about the meanings which their actions have for them, the phenomenology of their conduct.

Another exemplary study from this alternative tradition is Jerry Jacobs's study of suicide notes, from which he attempts to learn what is 'the common denominator in the personal situation of suicides' (Jacobs 1967: 60). Reviewing 112 suicide notes, he finds that in the most common type (which he calls 'first form notes', the other types being variants of this type) there are six recurrent themes, which, summarized briefly, are:

1   The problem is not of the suicide's own making.
2   A long-standing history of problems.
3   The escalation of problems beyond endurance (progressive social isolation).
4   Death is portrayed as necessary.
5   The writer begs the forgiveness or indulgence of those addressed.
6   The writer knows what he or she is doing, but knows that others cannot know.

Jacobs cites one such note, to illustrate the features or patterns which characterized these notes. This is shown, in full, as example (1).

(1)   (Jacobs 1967: 62)

It is hard to say why you don't want to live. I have only one real reason. The three people I have in the world which I love don't want me.

Tom, I love you so dearly but you have told me that you don't want me and don't love me. I never thought you would let me go this far, but I am now at the end which is the best thing for you. You have so many problems and I am sorry I added to them.

Daddy, I hurt you so much and I guess I really hurt myself. You only wanted the very best for me and you must believe this is it.

Mommy, you tried so hard to make me happy and to make things right for all of us. I love you too so very much. You did not fail, I did.

I had no place to go so I am back where I always seem to find peace. I have failed in everything I have done and I hope I do not fail in this.

I love you all dearly and am sorry this is the way I have to say goodbye.

Please forgive me and be happy.

Your wife and daughter.

This note very clearly illustrates the recurrent themes which Jacobs identified in suicide notes generally. I won't belabour this; you'll see very plainly how in these poignant final words to her family, the writer depicts her problems as long-standing and her death as necessary, begs the forgiveness of those whom she addresses, knows that others will not be able to understand what she is doing, and the rest. Jacobs's analysis offers considerable insight, therefore, into how individuals come to regard suicide as a reason-able or rational course of action for themselves. The analysis Jacobs offers consists of observations about the general meaning of sentences in this and other notes; so too Douglas and Katz formulate the meaning of sentences and entire paragraphs in a single thematic point, such as Katz's observation about an entire account of a killing that it illustrates how killers 'often postured as a defender of the children's moral sensibilities' (Katz 1988: 15). In Jacobs, as in these other studies, we don't find a close analysis of *how accounts are constructed* to have the meanings which they identify. I think we can see that if we move to another level of analysis and examine even more closely what the writer has said in this note, her use of language, we can find other salient and important features of her reasoning about what she intends to do.

Consider how she opens her letter, 'It is hard to say why you don't want to live'. We do not ordinarily use the construction *It's hard to say why ...* to depict what we have done or are about to do. For all those things we do, mundanely, like dressing in the morning, going to work, having lunch, talking to a colleague ... whatever ... we would not treat them as matters which are difficult to explain. They are all standard, routine and *expectable* activities. Of course if one decided *not* to get up and dress in the morning, or *not* go to work, then one might say, if asked, that it's hard to say why one didn't behave as normal, as expected – in other words, why one acted *improperly*. So in using this construction, speakers – and here the writer – treat what they are doing or about to do as contrary to expectation, not what one should properly do, and hence conduct which is accountable. Again, we do not offer accounts for routine, normal, expected behaviour; accounts are remedial devices through which speakers show that while they have acted/are about to act in ways which are contrary to social norms, nevertheless they understand the norms which apply and to which they generally adhere, except in these special circumstances (see Goffman 1971 on accounts in remedial exchanges). Notice in this respect that she says 'why *you* don't want to ...', her choice of pronoun (rather than '... *I* don't want ...'), constructing this in impersonal terms (in contrast to the next sentence, in which she changes to the first person, thereby turning from norms and expectations to her own reasons), so that her pronoun choice contributes to and enhances her orientation here to general social norms. In this way the writer begins her note by acknowledging that she is sufficiently of the society, sufficiently a member of society, to know the rules, and that what she plans is socially proscribed. In treating her conduct as accountable, she shows that she is not so heedless or 'anti-social' as to disregard the normative framework in which her action will be judged. Right at the outset, therefore, the writer displays that she knows what she is doing, and that what she is doing is contrary to some normative standards; and in this way her reasoning that *It's hard to say why ...* shows that she is rational, that she is not so far 'out of her mind' as not to recognize, and care about, what is expected of her.

Just parenthetically, we can notice also that she doesn't say something like *It's hard to say why you want to die.* Her use of *don't want to live* is less explicit, more allusive, about her intention to kill herself. Indeed, she is never explicit about her plan to commit suicide; in the only other direct reference to what she plans, 'I hope I do not fail in this', she does not name what she intends, but refers to it only through the deictic *this*. Her implicitness is consistent with Atkinson's report that in the notes he reviewed in his study of the work of coroners, only very rarely did writers state explicitly that they intended to commit suicide. Their intention was generally left implicit or alluded to in phrases of apology, of not being able to 'go on', of instructions ('Please look after my children') and the like (Atkinson 1978: 112–17).

A second feature of this note is that the writer addresses three people, whom she names as her husband, mother and father. She constructs her note as though directly speaking to each of them in turn (for example, she addresses each as 'you', and not in the third person). We might consider what she is doing in selecting these three people to address. I say 'select' because she has decided, or chosen, to 'speak to' these three, and not to others who might have been included. It may seem 'natural' to choose members of one's family, since the (membership) category 'family' seems so relevant to matters of love and support. She makes that explicit when she says 'The three people I have in the world which I love ...', but contrasts her loving them with their *not wanting* her. Of course there are many people who might 'not want' her, but these others are not treated as relevant (the absence of the love by others is not a relevant absence). Here again she is orienting to something normative about conduct, that one can expect that one's family will and should 'want' (love) one. Something else is implied in this, or is a corollary of it – and this is particularly important for what can be considered to be a *social structure* for love, help and support: in selecting these three people, and describing them as not wanting her, and referring to them explicitly as the three *I have in the world which I love*, she indicates that there is no one else who would care. As Sacks has pointed out, in such cases of someone considering suicide (for instance, speaking to a counsellor on a suicide helpline), determining that there is no one else to whom he/she could turn for help is not a matter of having to go through a list of all the people he/she knows, and asking about each one *Would she help?* (Sacks 1967). There is a range of people to whom a troubled person might turn, such as friends, colleagues, a priest (vicar, or rabbi), a doctor and so on. However, what is conveyed in 'the three people I have in the world which I love' is that it is unnecessary for her to consider all those others to whom she might turn for help. If these three don't want her, then no one else will. She draws this conclusion on the basis of the expectation, the norm, that is if anyone loves her, it is her family. So that if they don't love ('want') her, no one else will. The writer is invoking a social structure whereby not only can a population be identified as those to whom one might turn to for help (family, close friends, church, etc.), but the writer can know that if one of the categories in that population – family – cannot give her that help (*don't want her*), then none of the others (members of the other categories) can (for more about the use of membership categories in practical reasoning, including reasoning about suicide, see Sacks 1967; and the useful commentaries by Silverman 1998: Chapters 5 and 7, and 2001: 139–53).

A further point about the construction of the text to address her husband, father and mother. She selects *three* members of the category 'family'. We cannot know if she has siblings, or children (we would infer from this note, I think, that she does not have children, but on what basis might we do that? And why might we be more certain that she is childless than that she doesn't have siblings?). So we cannot know whether other possible family members have not been included. She could perhaps have addressed her mother and father together, rather than separately. Whatever the possibilities there might have been, her selecting *three* (and notice that she explicitly orients to there being three, in 'The three people I have in the world ...') has a particular 'meaning'. Jefferson has shown that when speakers produce lists in ordinary interaction, they most commonly produce lists of three items (Jefferson 1990). Here's an example from a telephone conversation in which Lesley has called a hospital to enquire about the progress of an elderly relative. The news from the ward sister is good.

(2) (Telephone conversation: call to a hospital)
```
      Ward:              Well she's (0.2) she's doing very well actually um she's
                         independent.
      Les:               Oh she is.
      Ward:      -->     Yes she's walking around uh washing n' dressing herself
      Les:               Oh good.
```

Having reported that the patient is doing well and is now independent, she lists (see arrowed turn) three activities which demonstrate her independence: *walking around, washing and dressing herself*. Jefferson further shows that not only are lists produced in three parts, but that speakers orient to lists as *properly* consisting of three items, in cases where they engage in a search for a third item.

(3)   (Jefferson 1990: 67)
      Mr B: It's not in the same league with adultery, and murder, and –and – <u>thie</u>very, but ...

This illustrates the general point that a list ought to contain three items in order for
it to be complete (and example (3) shows that this is not an analyst's stipulation of
a statistical deduction, but something to which speakers orient in their talk). The
same phenomenon of listing in threes, is to be found in all forms of interaction and
communication, for instance in political speeches (Atkinson 1984: Chapter 3). Here
are two examples, one from a consummate political orator, Margaret Thatcher.

(4)   (Thatcher: Conservative Party Conference, 1980)
      Thatcher: As you know we've made the first crucial changes in trade
                        union law
                        (0.4)
            1   in removing the worst abuses of the closed shop
                        (0.2)
            2   to restrict picketing to the place of work of the parties
                        in dis<u>pute</u>
                        (0.2)
            3   and to encourage secret <u>ba</u>llots
                        [Jim Prior has carried all these
      Audience: [XXXXXXXXXXXXXXXXXXXXXXXXXXXXXXX
      Thatcher: measures through with the support of the vast majority of
                        trade union memb[ers
      Audience: [XXXXXXXXXXXXXXXXXXXXXXX ....

(5)   (Alan Milburn, Health Secretary, Labour Party Conference, 2000)
      'We've made a start putting right what they did wrong. The internal market – gone. Waiting
      lists – down. Nurse training places – up,' he declaimed, to applause. ... 'More nurses, more
      power, more pay'. (From a report in the *Health Service Journal*, 5 October 2000)

In claiming to have 'made the first crucial changes in trade union law', Thatcher lists
three legislative measures (numbered for clarity) (notice that the audience begins
applauding, indicated by *XXXXXXX*, precisely after the third item, overlapping with
Thatcher's continuation about her colleague Jim Prior; for the significance of this, see
Atkinson 1984: 31–46). In example (5), the report in a magazine of Alan Milburn's
speech has selected two lists in which he cited three examples.

Three-part lists are used widely in advertising slogans, such as these.

LOOK WHAT YOU COULD SAVE WHEN YOU BUY A CAVALIER – YOUR TIME, YOUR CAR, YOUR LIFE
(A Cavalier is a kind of car)

LYCRA – COOL, CHIC, COMFORTABLE

ICI – WORLD PROBLEMS, WORLD SOLUTIONS, WORLD CLASS

COLLECT US COMMEMORATIVES – THEY'RE FUN, THEY'RE HISTORY, THEY'RE AMERICA
(about postage stamps)

CHALLENGE, VARIETY, LEADERSHIP. YOURS IN FIVE YEARS?
(Advertisement for Accelerated Promotion Scheme in the police)

I won't elaborate on the ubiquity of three-part lists in all areas of social, economic and political life (but for threes in courtroom cross-examination, see Drew 1990; and for a Freudian account of the convention of threes in children's fairy stories, see Bettelheim 1977). But I hope that from this brief sketch it will be clear that the particular property of three-part lists which all these uses draw upon, and which the writer of this note does also, is the sense of completeness which three items conveys – that the *totality* of something is represented by naming three items.[4] The writer makes this particularly explicit when she refers to them as *the three people I have in the world*, that is these are the only people she has. This works to consolidate her reasoning that if these (three) people cannot help her, no one can; that totality plays a part in her construction of a social structure of help.

Something else you may notice about the writer's account for not wanting to live is that at a number of points she describes her state of mind in terms of spatial metaphors, *let me go this far, I'm now at the end, I had no place to go* and *I am back where I always seem to find peace*. These are fairly idiomatic expressions (*I'm now at the end* probably referring to the idiom *at the end of my tether*, meaning exhausted, unable to take any more), which are very like the orientational metaphors (up, down, under, over, etc.) which Lakoff and Johnson show so commonly give emotional concepts a spatial orientation. Most familiar are expressions such as 'I'm feeling up' and to be 'buoyed up', and even 'up in the clouds', as versions of happiness; and 'feeling down', 'feeling low', 'down in the dumps', 'my spirits sank' and 'falling into depression' as versions of sadness or unhappiness (Lakoff and Johnson 1980: Chapter 4). Such metaphors structure how we perceive and think about the world. In describing how strongly someone feels, we refer to *depth* of feeling. Consider the power of *up* and *down* on our consciousness; doing better in the world is *rising*, doing worse is *falling*, orientational metaphors which structure the way economic and financial graphs are represented, and the way in which we think about the divine – heaven is generally represented as above, and hell (or its equivalent) as below. Such spatial/orientational metaphors provide a language resource for translating our emotions in ways we can describe, and in ways which can be understood by others. The point that these metaphors enable her to describe her state of mind in ways which can be understood by readers of the letter is particularly significant, because she is giving an account for concluding that she has no one to turn to, that there is no other way out for her (note again the spatial metaphor in *no other way out*). By translating her emotional state into these spatial terms, she constructs a version of the rationality of her conclusion, that she's taking this (unnamed) course of action because there is nothing else left for her to do. Through representing her state of mind in physical terms she avoids having to describe her emotions in a way which might admit some voluntarism, some choice or options. She depicts her state of mind as one in which she has no choice ('this is the way *I have to* say goodbye'). This is significant for her account for not wanting to live, since accounts are generally constructed in terms of constraints, of circumstances which compel or prevent us (Heritage 1988). She does this through metaphors which demonstrate to the reader that there is nothing else she can do. Of course using spatial metaphors as the writer does here provides a vocabulary with which to describe one's state of mind or emotions. These are the terms with which we've become accustomed when describing concepts (concerning emotions) which otherwise might be difficult to express, for which otherwise there's no easy or recognizable vocabulary. And this connects with the final observation I'd like to make about the writer's use of language in this text. She constructs her account through a series of paradoxes. Although she opens with 'It is hard to say why ...', in the next sentences she says why (gives an explanation): she loves her husband, he does not love her (as he should); her being 'at the end' will be the 'best thing' for him; she hurt her father, but in doing so hurt herself; her father wanted only the best for her, and this (her death?) is it; she has failed in everything she's done, but hopes she won't fail in this; she loves them dearly, but is leaving them, saying goodbye. Constructing a paradox is a way to describe something which cannot easily be described, which cannot easily be put into words. Macfarlane gives a rather clear example of this in his historical account of our (Western) conception and perception of mountains, and of mountaineering. In the section in which he traces the evolution of our fascination with the danger of mountain climbing and of the pursuit of fear, Macfarlane (2003: Chapter 3) cites a letter written in 1688 by John Dennis (a young Englishman who subsequently became a playwright) which provides one of the earliest modern memoirs of the pleasurable fear excited by mountaineering. Having just crossed the Alps, Dennis wrote home to a friend in England 'Tis an easy thing to describe Rome or Naples to you became you have seen something yourself that holds at least some resemblance with them: but impossible to set a Mountain before your Eyes, that is inaccessible almost to the sight, and wearies the very Eye to climb it' (Macfarlane 2003: 72). Macfarlane notes that Dennis faces the difficulty of

> 'how to say what something is like, when it is like nothing that your reader has ever seen'. Dennis first of all describes the mountains to his friend in physical terms; but when he 'tries to describe the exact feelings stirred in him as he reached a dangerously narrow part of the route, something unusual happens to his language:
>
>> We walk'd upon the very brink, in a literal sense, of Destruction: one Stumble, and both Life and Carcass had been at once destry'd. The sense of all this produc'd different motions in me, viz., a delightful Horrour, a terrible Joy, and at the same time, that I was infinitely pleas'd, I trembled.
>
> Against all his expectations, Dennis discovered that walking 'upon the very brink' – just one stumble away from violent death – brought him an odd pleasure. No vocabulary existed to describe what he experienced, so Dennis has to invent one using the artificial logic of the oxymoron. He has to resort to paradox – to allow each 'motion' its equal and opposite emotion, and say that he felt 'a delightful Horrour' and 'a terrible Joy'.' (Macfarlane 2003: 73)

Dennis's attempt to describe to someone who has never seen a mountain the 'infinite pleasure' he feels when faced with the dangers of climbing,[5] parallels the writer's attempt to give an account of why she doesn't want to live, to people who cannot understand (e.g. she *instructs* her father, 'you must believe this is it'). Each is describing emotions which are difficult to put into words, and which might seem irrational (to enjoy being frightened, to think that the only way to happiness is through killing oneself). Each of these writers uses the device of placing themselves between opposites, between two seemingly contradictory positions or feelings. They do so in order to express an emotion which is almost ineffable, too great for words. The emotions they are each describing do not lie between these opposites; rather, they consist of, or emerge out of, these opposites. So her use of paradox is yet another resource through which she constructs an account of why she does not want to live, and why she *has* to say goodbye.

What I have tried to show in this 'exercise' is that by examining in detail the language through which the writer constructs her letter, we uncover another level of 'meaning'. The recurrent themes which Jacobs identified in suicide notes (for instance, that writers portray their problems as having escalated beyond endurance, begs the forgiveness of those addressed, and knows that they know what they are doing even though others cannot know) certainly provide an insight into the 'common denominator' in suicidal persons' perspective. But by looking more closely at the language through which they reason about their intention to commit suicide, we learn a great deal more about how their (intended) conduct appears rational to them, and accountable to others – that is, that others can recognize the grounds or reasons for their suicide. The concept of rationality/rational action has long played a central role in sociological analysis (for a reflection on rationality in the work of Parsons, see Heritage 1984a: 22–7). Sociology has, I think, come to a position in which we have set aside external (e.g. Western scientific) standards of rationality. Instead, we are seeking to uncover how members of a society or culture, 'actors' or participants in social action regard what they do as rational. People's behaviour is based not on the perspectives of others, but of their own perspectives and perceptions. Therefore, if we are to understand what people are doing and why they are doing it, our aim should be to show how their conduct is *accountable* – how for them it makes sense to act in the way they do, and how they make sense of their behaviour for others. In these 'sense-making practices', we will learn what people's lives mean for them. And these sense-making practices consist of language and reasoning. In this brief examination of one suicide note, we can see that in her use of language the writer shows that she knows what society's rules are (normative behaviour), that she has no one left to turn to (if these three people can't help her, no one can), that she's left with nothing else to do. In other words, she constructs an account in which she's behaving rationally. She does this through certain conventional forms of reasoning (e.g. 'It's hard to say why ...'), through a three-part list, through spatial metaphors and paradox – all forms of language which are used in spoken language, in interaction, as well as texts.

Documents in interaction

I focused in the previous section on the use of language in a document. That document, the letter which came to be treated as a suicide note, played a role in the interactions associated with investigating that young woman's death, interactions between police and coroner, between the police and her family and so on (Atkinson 1978: Chapter 6). Though we do not have a record of those interactions, and therefore cannot say more about the role the note played, we do have access to the use of documents in other kinds of interaction. Here, for instance, is the transcript of the opening of a call made by the truancy officer of a large North American high school. Her job includes contacting the parents of children who are thought to be truant, as she does here (for an explanation of the transcription symbols used here, see the section on 'Transcription Symbols' at the beginning of this book).

```
(6)   (Arroyo Call 2) (Off = truancy officer)
 1    Mom:    Hello:
 2    Off:    .hhh Hello is this Missus Fieldwald?
 3    Mom:    Yes it is:
 4    Off:    .hhh This is Miss Medeiros from Redondo High School
 5            calling?,
 6    Mom:    Mm hm::,
 7    Off:    .hhh Uh I was calling about Michelle she has a couple
 8            a:bsences: since o::h las:t Thu:rsday,
 9            (.)
10    Off:    She's been reported absent (.) all day last Thursday,
11            (.)
12    Mom:    Uh huh well she hasn' been home i:ll.
13            (0.5)
14    Off:    We:ll, (.) she was absent Thursday, Friday, (1.0) .hh
15            an' again today.
16    Mom:    Are these all day absences? er are they (.) jus'
17            certain periods.
18    Off:    Uh:::: hhhhh .hhhhh (0.8) Well let's see it looks like
19            first second (.) third and fourth period for last
20            Thursday 'n Friday, .hhh an' here's sixth period an so
21            it's- (.) we'd have to assume that it's an all day
22            a:bsence, yes.
23    Mom:    Uh hmm,
24    Off:    .hhh And u:hh (0.8) you don't kno:w that she's been
25            home ill, huh?
```

You'll see that in response to the mother's enquiry in lines 16–17 about whether her daughter has been absent for entire days, or ('just') certain periods, the truancy officer *displays that she is referring to the document*. She does so both by explicit reference – 'let's *see* it *looks like*' and 'an *here's* sixth period' – and implicitly by audible indicators that she is having to read something, as in 'Uh:::: hhhhh .hhhhh' before she answers in line 18, and her hesitancy throughout, including her lengthy pauses in lines 14 and 18 and briefer pauses elsewhere (see also the delays which indicate she's reading from the record in line 8), so that she is conveying to the mother that, in order to answer her question, she is having to check the information in a document, presumably the record of attendance.

In circumstances such as this, someone may have a document of some kind in front of them, perhaps on a desk, available throughout an interaction (the truancy officer will have the record of attendance in front of her throughout such a call). The question then is: is there anything organized or systematic about the moments when reference is made to the document? At what points do speakers display to their recipient that they are reading some information from a document? Or is it random? Do they refer to a document just when they feel like? Well, there's a clue in example (6): the officer most explicitly refers to the attendance record (again, in 'let's *see* it *looks like*' and 'an *here's* sixth period') in response to having been pressed for accuracy by the mother. The mother hasn't simply accepted the officer's report; although she's not yet challenging the officer's claims, her enquiry is defensive. There might be an association, therefore, between citing the record and something slightly problematic in the interaction.

This is further substantiated in interactions in another educational setting, parent–teacher meetings. In a study of the meetings when parents come to talk to their children's teachers about SATS examination performance in a British primary school (these meetings concern results of the mock-SATS tests, which are rehearsals for the level 2 tests children take at age 11), Allistone (2002) showed that teachers commonly informed parents of the results in the following fashion.

(7) (Parent–teacher: Allistone 2002: 175) (T = teacher, P = parent)
1   T: Math<u>s</u>:
2   (1.4)
3   T: (tk) Level <u>four</u>,
4   (0.6)
5   T: >So we< want him to be a level four.

The teacher is the child's class teacher, and not the one who has actually taught the child maths. She is reporting the performance which another teacher has recorded for this child. Presumably during her silence in line 2 she is checking to see what result this child has achieved; but she makes *no explicit reference* to the document in front of her. I should explain that level 4 (line 3) is the expected level of achievement – anything better is very good indeed (the highest is level 6, but very few children get that), anything less is a cause for concern, both on behalf of the child and for the school (in terms of its performance targets). Anyway, the teacher announces the result directly as 'Level *four*' and then makes explicit that that is satisfactory.

However, in the following examples, the teacher is passing on not quite such good news.

(8) (Parent–teacher: Allistone 2002: 79) (T = teacher, C = child)
1   T: °<u>O</u>:kay°↑<u>ma:ths</u>:
2   (0.6)
3   T: >I- she's in Mrs G's set–<
4   (1.5)
5   T: (tch) .hhh A::::Nd (0.9) (u)national average (.) is
6   a level fou:r
7   (0.8)

```
 8    T:    (tk) for these SATS.=↑now this says level ↑three::.
 9          (1.6)
10    T:    ↑Is that ri:ght?
11    C:    I'm bad int I, (hhh)
```

```
(9)   (Parent-teacher: Allistone 2002: 63–64) (T = teacher, P = parent)
1     T:    >If: we,< (0.7) talk about her maths: first
2     P:    °Yea(h)°
3     T:    .hh Okay so she's in: Mr D's set (0.8) y[eah?
4     P:                                            [°yeah°
5     T:    .hh urm and he says that- (0.4) >she's working at-< (0.9)
6           .h level three
7     P:    Yea::h.
8     T:    The::: national average, (0.7) is level four
```

In each case, the child has, as the teacher remarks (line 5 in example (8), and line
8 in example (9), performed below average. In example (8) the child shows that he
knows the news is bad (line 11). The difference between the teacher's unelaborated,
direct announcement of the satisfactory 'no problem' result in example (7) and these
announcements of below-average performances is that here the teacher is explicit
about the *source* of the information she has ('She's in Mrs G's set' and 'So she's in:
Mr D's set', respectively), and then makes explicit that she is reading this information from a document: 'this says level three::.' and 'he says that–'. Notice also the
same kind of indications or *display* that she's reading that were evident in example (6) –
similar 'turn holding' expressions (e.g. 'urm' in example (9) line 5, and stretching
'A::::Nd', in example (8) line 5) and other delays and pauses. This was fairly systematic across Allistone's corpus. When the teacher was announcing a satisfactory performance,[6] she almost always did so without referring directly to the document.
However, when the score was below the expected standard, the teacher would format
the announcement in the fashion illustrated in examples (8) and (9), as the result
recorded by another teacher.

We see in these examples that only when a teacher is reporting something problematic – a test score below expectations – does she make explicit reference to the
document, attributing the bad news to what the document says. In this way she represents the news as coming not from herself, but from what's in the record (from
another teacher), and only through her indirectly;[7] contrast that with her unelaborated announcement of good news.

This corresponds with the findings of a study by Boyd (1998) of interactions
between doctors in the US medical system. When a child has been referred for a
minor surgical procedure to relieve middle ear infection (tympanostomy), a doctor
working for the insurance company will prospectively review and evaluate the recommendation by the child's doctor, in order to decide whether or not the insurance
company will pay for the procedure. They do this by speaking to the recommending
doctor on the phone. Boyd points out that there is an inherent tension in the form
of peer review, as it requires one physician to evaluate the recommendation of

another. When they talk, the doctors are attempting to preserve professional autonomy, while simultaneously compromising that autonomy in the review process itself (Boyd 1998: 202). Anyway, the physician-reviewer consults the 'paper trail' from the doctor's recommendation and case notes, through a preliminary review by a nurse. He or she then calls the child's doctor, who has the child's medical record to consult. Boyd identifies two formats which the reviewing physicians may adopt when initiating these review calls – a bureaucratic or collegial format. In the *bureaucratic* format, the reviewer's enquiries focus initially on 'some documentary or clerical aspect of the case (which characterizes it) as problematic. Typically it contains a reference to some inconsistency, omission or other problem, as recorded in the first-level review' (Boyd 1998: 205). Here is one such typical bureaucratic opening by the reviewer:

The information I have is he's six an'-=with a history of recurrent uh otitis and (1.0) uh I think 'e had previous tubes, (0.5) but according to the information we got from a doctor (Katz), (.) the pediatrician's office, (.) He has uh- (0.2) they I- I don't get any documentation of any problems at all in the last year. (Boyd 1998: 206)

In such cases, Boyd reports, the reviewer indicates that there is a problem. By referring to what the documents show or do not show (here, they do not show any problems in the last year), the reviewer is formulating an inconsistency between the other doctor's recommendation and the medical evidence in the case notes/paper trail. And this is done by explicitly citing the documentation (again, notice the indications that the reviewer is displaying that he is looking at and reading from the documents). Initiating the review in a *collegial* format, by contrast, reviewers do *not* refer to or cite the documentation, but open directly by asking the child's doctor for information about the case:

.hh Uh can you tell me something about this youngster? (Boyd 1998: 209)

The parallels between these bureaucratic and collegial opening enquiries, and the different ways in which teachers announce SATS tests results, will be obvious. What is most germane here, though, is that Boyd reports that when reviewers open with the bureaucratic format, and explicitly refer to the documents in the paper trail, this projects a problem with the case, and they generally do *not* confirm the case doctor's recommendation and deny subsidizing the cost of surgery through the health plan. When the reviewer opens with a collegial enquiry, by contrast, they generally find no problem with the recommendation and approve a financial subsidy for the surgery.

So at least one systematic basis for referring to or citing a document in interaction is that speakers may refer to documents when they are managing something which is potentially problematic (responding to a defensive enquiry, announcing scores which are below expected standards, anticipating that a doctor's recommendation may be faulty). The document stands as an objective record, de-personalizing the bad news to be delivered by attributing the news, or the evidence for the news, to the document and not to the speaker. We begin to see how documents can play a part in interaction, in managing specifically tricky, awkward or difficult matters.

─────────────────────── **Summary** ───────────────────────

I have tried to do three things in this chapter. First, my aim has been to highlight the importance of documents as a source of data in sociological research. Documents may not be as familiar a part of the methodological canon as, say, (survey) interviewing. Nevertheless, they are a tremendously valuable source of information about the social world, in a wide variety of substantive areas.

Second, I have outlined and exemplified two analytic approaches which contrast with the orthodox tradition, in which the contents of documents are regarded as containing objective, factual information. The *interpretative* approach treats documents as reflecting the meanings which people, either types of individual (e.g. murderers) or groups, attribute to their experiences, and the perspectives through which they define their social realities. On the other hand, documents may also be used as an *interactional resource* by participants; in this way documents play a significant and systematic role in interaction.

Third, through these exercises involving the textual analysis of a sample document (a suicide note), and comparative sequential analysis of interactions (in educational and medical settings), I have outlined something of the methodologies which we can use when analysing language and interaction in close detail. Added to this, I have tried to demonstrate what we can uncover through such analysis, and to show how novel and illuminating the results of such analyses can be (for instance, about the way the writer constructs her note in such a way as display the *accountable rationality* of her conduct).

Finally, I have focused here on *textual* documents because they are perhaps the most widely used in, and relevant to, sociological research, and also because they relate most directly to the subject of this book – language and interaction. In doing so, I have not considered forms of graphic representations (e.g. charts, work and incident records, colour codes, photographs and film, advertisements, tables, computer screens). A particularly vivid and powerful demonstration of how graphic representations can feature in interaction in social settings can be found in Goodwin's account of the use made of colour charts and graphic records, and video film, in the work settings of an archaeological field excavation and a courtroom, respectively (Goodwin 1994).[8]

─────────────────────── **Notes** ───────────────────────

1. On the distinction between topic and resource, see Zimmerman and Pollner (1971).
2. I had another, larger aim in view, which was to look for any connections (correlations) there might be between the escalation of violence during those years and socio-economic factors and indicators – along the lines suggested by research in international relations.
3. In John Dewey's famous phrase, 'Things … are what they are experienced as'.

4. It might seem puzzling that listing (only) three items can suggest completeness, a totality. Putting items together in a list suggests a pattern, the collection of which these items are members. If you are told that two members of a collection are 3 and 9, and asked what the pattern is, that might be squaring the previous number, adding 6, or multiplying by 3. With just those two numbers, it's difficult to deduce the pattern. But given a list of 3, 9 and 27, one can now see that the pattern is that each prior number is multiplied by 3. Three is, therefore, the minimum number of items required to determine a (mathematical) series, and hence establish the pattern which conveys completeness.

5. The paradox of the joy to be experienced in pain is known as algolagnia (see Praz 1970).

6. This was adapted to the level of ability of particular children, so if a child had performed well above expectations, even if below the level 4 national average, then the result was announced in the 'no problem'/good news form shown here.

7. This brings to mind Goffman's observation that speakers may take different stances, or 'footings', in regard to what they are saying, particularly whether they are the author, animator or principal of what is said (Goffman 1981b). For an explanation of these distinctions and their application in the context of news interviews, see Clayman (1992).

8. 'A theory of discourse that ignored graphic representations would be missing both a key element of the discourse that professionals engage in and a central locus for the analysis of professional practice. Instead of mirroring spoken language, these external representations complement it, using the distinctive characteristics of the material world to organize phenomena in ways that spoken language cannot ...' (Goodwin 1994: 611).

CHAPTER SIX

•••••••• # Observation, Video and Ethnography: Case Studies in Aids Counselling and Greetings

Anssi Peräkylä

In this chapter, I discuss some ways in which the micro-analysis of video recordings can contribute to the understanding of social action. I will focus on two kinds of action, professional and mundane. The first part of the chapter deals with professional action. Using my own study on AIDS counselling as an example, I will show how the micro-analysis of video recordings enriches the understandings offered by the practitioners' own accounts and theories concerning their work. The second part of the chapter deals with mundane, everyday action. There, I will take greetings as an example, and will show how the micro-analysis of video recordings can help the researcher to ask questions that go beyond those arising from more ordinary (ethnographic) methods of observation.

In both parts of the chapter, I will contrast and compare two modes of description of social action. In the first part, which deals with professional action, the modes of description involve practitioners' own theories on one hand, and the micro-analysis of video recordings of their practice on the other. In the second part, which deals with everyday action, the contrasted modes of description involve ethnographic observations on one hand, and again, the micro-analysis of video recordings on the other. To put it simply, the main message of the chapter is this: there is much to gain in using video recordings in researching professional and mundane social action.

I will use the term 'micro-analysis' (see Goffman 1983) to refer to qualitative analysis of behavioural segments. Conversation analysis (CA) is a typical, but not the only, representative of micro-analytic techniques. One of the micro-analytic studies that I use as an example (AIDS counselling) involves CA research, whereas the other (greetings) involves another kind of micro-analytic approach. This difference is not important in the context of this chapter: I am focusing on what the video recordings can offer as data, not the specific analytic techniques.

——————— **Video recordings in the analysis of professional action** ———————

In this section, I want to show what the use of video recordings can contribute to the observation of professional action, focusing particularly on professionals interacting with their clients – although the perspective adopted here can also be applied to other kinds of professional work (e.g. see Heath and Luff 2000). As my primary example, I will use my own research on AIDS counselling (Peräkylä 1995). I will compare the picture of professional action given in the practitioners' own theories with the picture that the analysis of video recordings yields. My main argument is that micro-analysis of video (or audio) recordings gives the researcher access to layers of organization that are critical for successful professional conduct but which may remain unrecognized in the practitioners' own theories.

Practitioners' theories of their action

One distinctive feature of professions is that at least some aspects of the professional conduct are codified in written texts – in textbooks, professional journal articles, training manuals and the like (Peräkylä and Vehviläinen 2003). Some of these texts are normative, constituting standards of good practice, whereas others are descriptive, conveying to trainees and outsiders what the professionals actually do in their profession. In professions where the practitioners deal with clients, these texts also describe and/or prescribe standards for the conduct of professional–client interactions.

If a social scientist is doing research on professional work, such texts are an invaluable resource. It is impossible to understand properly, say, therapeutic encounters, without knowing about the therapeutic theories that inform the therapists' work (see Arminen 1998; Arminen and Leppo 2000). By using video or audio recordings, however, the researcher can also 'go beyond' what is described in professional texts. In a recent paper, Sanna Vehviläinen and I argued that conversation analytical (CA) research can take different relations to the practitioners' own theories of their action. Sometimes CA studies simply *falsify* assumptions that are part of professional theories, but they may also *provide a more detailed picture* of practices that are described in such theories. They can *add a new dimension* to the understanding of practices described by a professional theory, or *provide the description of practices* that are not at all recognized in the professional theory (Peräkylä and Vehviläinen 2003).

In what follows, I will take AIDS counselling as an example through which I will try to illustrate the relation between professionals' own theories concerning their action and what the analysis of video recordings made of the professional practice. In the 1990s, I conducted a study on AIDS counselling at the Royal Free Hospital, London (Peräkylä 1995; see also Silverman 1997). The counselling practice that I analysed was based on a particular therapeutic theory, known as *Milan School Family Systems Theory*. I will first explain some of the basic assumptions of this therapeutic theory, and then go on to show how the micro-analysis of video recordings enriched the understanding of practice provided by the theory.

Family Systems Theory

Family Systems Theory thinking was initiated in a private clinic in Milan, Italy, when Mara Selvini Palazzoli, a child psychiatrist, together with her colleagues, started 'The institute for family study' (in 1967) and thereafter 'The centre for the study of family' (in 1971). Disillusioned by the ineffectiveness of psychoanalytic therapy, Selvini Palazzoli became interested in the family therapeutic and cybernetic ideas. Instead of considering behavioural symptoms as indications of intra-psychic conflicts of the individuals involved, the Milan associates started to view the manifest problems as parts of the unacknowledged 'games' that the families were playing.

Individual symptoms were seen as a part of a 'system' comprising the whole family. Given this new psychopathological understanding, the aim of the therapy is to make the families aware of their games, and of the functions which the behaviour labelled as a problem serves there. The game is interrupted, and the family is helped to acknowledge the systemic functions of their problems (Hoffman 1981). This is achieved by the therapists using specific interactive techniques. They include, for example, 'circular questioning' and 'live supervision'.

'Circular questioning' is a way of soliciting information in such a manner that differences between the family members' perspectives and experiences are brought into focus (Feinberg 1990; Fleuridas et al. 1986; Mauksch and Roesler 1990; Penn 1982). The therapist typically asks one member of the family to comment upon the relationship of two others in their presence. The questions are preferably so constructed that they focus on differences, for example 'Who is closer to father, your daughter or your son?' Sometimes the circular questions are asked in a hypothetical manner, for example 'If you had not been born, what do you think your parents' marriage would be like now?' (Hoffman 1981). This kind of questioning is efficient in engaging the family in talking, and helps them to realize how the problem of one member affects all others, that is, the 'systemic' character of their problems.

In 'live supervision', one (or sometimes two) of the therapists converses with the family members, while the rest of the team follow the session behind a one-way mirror. The team can communicate with the therapist during breaks in the session or, in some cases, using a telephone. These arrangements make it possible that the functioning of the family and that of the family-plus-therapist system is attended to and reflected on by the whole team. Because the team members behind the screen are not actively involved in the interaction, their perspective is different from that of the therapist. This enables the team to see and think differently about the family and about the process of the interview (Selvini and Selvini Palazzoli 1991).

Milan School Family Systems Theory was developed in the context of psychiatric treatment of severely disturbed patients. Later on, it has been applied in a wide variety of therapeutic and counselling settings. The AIDS counselling that I observed was one of its applications. My study focused in the key practices of circular questioning and live supervision, seeking to show how these theoretical ideas are translated into interactional practices. In doing this, video recordings of the actual counselling sessions turned out to be invaluable materials.

Circular questioning in practice

In the video recordings of AIDS counselling sessions based on Family Systems Theory, I found the counsellors regularly asking 'circular questions' of their clients. For example, the counsellor asked one client to describe the thoughts or experiences of another one. Thus, the counsellor could ask the mother of a HIV positive patient to describe what her (co-present) son's greatest concern is. The person whose thoughts and experiences were described by others was sometimes the patient, sometimes a 'significant other' accompanying the patient – spouse, parent, boy- or girlfriend or the like. In my analysis, I showed how such questioning sequences were practically accomplished. This amounted to showing the practical ways in which the clients were helped to understand each others' perspectives on their shared problems, that is to understand the systemic nature of their problems.

However, there also seemed to be something more at stake in circular questioning. In addition to showing the systemic nature of the problems, the circular questions seemed to have a more 'primordial' task or function. The examination of the video recordings led me to the conclusion that circular questioning involves a powerful practice to incite the clients to speak about matters that they otherwise would be reluctant to talk about. Most importantly, in circular questions, it was not only the counsellors who encouraged the clients to talk about the fears and worries. A local interactional context was created where the *clients* encouraged *each other* to talk.

One type of evidence for this function of the circular questions comes from the structure of such questioning sequences: without exceptions, circular questions were followed by the person whose experience was described him- or herself giving an account of the experience in question. In most cases, the counsellor asked directly this person's own view after having heard the co-participant's version; sometimes he or she volunteered his/her view. In both cases, the pattern of questioning made the person concerned speak about his or her fears and worries. Extract (1) below provides an example of such a sequence. The participants are an HIV positive patient (PA), his partner (PRT), and the counsellor (CO). Arrows (1)/(4) stand for the initiation of key utterances: (1) for the counsellor's 'circular' question, (2) for the partner's answer, (3) for the follow-up question to the patient, and arrow (4) for his response. Here, as in many other cases that I analysed, the circular question leads the person whose experience is discussed to disclose his deep worries (see especially lines 45–55). (Explanation of the transcription symbols is to be found in the section on 'Transcription Symbols' at the beginning of this book.)

```
(1)   (Peräkylä 1995: 110)
1       CO: (1)->    What are some of things that you think E:dward might
2                    have to do.= He says he doesn't know where to go from
3                    here maybe: and awaiting results and things.
4                    (0.6)
5       CO:          What d'you think's worrying him.
6                    (0.4)
7       PRT: (2)->   Uh::m hhhhhh I think it's just fear of the unknow:n.
8       PA:          Mm[:
```

```
9    CO:           [Oka:y.
10   PRT:          [At- at the present ti:me. (0.2) Uh:m (.) once: he's (0.5) got a better
11                 understanding of (0.2) what could happen
12   CO:           Mm:
13   PRT:          uh:m how .hh this will progre:ss then: I think (.) things will be a little more
                                    [settled in his=
14   CO:                             [Mm
15   PRT:          =own mi:nd.
16   CO:           Mm:
17                 (.)
18   PA:           Mm[:
19   CO: (3)->         [E:dward (.) from what you know:: (0.5) wha- what- what do you think could
20                 happen. (0.8) I mean we're talking hypothetically [now because I know=
21   PA:                                                              [Mm:: (well)-
22   CO:           =no [more than you do about your actual state of=
23   PA:               [uh::
24   CO:           =health except that we do: know,=
25   PA:           =uh
26   CO:           .hhh you're carrying the virus::, (.6) as far as- (.3) the- that first test is
                   concerned.
27   PA:           Umh
28                 (1.4)
29   PA: (4)->     (Well I feel) I see like two different extremes.=I
30                 see [that I can just- (.8) carry on (in an)=
31   CO:               [umh
32   PA:           =incubation state:, [for many years [and (up)=
33   CO:                               [umh           [umh
34   PA:           =.hhhh you know just being very careful about (it) [sexually:.
35   CO:                                                              [uhm:
36                 (.4)
37   PA:           [and: er (.3) can go on with a normal life.
38   CO:           [umh
39   CO:           umh
40   PA:           And then I get my greatest fears: that- (.2) you
41                 know just when I've get my life go:ing: you know a
42                 good job=
43   CO:           =um:h=
44   PA:           things going very well,
45   CO:           uhm::
46                 (.3)
47   PA:           that (I[::) er:: (.2) my immunity will collapse,
48   CO:                  [umh
49   CO:           um[h
50   PA:             [you know: (and I will) become very ill:: (.2) >quickly?<
51                 (1.0)
52   PA:           .hhh [hh an ]d lose control of th- the situation,
53   CO:                [um::h ]
54   CO:           umh:
55   PA:           That's my greatest fear actually.
```

The frequency of this sequence structure in circular questioning posed a kind of a puzzle for the researcher: how come the participants whose experience is discussed always give their authoritative versions after their experience has been described by somebody else, often even without the counsellor having asked for it? The inner experience of somebody is a very special object: as a speaker or as a hearer, the person whose experience is described is treated as the *owner of the experience* (see Sharrock 1974). The owner says the last word about his or her experience. In psychological terms, ownership arises from a person's privileged position as the observer of his or her subjective states of mind. However, ownership of experience is not a private matter: it is realized, and oriented to, in the details of social interaction. This could be observed in the AIDS counselling sessions where 'circular questioning' was done.

There relevance of the person's authoritative version of his or her experience arises from his/her ownership. By examining the recordings in their minute detail, I started to grasp how a person's ownership regarding his or her experience was collaboratively and consistently built up. Perhaps the most straightforward means of building up the owner's authoritative status in describing his/her experience (and the relevancy of his/her utterance arising from that status) involves agenda statements. Sometimes the counsellors couched their circular questions with statement components where they indicated that they are going to ask the 'owner's' view after having heard the other client's answer (Peräkylä 1995: 115–16). Regularly, the counsellors and/or the clients indicated, through the design of their questions and answers, that the person who is describing the 'owner's' experience is not talking in an authoritative position. This could be done, for example, through 'you think' or 'I think' formulas, such as in lines 5 and 7 in extract (1), reproduced below:

CO: What **d'you think**'s worrying him.
      (0.4)
PRT: Uh::m hhhhhh **I think** it's just fear of the unknow:n.

The owners themselves also contributed to building up their special authoritative status *vis-à-vis* the descriptions, and, thereby, to the relevancy of their own subsequent utterance. This was done, for example, through acknowledgement tokens. Acknowledgement tokens are particles through which the receivers of utterances can 'receipt' what they have heard and, among other things, indicate that they have no need to ask for clarification or initiate other kind of repair, thereby 'passing back' the turn at talk to the initial speaker (see Schegloff 1982; Sorjonen 2001). Usually in question–answer sequences, acknowledgement tokens would be produced by the questioners. However, in circular questions, the 'owners of the experience' regularly produced acknowledgement tokens when their significant others were describing the owner's mind and circumstances. In this way, owners indicated their special involvement in the matters that were spoken about. That was also the case in extract (1): in lines 8 and 18, PA responds to PRT's answer to CO's questions through 'Mm:'s. He shows his ownership of the matters spoken about, thereby also building up the relevance of his own description of them.

The same orientation is shown by the participants through their body posture. The clients who answered the circular question regularly shifted their gaze to the 'owner' at the beginning of the answer and only towards the end of it gazed at the counsellor (to whom the answer is given). This organization of gaze contributes to the relevancy of the owner's utterance where she/he eventually describes her/his concerns. A segment from extract (1) shows this pattern. Please note the special organization of the transcript here: the three lines (one for PRT, the other for CO and the third for PA) are synchronized, that is the movement from left to right in the three lines represents simultaneous temporal progression.

(2) (segment of extract (1); Peräkylä 1995: 125)

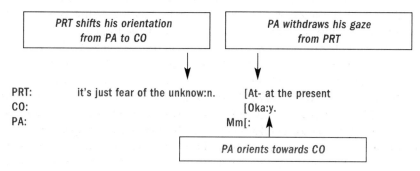

At the beginning of his answer, PRT is not oriented to the questioner (the counsellor) but to the person whose mind he is describing (PA). Likewise, PA is gazing at PRT; thus they are in a mutual gaze contact. PRT, the speaker, turns his gaze to the counsellor at the end of the first sentence of his answer, and shortly after that, PA withdraws his gaze from the speaker and turns also to the counsellor. Through these actions, PA's special status *vis-à-vis* the things spoken about is collaboratively recognized.

The analysis of circular questioning led me to conclude that in this way of asking questions, a special context was created for the clients' talk about sensitive issues. Unlike 'direct' questions, circular questions mobilize *the clients* in the work of eliciting and encouraging each others' talk. The co-client (e.g. partner) describing the owner's mind is under a moral pressure to show companionship by describing the other's mind in a caring and sensitive way. This co-client's version of the 'owner's' experience then works as what Pomerantz (1980) called a 'fishing device', inviting the owner to produce the authoritative version of his or her mind. Detailed analysis of video-recorded interaction made it possible to examine this elicitation in detail.

Video analysis and the practitioners' theories

Let us now return to the ideas presented in the Family Systems Theory. According to the theory, the main function of circular questioning is to help the clients to realize how the problems of one individual are embedded in his or her social relations. Circular questions are asked in order to help the clients to realize the systemic character of their problems. The empirical analysis of video recordings shows how this is done in practice. However, the empirical analysis gave a special emphasis to another function of circular questioning: these questions are a powerful device for engaging the clients in the talk. By asking a circular question, the counsellor initiates a trajectory of interaction which most likely leads one client to elicit self-disclosure of the other, and eventually, the client whose experience is discussed to disclose his/her fears and worries. In my data, the clients did not resist this trajectory. This function of circular questioning is not much discussed in the Family Systems Theory texts. The empirical analysis of video-recorded data suggests that it is an even more primordial function of circular questioning. In order to be able to do anything at all with the clients, the counsellors have to, in the first place, engage them into the talk, into answering the questions. The full appreciation and the detailed understanding of this more primordial task was made possible through the analysis of video recordings.

In describing professional action, a distinction can be made between 'what' and 'how' questions (Silverman and Gubrium 1994). Micro-analytical research based on video or audio recordings has a different role regarding these two types of question. 'What' questions concern the general regularities in interaction: what is done by the participants. In the case of AIDS counselling, many of the 'what' questions are answered in the counsellors' theories, where techniques like circular questioning and direct open supervision are discussed. To find them from the video-recorded data does not necessarily add anything to what the counsellors already know, or what anybody can learn from the professional texts. However, there are other professional contexts, such as career guidance counselling (Vehviläinen 1999, 2001), in which the practitioners' own theories are much patchier. In such contexts, research based on video recordings may also find practices that are not at all recognized in the professionals' theories. Thus, Vehviläinen (1999, 2001) found advice regularly being given by the counsellors to their clients, in spite of the fact that according to the career guidance counselling theories, no advice should be delivered in such counselling (for a more thorough discussion, see Peräkylä and Vehviläinen 2003).

'How' questions concern the *techniques* of doing what is done in the interaction. In the study on AIDS counselling, this involved, for example, the precise ways in which circular questions are asked, received and responded to, and how direct open supervision works. In another kind of therapeutic setting, 'how' questions pertain to issues such as the ways in which psychoanalytic interpretations are prepared for (Vehviläinen 2003) and designed (Peräkylä 2004). In dealing with 'how' questions, it appears, research using video (or audio) recordings as data operates on an entirely different level of precision from that of the practitioners' theories. Usually, even the practical guides and training materials for professionals discuss 'how' matters only at a very general level, for example by giving a paraphrased example of a certain type of question. The implicit assumption seems to be that as members of the common-sense world, readers have the knowledge and skills needed for the comprehension and application of the patterns presented. This is, of course, a reasonable assumption. Therefore, issues like the participants' postural orientation during the delivery of a question or an answer, or specific lexical choices indexing the epistemic framework of questions, need not be addressed in the practitioners' theories.

Micro-analytical research based on video or tape recordings, however, is concerned with exactly these kinds of phenomenon. By studying them, it seeks to explicate the interactional competencies that the professionals and the clients mobilize when accomplishing their tasks. There is probably a vast array of skills of being a professional or being a client that are common to many institutional settings. But specific settings, such as medical consultations (e.g. Heritage and Maynard 2006), psychotherapy (e.g. Peräkylä 2004; Vehviläinen 2003), news interviews (e.g. Clayman and Heritage 2002a) or juridical settings (e.g. Drew 1992), also require specific skills from their participants. In research referred to above, some of the skills of 'being a counsellor with Family Systems Theory orientation' were explicated. Unravelling such specific skills can be considered as one of the main contributions of video-based analysis of professional action.

Greetings: ethnographic observation and video analysis

In the preceding section, we examined the ways in which the micro-analysis of video recordings can enrich the description of professional activity. It was shown that the analysis of video recordings added significant new dimensions to the understanding of AIDS counselling that is offered in the practitioners' own theories.

In this section, we will focus on the description of mundane, everyday action. Let us take as an example *greeting*, which is a most ordinary routine action that most of us are engaged with numerous times a day. Despite the fact that there is relatively little sociological literature on the topic, greetings can be regarded as a locus action where social organization and social relations are expressed and managed in a very dense ways (see Duranti 1992: 660). Goffman (1971: 79) points out that greetings are rituals that 'mark the change of degree of access' between persons at the beginning of an encounter. They also display and maintain continuity in social relations and manage affect (Goffman 1967: 41). Anthropological studies offer detailed accounts on the ways in which participants' relative status is negotiated in greetings, through the organization of verbal exchanges (e.g. Irvine 1974) as well as body movement and spacial arrangements (Duranti 1992). As all patterns of behaviour, greetings are subject to cultural variation. Still, the existence of a greeting ritual is universal, not only among humans but also among many other animals (e.g. Colmenares 1991; de Waal 1996: 191–3). Therefore, the study of greetings may give us access to some of the core properties of social life.

Again, we will juxtapose two descriptions of a practice. This time, we will examine how the descriptions of greeting proffered by micro-analysis of video recordings differ from descriptions based on *ethnographic observation*. As Duranti (1992: 659) points out, most studies on greetings are 'based on the researcher's field notes or recollections of actual greetings and his or her discussions with a few informants'. Basically, what we want to explore is the ways in which video analysis can enrich the understanding of ordinary action offered by more traditional ethnography.

Ethnographic observation of greetings

As a part of a course on qualitative methods, I gave third-year sociology students an assignment in which they had to do a small-scale ethnographic study on greetings. In what follows, I will first describe the students' findings, and then compare them with those reported in a classic video-based study on greetings by Adam Kendon (1990).

The lectures that preceded the assignment on greetings dealt with the principles and practices of ethnographic research (see e.g. Hammersley and Atkinson 1995). The examples of ethnographies that were referred to came mostly from medical, social welfare and educational settings; no studies on greetings were discussed in the lectures. Thus, the idea of the assignment was that the students would test and practice their emergent ethnographic skills with a 'fresh' substantial topic which was nevertheless one that they were well acquainted with through their everyday life. The students worked in groups of three members and each group was asked to make observations on greetings in public or private spheres in Helsinki, and to report their observations in a short article.

The results were astonishingly detailed, given the brevity of their training in ethnographic observation, and the compressed schedule for doing the observations and reporting them. In many papers, greetings were divided into different types, such as embrace, handshake, wave and verbal greeting. Some papers discussed the 'distribution' of these types of greeting among different kinds of person, pointing out, for example, that embrace typically takes place between female subjects, whereas shaking hands is more typical between male greeters and in male–female pairs. The import of status differences to the type of greeting was also discussed by some groups. One group noticed how the degree or intimacy not only 'predicts' the choice of the type of greeting (embrace indicating most intimate relation), but is also a 'result' of this choice: by choosing to embrace somebody and shake hands with somebody else, a person entering a company can display her or his different relation to different members of that company. However, it was also pointed out by a couple of groups that the *social situation* in which the greeting occurs (e.g. whether the meeting is expected or unexpected, or whether it takes place in a party, in a meeting or in classroom) may be more important in terms of the choice of the type of the greeting than relational variables as such.

Some groups pointed out that greeting is in fact a *sequence* of actions, rather than a singular action. They described a progression from the initial noticing to the 'greeting proper'. The most detailed description of this progression named the following phases. 'Optional' phases which are sometimes skipped are indicated by square brackets.

1   Gaze contact (continues until verbal greeting)
2   Smile (continues until verbal greeting)
3   [Wave]
4   Approach
5   Verbal greeting
6   [Physical contact]
7   Beginning of discussion

The group that outlined this sequence also pointed out that it is characterized by a gradual intensification of the bond between the greeters. This intensification requires reciprocal action by both parties.

In outlining greeting as a sequence of actions rather than as a singular act my students hit upon something that Goffman, one of the few sociologists who have studied greetings, left unnoticed or at least unelaborated. Goffman (1971: 74) does recognize the different elements out of which the greeting is built (gaze, smile, wave, words, physical contact). However, in his analysis, he more or less treats the greeting as one unitary event, the social functions of which he then ingeniously discusses. My students, on the contrary, pointed out that the 'greeting proper' (verbal exchange and possible physical contact) is preceded by an elaborate interactional dance in and through which the participants negotiate their relation and also arrive at a decision about the relevancy or non-relevancy of the greeting proper. This sequentiality of greetings has been emphasized, among others, by Duranti (1992).

Sociology students are not professional researchers. An experienced ethnographer would most probably make even more detailed observations on greetings than my students did. However, I was impressed by what my students found. Even if their observations would not exhaust the topic, I do consider them as indicative of the possibilities of ethnographic observation: it is these kinds of issue that ethnographers would pay attention to when observing greetings.

Micro-analysis of video-recorded greetings

Now, let us consider observation based on video recordings. How would the use of video recordings enrich the observations made on greetings? Luckily enough, there is a compact and well-known study on greetings among English-speaking North Americans by Adam Kendon (1990: Chapter 6). By examining Kendon's study, we can gain some understanding on how the use of video can help the analysis of mundane practices.

In his video-based micro-analysis, Kendon has paid attention to many issues that were also noticed by my students in their ethnographies. For example, the 'relational' functions of greetings, having to do with status and emotional closeness between the parties, were discussed by both. The main focus of Kendon's observations, however, is precisely the *sequence* of actions that constitutes the greeting exchange. Basically, Kendon's observations are in line with those made by my students. But there is a significant difference in the degree of detail of the description. I would like to suggest that the difference arises from the basic medium of observation (ethnographic fieldnotes versus video) rather than from the training and the previous experience of the researchers.

Kendon's description of the greeting sequence consists of six phases. Each phase is characterized by the typical behaviours that occur in it.

1. Sighting, orientation, and the initiation of approach

Kendon points out that practices of beginning the greeting vary. A person may begin greeting as soon as he/she perceives the other, or he/she may wait in orientation to this other party until this other party has indicated (through his or her gaze) that he/she also has observed the other and is ready for greeting. Through these choices, the participants indicate the urgency of the greeting and, thereby, their respective roles, for example, in terms of status or in terms of being the host and a quest. For eliciting the other's gaze before beginning the greeting, different practices are used. A person may orient himself towards the other; this is often done by turning head only, the rest of the body being retained in other orientation. Kendon suggests that this serves to give the initial move 'certain tentativeness' (1990: 170). An even more tentative practice involves that the person who is about to initiate the greeting 'avoids catching the eye of the other, but at the same time [...] synchronizes his movements with those of the other and [...] may also glance at the other fleetingly, looking away each time the other looks towards him, until the other actually directs a salutation display to him' (p. 171). Kendon suggest that this indirectness in the initiation of the greeting is a way of dealing with the risk that the other would not wish to reciprocate the approach. Should the other not make a move towards an explicit contact, 'one can continue to go about one's business as if one had not made the initiation attempt' (p. 171). In other words, considerations of face (Goffman 1955) seem to be particularly salient here.

2. Distance salutation

When the persons have established mutual orientation, the distance salutation is usually the first action whereby they indicate to each other and to others present that they are engaged to greet one another. Kendon (pp. 173–7) reports that there are several forms of distance salutation. He focuses on body movement but points out that these are usually associated with a smile and a call. In *head toss*, the person tilts his/her head rapidly backwards and then brings it back again. Typically, head toss is *not* reciprocated with a similar movement. *Head lower* is the typical response to head toss. In head lower, the head is tilted forward and held in that position for a while before returning it to the normal position. Kendon suggests (p. 175) that as an initiatory greeting, head lower embodies status distance (adult greeting a child, or older man greeting a much younger woman). *Nod* and *wave* are other forms of distance salutation.

3. Head dip

In many cases, the distance salutation is followed by one of the parties lowering his head by means of forward bend of the neck. Kendon suggests that the head dip operates as means for shifting 'attention gear', that is as a way of marking the greeter's shift from other involvements to fully attending to the person he has just saluted.

4. Approach

If the parties are going to engage in a 'close salutation' (see below), they will have to move closer to one another. Kendon points out that in choosing the distance each will move towards the other, the participants yet again display what kind of relation they have, for example in terms of status (see Duranti 1992; Irvine 1974). During the approach, distinctive behaviours occur. One has to do with *gaze*. At the distance saluta-tion, the parties typically gaze at each other. After that, however, 'one or other of the greeting pair, or sometimes both, look away, and they may continue to avoid looking at the other until they are almost close enough for the close salutation' (Kendon 1990: 180). Kendon (pp. 183–5) points out that the party who moves most, that is the one who enters the other's physical territory, is even more likely to look away than the other party, suggesting that the aversion of gaze may help to decrease the input of stimulus and threat that otherwise could be experienced by the one who is approached. Another recurrent behaviour involves what Kendon (pp. 185–6) calls *body cross*. Recurrently, one of the greeting partners 'brings one or both of his arms in front of him, "crossing" the upper part of the body' (p. 185). Kendon suggests that the party who does this is the more vulnerable of the participants – the younger, the one who is entering the territory from outside (like a guest), or the one who covers most distance in his approach. If body cross is associated with vulnerability, he goes on to propose, it may be a protective move-ment, and it may also communicate non-aggressive intent to the other party.

5. Final approach
The greeting partners re-establish mutual gaze when they are rather close to one another (about 3.5 metres or less). At this point, some vocalization (verbal greeting) takes place. *Smiling* reappears in the greeting partners' faces. (The parties frequently smile during the distance salutation but not during the approach.) Now they also adopt a distinctive *head position*, with females most often having their head cocked to one side and males their head cocked forward. A distinct hand gesture often occurs: the person 'presents' his/her palm to the other party, with the arm extended forward or laterally. Kendon (p. 191) points out that this gesture has previously been identified in earlier, cross-cultural research and suggests that it may signal openness to social contact with the other party.

6. Close salutation
Finally, the parties stop their approach, come to halt facing one another and engage in greeting ritual. It may involve no body contact but just head movement. Sometimes it involves handshakes (usually three up-and-down movements) which may be combined with other gestures, such as head nodding or cheek kiss. Embracing is yet another frequent form of greeting ritual. Quickly, after performing the ritual, the parties withdraw from the facial orientation. In Kendon's data, the dis-tribution of different forms of close salutation was associated with the gender of the greeters, no contact greeting being the most frequent in female–female pairs, hand-shake in male–male pairs and embrace in male–female pairs.

Comparing ethnography and video-based micro-analysis

Now, we are in a position to compare the two descriptions of greeting based on dif-ferent modes of observation: ethnography (by my students) and video (by Kendon).

First of all, it has to be pointed out that they have very much in common. Basic modes of greeting (or to use Kendon's terms, of *close salutation*) were acknowledged in both. The relational work, having to do with affect and status, that is done in and through greetings was acknowledged and analysed in both. The sequence of actions that precedes the close salutation was identified and described in Kendon's video-based analysis, and in some (most well developed) ethnographies of my students. The gender differences associated with modes of greeting were also acknowledged in both types of observation. There was an interesting contrast between these two data sets: in Kendon's data (from the USA in the 1960s and 1970s) embracing was most often used in male–female greetings, whereas in the Finnish data from 2003, it was most often used by female–female pairs. Both samples are very small but, nevertheless, this raises comparative questions about changes in gender relations and/or cultural differences between the USA and Northern Europe.

However, there were also significant differences between the ethnographic and the video-based descriptions of greetings. The most important difference between Kendon and my students has to do with the degree of detail of description. The basic phases of the greeting sequence were outlined in rather similar ways in the best ethnographies and in Kendon. However, Kendon's video-based description yielded a rich depiction of the variation of the gestural and other physical actions associated with each phase. Video-recorded data afforded a more detailed representation of the head positions, the movements of hands and arms, the gaze and the facial expressions of the participants that clearly would have been inaccessible for any other mode of observation.

The details that Kendon's study provides seem to me extremely fruitful for the enhancement of the social scientific understanding of greetings. Consider, for example, two central behavioural details during the approach, *avoidal of gaze* and *body cross*. Noticing and describing these behaviours would certainly be worthwhile in itself, as they are central parts of the greeting sequence. (You can get a 'feeling' of how powerful the norm of gaze avoidal is during the approach by trying to hold the other's gaze throughout this phase: you will be feeling very uncomfortable and possibly losing friends![1]) Kendon, however, goes further, as he asks what the communicative tasks are that these behaviours help to accomplish. As mentioned above, he suggests that they may have to do with the minimization of *threat* imposed by one party upon the other in the encounter. Therefore, greetings, which certainly constitute a major mechanism for the display and maintenance of social bonds, also involve a 'darker' side, which has to do with the regulation of aggression. Bonding probably would not be possible without that regulation. The observation of the subtle gestures, the identification of which is possible for the researcher probably only on the basis of video-recorded data, seem to open a whole new dimension for analysis in greetings.

As another example, consider the practices of eliciting the other's gaze at the first phase of greeting. Kendon showed the subtle indirect practices involved in this (e.g. adopting the rhythm of the other's movement without looking at him/her). Thereby, he showed how carefully the interactants work to avoid having their initiatives for approach openly being turned down. This, in turn, opens up new avenues for the understanding of 'face' (i.e. the worthiness of the self that is presented by participants: Goffman 1955) in social interaction. It shows the interactants' tacit orientation to the possibility of rejection and the possibly ensuing shame (Scheff 1990) and embarrassment. And as yet another example, consider Kendon's observations about the head position in final approach. He pointed out the regularity in which females and males adopt different head positions here. By pointing out this difference, Kendon has obviously located one practice of *doing gender* in social interaction (see Garfinkel 1967b; C. Kitzinger 2000).

So, in research such as Kendon's, the description of behavioural detail, made possible by the micro-analysis of video-recorded data, led to theoretical and other questions that could not have been raised without this level of detailed description.

Conclusion: the place of the video-recorded data

In this chapter, I have explored some ways in which the micro-analysis of video-recorded data can contribute to the understanding of professional and mundane social action. In discussing the analysis of professional action, I compared the descriptions of AIDS counselling offered in the practitioners' theories with the descriptions that arise from conversation analysis of video recordings of the actual counselling sessions. In a similar fashion, when discussing the analysis of a mundane action, descriptions based on ethnographic fieldnotes and descriptions based on video recordings were compared. In both cases, my suggestion was that the micro-analysis of video-recorded data offers access to aspects of organization that the other forms of description do not reach.

The upshot of this, however, is *not* that micro-analysis of video recordings would have rendered the other forms of description useless. Practitioners' theories and accounts of professional action are necessary, for example, in the training of professionals and in the evaluation of the professional action. Micro-analysis of video recordings can be useful both in training and evaluation, but it cannot supersede the practitioners' own theories here, because these theories incorporate the practitioners' own way of thinking and talking about their work. Likewise, traditional ethnography certainly has its uses in social science. For example, in the description of organizations, such as school (Gordon et al. 2000) or hospital (Strauss et al. 1985; Timmermans 1998), an ethnographer can arrive at such an overall understanding of the setting that would be difficult to gain using video or tape recordings only as data (see also Chapter 7 in this volume).

Having said this, I want to return to my main point: there is much to be gained by using micro-analysis of video recordings in researching professional and mundane social action. In both examples that I discussed in this chapter, the key advantage of the use of video-recorded data was the access to *behavioural detail* that it offers to the researcher.

Is a high degree of detail a virtue in social science? The answer depends on the type of text that we are dealing with (see Chapter 7 in this volume). In general theoretical texts, for example, references to behavioural details may not be needed. However, even in texts that deal with empirical phenomena, the description of all details is not necessarily useful. In assessing student papers and in reviewing journal submissions, I find myself every now and then suggesting that a particular section, in which some details of the data are described, is not useful for the overall argumentation presented in the paper. Sometimes meticulous description of details may become an obstacle for the researcher understanding the very phenomenon that he or she should be focusing on.

So, the significance of detail can only be judged on the basis of what the details contribute to the understanding of the phenomenon that is investigated, in the context of the questions asked and arguments put forward in the paper. It is exactly from this perspective that the behavioural details offered by the video recordings in my study on AIDS counselling, and in Kendon's study on greetings, turned out to be extremely useful. The examination of the organization of gaze and the use of acknowledgement tokens, as well as features of turn designs and sequence organization, led me to ask questions about the uses of circular questions in eliciting the clients' talk in AIDS counselling. Likewise, the observations on gesture and gaze positions led Kendon to ask questions pertaining the normative structure of the greeting sequence, as well as the management of face, regulation of aggression and gender performance in greetings. These questions have to do with the core properties of social action and social relations, and in the case of studies that we have used as examples, they were raised through the micro-analysis of video recordings.

Note

1. This exercise has been used by and was suggested to me by Paul Drew.

CHAPTER SEVEN
•••••••••

Language, Dialogue and Ethnographic Objectivity

Darin Weinberg

Ethnographers are fond of admonishing one another against the evils of reification. Social life, we are very often told, is not really a *thing*,[1] or even a collection of things, but a complex of *processes*. It is not eternal and unchanging, but dynamic, evolving and, most fundamentally, *achieved* through the creative interaction of sentient, intentional and knowledgeable actors (see Blumer 1969; Bourdieu 1990; Collins 1981; Garfinkel 1967a; Giddens 1984). Hence, to presume that we can speak directly to the nature of such things as states, markets, social organizations, or social movements – let alone such things as social roles and rituals – is, according to this line of argument, to commit ourselves to a misplaced 'positivism' or 'scientism'. Insofar as they possess a genuinely *social nature*, such things must be studied as artefacts of the artful human interactions that give them their distinctive empirical forms. In short, ethnographers ubiquitously encourage us to avoid reification in social research by focusing our analytic attentions on the empirical details of the specific organizational and interactional practices through which social things are realized (literally, made real).

Though I accept this advice in spirit, there is a niggling problem with it that has often troubled me. That problem may be introduced with this question: Are social processes like organizational and interactional practices not also *things*? The ethnographic admonition against reification seems to trade on the implication that they aren't. After all, if we avoid reifying things precisely by looking at how social processes create and sustain them, then how could these very social processes themselves be things? A moment's reflection reveals that those who would proclaim that social processes are things appear less like anti-reificationists, and more like plain old-fashioned reductionists – simply installing one set of empirical objects (i.e. social processes) as analytically more fundamental than any other (e.g. nations, ethnicities, classes, genders, families, etc.). Positing that social processes are things seems not to avoid reification but only to trade one form of reification for another.[2]

On the other hand, if they are to be rigorously studied, presumably social processes must be understood as amenable to observation, description, measurement, explanation, and/or the other practices through which we normally distinguish the real from the hypothetical, mythical or illusory. To the extent we would wish to identify and describe them, we quickly find it is impossible not to presume that social processes are things. While some radically postmodern ethnographers have side-stepped this dilemma by forsaking the very prospect of objective description itself, most of us recognize that such an unbridled epistemological scepticism renders the very idea of ethnography itself untenable (see Hammersley and Atkinson 1995; Silverman 1993). It is one matter to recognize that the achievement of ethnographic objectivity is always historically, culturally and interactionally situated, it is quite another to forsake the reality of that achievement altogether (Weinberg 2002).

It would appear, then, at least on first glance, that there is a rather serious analytic antinomy here. On one level we wish to defend against what we view as the reifying and reductionist tendencies of 'scientism' or 'positivism', but we also wish to preserve some sense for the idea that our writings are not merely imaginative exercises but do actually describe the worlds inhabited by those we study. In this chapter I take up the question of how this antinomy might be resolved through a discussion of the various ways in which language use has been found to figure in social life. As I will show, the study of language use offers a perspicuous case study for how ethnographers, and other social scientists, might combine a sense of our own objectivity with an emphatic rejection of the 'scientism' or 'positivism' that effectively occlude the central importance that questions of meaning and inter-subjectivity have for the understanding of human social life.

Analytic domains, dispute domains and research objects

In this section, I distinguish two approaches to the understanding of ethnographic research, analytic and reflexive, and indicate their consequences for the way we think about the things we study. The *analytic approach* posits a distinctive domain of empirical phenomena, the essence of which ethnography is uniquely equipped to grasp. The *reflexive approach* posits a provisional self-understanding of ethnographic research itself and construes its research objects as inextricable from the specific nature of that work. While many have argued that the reflexive approach can only end in a nihilistic relativism, I indicate why this is mistaken. The discussion is couched in a brief and rather selective historical survey of ethnography as an academic discipline with particular attention given to the significance ethnographers have found in language as both an empirical phenomenon and a medium of work.

Ethnography as we now know it emerged in the late nineteenth century as a scientific regimen through which to discern humanity where others had failed to do so. Early ethnographers, most notably Franz Boas and his students, argued that through the impartial exercise of scientific data collection and analysis, social practices once widely held as evidence of savagery would be transformed into evidence of the awesome depth and variety of human experience and expression. Through ethnography, parochialism would be shed for cosmopolitanism, prejudice for enlightenment, derision for appreciation, and fear for respect. Hence, not only would the status of non-Europeans be raised to its rightful place on a moral and intellectual par with Europeans. But the humanity of Europeans themselves would also be exercised and extended through ethnographic encounters with the worlds of others (Stocking 1990). Through ethnography would be revealed the vast treasury of non-Western human achievement and we would all be richer for it.

This project had two core elements. One was to establish ethnography on a secure scientific footing by demonstrating its possession of a distinctive empirical domain and a systematic and theoretically rigorous approach to the analysis of that domain. The other element was to discredit the overtly racist strains of anthropological thought that had taken root earlier in the nineteenth century. These two elements were intrinsically linked. The Boasian approach to securing a distinctive empirical domain for ethnographic research was also a method for discrediting scientific racism. Boas and his students argued against the view that biological inheritances govern human behaviour by producing empirical research suggesting that human behaviour was a function of human *cultural* rather than biological variation. Hence, Boasians simultaneously made a case for distinguishing the empirical domain of cultural anthropology from that of biology and cast aspersions on the idea that there exists an intrinsically, or biologically, 'primitive mentality' distinct from the civilized and more rational mentality of white Europeans.

As his ideas took root in American anthropology, Boas and his students produced more explicit specifications of the concept 'culture' and sharper arguments to the effect that this concept referred to an empirical domain over which cultural anthropology, and the ethnographic method, ought properly to be held as sovereign (see Herskovits 1947). At the same time, intellectual movements abroad were travelling in confluent directions. In Britain, figures like Branislaw Malinowski and A.R. Radcliffe-Browne were systematizing and successfully promoting a functionalist approach to the ethnographic understanding of 'primitive societies' that all but analytically outlawed reference not just to the biological inheritances of their research subjects but to their putative histories as well. Building on Saussurian structural linguistics, Claude Levi-Strauss also developed an immensely influential and largely synchronic approach to ethnographic research. These approaches converged to produce by the mid-twentieth century a powerful international consensus that conceived ethnographic research as a relatively ahistorical analysis of data one had personally collected during a stint of fieldwork conducted among some fairly small population. Thus, human cultures came to be construed as historically enduring, autonomous, and distinctive social worlds. And ethnography was widely recognized as the scientific discipline concerned with such things, the sum total of which comprised its distinctive analytic domain.

Prominent among the mid-twentieth-century systematizers of Boasian thought must be counted one of Boas's star students, Edward Sapir. Sapir is particularly important for our purposes because he eventually moved away from considerations of culture as such and towards the formal characteristics of language specifically. Sapir argued that human thought is channelled in systematic sorts of ways by language. Hence, insofar as different cultures possessed distinctive languages, they could also be expected to exhibit systematically different sorts of cognitive orientation to the world (Lucy 1992). This idea was developed by Benjamin Lee Whorf, who insisted that languages, understood as coherent symbolic systems, not only channel our thoughts but effectively integrate them as well. Hence human collectives, by virtue of sharing a language, also share a distinctive and relatively coherent worldview.

This analytic claim proved a compelling one for legions of ethnographers insofar as it provided a reasonably straightforward recipe for empirical research. Ethnography, by these lights, entailed gathering indigenous materials through participant observation and interviews with local informants and using these materials to reconstruct one's research subjects' collective worldview. Worldviews, understood as analytic wholes with their own distinctive properties and forms of internal integrity, thus became new types of *things* that ethnographers were uniquely equipped to understand. Obviously, linguistic materials figured very prominently in this effort. Local lexicographies were produced, narratives of one kind or another were elicited and collected, grammatical forms were scrutinized, all in the interest of recovering what was variously referred to as 'the native's point of view', 'local belief systems', 'conceptual schemes', 'conceptual frameworks', 'stocks of knowledge', 'local knowledge' or indigenous theories of this or that. This approach to the analysis of linguistic materials remains as a resource in contemporary ethnography and there is no reason to my mind why it should not continue to do so. However, it has also met with some rather fundamental criticisms that ought to be taken seriously.

One important difficulty that has been raised with respect to this sort of research concerns its failure to address the actual conduct of language use. Instances of language use are employed to construct a theoretical model of the cognitive contents of some bit of culture, but the activity of language use – most emphatically, its *interactional* dimensions – appear almost entirely neglected. It must be said that this neglect is not, by itself, a fatal flaw. No analytic approach can pretend to a comprehensive coverage of its phenomenon (see Schegloff 1987). However, many ethnographers have sought to transcend this limitation and to consider language less as a fixed form of social structure and more as a dynamic form of social interaction. During the 1960s, innovators in linguistics, anthropology and sociology began to demonstrate how language use is interactionally organized with respect to specific practical activities. This approach has borne fruit in a number of ways and, thereby, profoundly humbled the prospects of anyone who would hope to explain language use exclusively with respect to invariant linguistic structures.

Another, perhaps more damaging, criticism of the Sapir–Whorf approach pertains to the legitimacy of the presumption that language community members' cognitive commitments are either as identical or as conceptually coherent as this approach implies. It is one matter to suggest that language communities tend towards certain cognitive habits compared with other language communities, it is quite another to suggest they share a coherent 'belief system' or an identical stock of knowledge in common (Turner 1994). Much ethnographic research suggests that even the smallest and seemingly homogeneous communities are rife with ideological (among many other) conflicts and that people's 'belief systems' are not necessarily as 'systematic' or conceptually coherent as this approach often implies. Moreover, the very ideas that languages are mutually exclusive or that there are reasonable ways of decisively demarcating language communities from one another or of indicating what exactly language communities share in common have been found analytically wanting on a number of scores (Duranti 1997: 68–83). More than merely indicating limitations in the analytic scope of the Sapir–Whorf approach, these critiques have questioned the extent to which it is at all reasonable to think about belief systems, languages or language communities as integral things-in-themselves.

These sorts of observation have lent momentum to the view that such holistic renderings of the structural characteristics of languages or language communities may be rather seriously misleading. They have encouraged ethnographers to look beyond the idea of shared linguistic structures to account for the apparent orderliness and/or coherence of human communities. But holistic and structural approaches to the study of language and culture have also been criticized on ethical/political grounds. By reifying the characteristics of language, language communities and/or linguistic practices, we analytically render them beyond the influence of factors external to them. Not only does this prevent us from appreciating the extent to which language interacts dynamically with other elements of social life (Goodwin 1994, 2000), but it prevents us from seeing how our own analytic regard for languages, language communities, and linguistic practices is itself the product of a kind of interaction with them.[3] This in turn prevents us from appreciating the various and ever-changing ways in which ethnographic research and the wider social world mutually influence (and indeed *change*) one another. While we might learn by unilaterally observing each other, there is no element of actual dialogue, or mutual *instruction*, between researchers and research subjects in this picture at all.

Increasingly, ethnographers have come to appreciate that social scientists do not hold an unrivalled interest in the production of true descriptions of the social world. We have come to appreciate that our research subjects themselves often have a great deal to say to us about the nature of their own lives, and that their accounts may bear a fairly wide variety of relationships to the descriptions we ourselves proffer. Whereas ethnographers in earlier eras once easily alternated between treating members' accounts of their lives as either objective testimony regarding local affairs or as analysable phenomena in their own right, today we are confronted with the complex and ongoing task of navigating between these two poles (DeVault 1999; Gubrium and Holstein 1999; Pollner and Emerson 1988). In place of images that construe our subject matter as hermetically sealed analytic domains towards which we are entitled to a posture of analytic and 'value-free' detachment, ethnographers are now more often confronted with images that construe our subject matter as comprised of diverse interlocutors with whom we must inevitably engage in serious dialogue. We must now continuously ask ourselves whether, and *why*, we wish to accept, critique, or ignore the accounts of their worlds proffered by those we study.

Moreover, there is yet another layer of complexity with which we must contend. In addition to the assorted descriptions of social reality produced by those we study, we must also consider the various relationships our own descriptions may take to those proffered by other social scientists. We mustn't forget that the social sciences are themselves heterodox fields of activity made up of diverse researchers often working in relative indifference or even conflict with one another. Just like the cultures of those we study, our own analytic cultures are often marked by dynamism, disunity and widely divergent concerns. In the same way that we must do so with respect to those we study, we must also continuously ask ourselves whether, and *why*, we wish to accept, critique, or ignore the accounts proffered by our social scientific colleagues. In place of images of scientific work that suggest a unity of method and theoretical outlook among colleagues, we are increasingly confronted with the reality of differences among ourselves and of the unavoidable necessity for dialogue across these lines of difference.

I have belaboured these points because they powerfully illustrate the extent to which language use is more than just an ethnographic *topic*. It is also a constitutive element of ethnographic practice. In the conduct of ethnographic research we inevitably engage in ongoing dialogue both with members of the communities we study and with those who make up our own professional communities. These dialogues profoundly shape the nature of our analyses. Hence, our analyses of how language use figures in social life inevitably carries implications for how we understand the nature of those analyses themselves. If we find that holistic renderings of the structural characteristics of languages or language communities often fail to describe adequately the social lives of those we study, we might be well advised to consider whether they are any more adequate to the task of describing ethnographic research itself. If we find it is unwise to dissociate the logic of language use in the communities we study from the logic of the social activities within which language use participates, perhaps similar points might be made with respect to the relationship between our analyses (be they rendered in verbal or textual form) and the wider round of organizational activities that make up our professional lives.

These kinds of consideration figure centrally in what has been called the 'reflexive turn' in ethnographic research (see Emerson 2001; Hammersley and Atkinson 1995). The proponents of reflexive ethnography are a diverse lot but they are agreed on the principle that ethnography is made a subtler and more valuable craft through attention to the worldly circumstances of its own accomplishment. While early proponents of the reflexive turn focused largely on the literary devices through which ethnographic authority is accomplished (see Atkinson 1990; Clifford and Marcus 1986; van Maanen 1988), later contributors have opened the discussion to the whole spectrum of mundane practices that constitute qualitative data collection and analysis (see Bourdieu 1996; DeVault 1999; Emerson et al. 1995; Gubrium and Holstein 1997; Katz 2001, 2002; Pollner and Emerson 1988, 2001). Lending my own voice to this chorus, I have argued that scientific research – including, of course, ethnography – ought to be conceptualized in terms of the *dispute domains* within which it occurs (Weinberg 2002). In place of formal analytic specifications of the *topical* domains addressed by scientific disciplines, we should empirically specify the *practical/dialogical* domains within and for which our analytic disputes occur.

The reflexive approach insists that the research objects that concern ethnographers are not entirely independent of the practices through which ethnographers work. Hence, for example, many critical anthropologists have argued that the very idea that there are bounded cultures in the world is a product of the colonial enterprise within which ethnography first took form (see Asad 1973). According to this argument, 'cultures' were established as researchable objects largely by virtue of the fact that colonialists had a stake in classifying the properties of foreign populations for the purpose of imperial administration. Analogous arguments have been made regarding any number of ethnography's research objects. Instead of regretting the fact that ethnography's objects are, in some senses, artefacts of the research enterprise, reflexive ethnographers tend to see it as inevitable. The interesting question is not how we might transcend the perspectival standpoints from which we work, but how we might better grasp the relationship between diverse perspectival standpoints and the practical circumstances that condition them.

This interest has very often rendered reflexive ethnographers vulnerable to the charge of relativism. If the research objects we claim to describe are in some senses artefacts of the theoretical and methodological commitments with which we approach the research enterprise, then what hope do we have for transcending those commitments? Some reflexive ethnographers accept that indeed a thoroughgoing relativism is entailed by their reflexive commitments. They claim that there are various forms of knowledge in the world and that we must simply make our choices and live with the consequences (cf. Collins and Yearley 1992). Others, though, are not convinced that relativism is a necessary fate. I am, myself, convinced that it is only by embracing reflexivity that we may hope to establish a stable footing from which to arbitrate the comparative objectivity of competing accounts. I will finish this section with a brief defence of this position.[4]

According to the classic conception of the analytic approach to understanding ethnography, the whole point of empirical research is to forge valid links between our conceptual generalizations and the intrinsic essence of the things we are conceptualizing. By this view, it is only if our data can be gathered entirely free of conceptual taint, that it can genuinely confirm or refute the correspondence of our concepts with anything that exists entirely apart from them. But as it has turned out, all efforts to formulate the nature of data in some sort of conceptually neutral 'observation language' have been soundly discredited (Gibson 1979; Hanson 1958). Hence, for example, collecting data using attitude scales must prejudicially presume the existence of things in the world that warrant use of the concept 'attitude'. Though such data may help us arbitrate between theories presuming different attitudes in a given population, it will be of little use in deciding between these theories and theories that altogether reject the independent existence of anything warranting the concept 'attitude' in that population. One must believe there are such things as 'attitudes' in the first place for this sort of data to be meaningful. This same point holds generally because all data must always be about a given subject matter before it can confirm or refute specific theories concerning that subject matter. Scientific research is, then, always based on a foundation of provisional assumptions regarding the basic characteristics of one's subject matter. And, by necessity, it will always provisionally presume, rather than prove, the existence of certain basic facts about the world. These presumptions profoundly affect how researchers decide to accept, critique, or ignore the accounts proffered by both members of the communities we study and by our social scientific colleagues.

Scientific assessments of objectivity must be made in light of the substantive assumptions current in particular scientific communities. And, at least in some respects, the authority of these assumptions is always contested. Hence good scientific researchers must do more than blithely conform to a fixed set of canonical assumptions regarding the nature of our phenomena. We must address the critiques of our assumptions. Answers to questions regarding the comparative objectivity of competing accounts of the social world cannot, then, be settled with respect to some fixed criteria for scientific excellence. They must be sought in light of detailed *reflexive* consideration of the unique constellation of discursive (and other practical) challenges that confront any particular research project. This is not in any way an apologia for relativist resignation. It is a call for vigorously reflexive and critical *dialogue* across lines of theoretical and methodological difference. Far from entailing relativism itself, this kind of reflexive ethnographic research and dialogue is, to my mind, the *only* way the orthodoxies that embody our partisan prejudices can be effectively unearthed and overcome.

Ethnography, language and social action

In this section I move from the general to the particular in an effort to provide more detailed empirical grounding for my argument. Ethnography has matured and developed in the many decades since it first emerged as a force to be reckoned with on the academic landscape. It is now many things to many people (see Atkinson et al. 2001; Denzin and Lincoln 1994). We are well past the time for totalitarian pronouncements on the proper methods or topics of ethnography. Our interests, alliances and opportunities are diverse, provisional and in flux. And it is within this environment that we must make our choices regarding who and what to take seriously and why. I raise these points only to reiterate that my own views are inevitably informed by the unique sets of challenges and issues that have arisen in my own research and by virtue of my own trajectory through our fragmented and often fractious professional culture. Hence, I do not presume to speak for everyone, nor that my comments will be equally germane to all who read them.

I have done the bulk of my own ethnographic fieldwork in therapeutic communities designed for homeless people diagnosed with various mental health problems. Talk figured centrally in these programmes and, judging from the ethnographic literature pertaining to these kinds of setting, language enjoys a position of perhaps unrivalled theoretical interest among ethnographers who study them. One reads routinely of the centrality of language, dialogue and narrative, both with respect to more established forms of dyadic 'talk therapy' (Klienman 1988; Labov and Fanshel 1977) as well as forms like family therapy (Gubrium 1992), brief therapy (Miller 1997), Alcoholics Anonymous (Denzin 1993; Pollner and Stein 1996; Rudy 1986), and others (Frank and Frank 1991). This literature has revealed much more than I can summarize here about the variety of ways in which language use figures in these sorts of therapeutic work. In lieu of a general summary, I will focus on a few illustrative themes that arose in my own research. My effort will be to demonstrate what I take to be some of ethnography's distinctive capacities for contributing to the study of talk in therapeutic communities and similar settings.

My field experience largely confirmed the critiques mentioned earlier regarding holistic or structural renderings of cultures, languages, language communities, belief systems, and the like. Rather than finding variations on a single symbolic 'system' or 'structure' underlying programme practice, I found my settings to be idiomatically eclectic. Unlike other programmes that embrace some particular treatment model, my programmes made use of a variety of conceptual resources drawn from diverse sources, including Alcoholics Anonymous, psychiatry, social work, Christian theology, and others. Moreover, I could find no algorithm that explained if, when, or how these various idioms were invoked in the course of programme practice. Hence, rather than focusing primarily on the ways these idioms were articulated, modified or resisted in the talk I observed, I focused more closely on the practical work that seemed to be getting done through talk.

I was not always able to tape-record the events I observed and was, at any rate, more inclined towards ethnographic investigations of my settings as distinctive sorts of 'going concerns' (Hughes 1971) than generic aspects of talk-in-interaction or in the ways in which my settings exhibited variations on more ubiquitous patterns of talk-in-interaction. Hence, I must confess, the scientific sensibilities I took into the field were of a classically ethnographic, rather than conversation or discourse analytic, sort. I sought to understand my settings more or less holistically, as social *things* marked by distinctive characteristics and forms of internal integrity. And while I was suspicious of the hypothesis that their integrity, as social things, could be explained solely as a product of a putatively shared belief system or symbolic structure, I was nevertheless convinced that it was not sociologically misguided to consider them as scientifically describable objects and to investigate the various forces that contributed to their stability. In what follows I sketch one piece of this research enterprise in an effort to demonstrate what I suggest is: (1) a uniquely *ethnographic* analysis of the talk I observed in my settings, and (2) one which possesses a form of scientific objectivity that is not borne simply of its correspondence with that which it seeks to describe, but is thoroughly nested in a particular scientific dispute domain.

After having spent considerable time in the field and having reviewed a great deal of the ethnographic literature concerning 'street addict culture', 'bottle gangs', and homeless street life, I came to notice a rather sharp inconsistency between the descriptions of street life and of street drug users I was hearing from my research subjects and those I was reading in the literature. Whereas the ethnographic literature tended overwhelmingly to portray the street drug scene as eminently socially organized and active drug users as rational actors (see Agar 1973; Finestone 1957; Stephens 1991), my own research subjects tended to describe street life and active drug users in terms of chaos, savagery and irrationality. I began to wonder what might explain this.

One possibility was that my subjects were systematically exposed to a more chaotic, and savage, side of street life than were those studied by other ethnographers. After all, insofar as they were now in treatment, presumably they were more traumatized by the drug life than those who remain in it. Two empirical points inveighed against this explanation. One was that my subjects' accounts were not at all limited to their own behaviour and experiences, or even those of known associates, but were routinely made generically of the whole world of street drug use. If they were simply describing their own particular experiences, then why did they cast such a wide swathe? Second, if they were simply describing their own particular experiences, it was also puzzling that their accounts exhibited such a high degree of conformity. Could it be that so many of my research subjects shared a common experience of the street drug scene that was so systematically out of step with those I read of in the ethnographic literature? This didn't seem very plausible. Having lost faith in the proposition that these accounts could be understood simply as more or less accurate descriptions of people's experiences, I considered what sorts of work they might be doing for programme members.

I began to look more carefully through my fieldnotes and to pay more serious attention in the field to people's descriptions of street life and street drug use. What specific things were being said? How were they being said? When? By whom? Slowly, some clues began to emerge. Often these descriptions were made to provide explicit contrast to the lives of programme members, as in the following remark made by a client during group therapy in a skid row drug rehabilitation programme:

> We're all on the programme. At least we've begun to see. Now I've been on the programme before and I relapsed before, but at least I know what I need to do. These brothers out there? They don't even KNOW what they're doin' to themselves.

More than merely distinguishing themselves from programme non-members on the street, I observed a ubiquitous expectation among programme members that distinctions between themselves and street denizens pertained specifically to drug use. This can be seen in the following data excerpt from an out-patient programme on the west side of Los Angeles. After venting in group therapy about a recent run-in with an aggressive panhandler, Charlie[5] shared as follows:

> 'These people don't care about keepin' clean or keepin' any kind of self respect about themselves. I'll tell ya, stayin' clean and healthy and keepin' my clothes lookin' alright is important to me. If ya don't try and distinguish yourself from the scum, then you'll turn into the scum. If you don't try to get yourself outta the gutter, you'll become part of that gutter. And that's what a lot of these people out there are. They don't got no principles. They don't demand anything from

themselves.' Mack laughed and added, 'They'd literally kill their own grandmother to get a hit [of crack cocaine]'. Charlie said, 'Yep, it's all about the drugs. That's all it's about. People don't care about anyone or anything. They have no respect for themselves, no respect for other people, and no respect for their environment.' Mack, Del, and Clarise were nodding fiercely in agreement. Others were also doing so occasionally.

Here, Charlie opposes his own conscientious efforts to '[stay] clean and healthy' to the profligate dirtiness, degradation, and amorality of 'these people out there'. The narrative linkage of this general degradation and drugs in particular can be seen in Mack's taking up of Charlie's lament with an unprecedented invocation of drug use ('they'd literally kill their own grandmother to get a hit'). Evidently, Mack understood Charlie's complaint as one specifically about drug users and, indeed, Charlie confirms Mack was correct in his next remark ('Yep, it's all about the drugs …'). Beyond these points, though, one can begin to see in these passages what I came to believe was another, perhaps even more significant, element of the descriptions programme members made of life on the street.

In the first excerpt inhabitants of the world 'out there' are cast specifically as *unconscious* of the damage they are doing to themselves. And in the second excerpt, drug use is held to reflect personal lapse and dissipation rather than self-governed activity. A linkage between life 'out there' and the absence of self-control was also evident in many of the other accounts of the street drug world that I collected (see Weinberg 2000). And, it was very often made in direct contrast to the conscientiousness said to be found among programme participants. This began to suggest to me that there might be more to these descriptions than a simple Durkheimian dichotomy between us-good-insiders and them-bad-outsiders. I began to suspect that members of my programmes were doing more than merely affiliative work with these descriptions, but what exactly?

Eventually a few more clues emerged. I found that programme members' descriptions of street life were not always made in *contrast* to themselves at all. Indeed, sometimes they were very clearly self-implicative. In the following passage, Ian describes the effects that street life had on his own behaviour:

People don't even know what it's like to be homeless now. A lot of people think it's still like the sixties, you know, where everybody helps each other out. I mean, I wasn't around that far back, so I don't know if it was ever like that, but it sure as hell ain't like that now. I remember when it used to be you'd get the rockheads all hangin' out in one place and all the drunks here, and all the junkies some place else, and then maybe you had a little bit of people lookin' out for each other. I mean a LITTLE bit. You know if you got somebody high, then they figure they owe you one and they'd do you a favour or somethin', but even that'd only go so far. I mean you still got ripped off a lot even then. But now there ain't even none of that anymore. Everybody just lookin' out for themselves and nobody can't do nothin' for nobody else. Nobody trusts anybody and nobody can be trusted. People rip off anyone; it don't matter who you are. It's pure shit. I used to use behind that shit all the time 'cause I just couldn't take it.

Here Ian offers a description of collective descent into a quasi-Hobbesian order that culminates with the statement that his drug use was a product of defeat ('I just couldn't take it') and not deliberate or rational adjustment. The phrase 'I couldn't take it' reflects a very different vocabulary of motives (Mills 1940) from 'using drugs seemed sensible given my dire circumstances'. Hence, Ian explains his drug use as an environmentally induced relinquishing of self-control, rather than a deliberate exercise of self-control. This same usage of a description of street life can also be seen in the following remarks made by Lee in group therapy:

> 'I've had periods in my life when I was really lonely, REALLY lonely, like when I decided to bum it last time and those were bad times ... 'cause I didn't know anybody and I couldn't meet anybody. That was the worst part about bein' homeless (laugh). It's funny, too, 'cause I used to always go and sit on a bench out in Palisades Park and there was this other homeless guy who used to sit across from the bench I sat on, and one time, he came over to talk to me, but I said, 'Hey, I don't wanna talk to you, get outta here."' Claire, a counsellor, asked, 'Why'd you do that?' Lee replied, 'I don't know why. Maybe I thought I was better than him unconsciously or somethin'. Maybe I was scared he was gonna con me or rip me off. I dunno.' Tanya, a client, laughed. Both she and another client, Neil, nodded in recognition of the sentiment Lee expressed. Lee spoke again, 'I get lonely though. It's bad. That's the worst feeling I know – loneliness. That's when my worst depressions would set in and when I got depressed, that was when I'd relapse. You know you just start thinkin', like, nobody cares, so you say, "Why should I care? I don't care either".'

Similar to Ian, Lee attributes his relapses to the demoralization and loneliness he suffered while living on the street. Relapse is thusly described not as a deliberate act of self-control, but as a relinquishing of self-control in the face of overwhelming adversity ('You know you just start thinkin', like, nobody cares, so you say, "Why should I care? I don't care either".') Data like these indicated that members of my programmes described the street in such disparaging terms, in part, to assign responsibility for their relapses to the overwhelming pressures they found there. But more than this, these descriptions of street life gave contour, through contrast, to the precise dimensions of life *in* the programme that were held to possess medicinal force. If relapse could be triggered by the hazards, demoralization and loneliness of the street, then recovery could be fostered through the security, moral inspiration and community that was presumed to be available in the programme. Ultimately, I came to see that these descriptions of life 'out there' effectively dissolved what many have called *the* basic paradox underlying contemporary drug abuse treatment discourse – namely, they reconciled the paired propositions that programme participants: (1) suffer from a disease, addiction, that is genuinely beyond their control, but (2) can, nonetheless, be empowered to master this disease through participation in a recovery programme.

My research subjects inherited these two propositions as non-negotiable institutional structures that had to be honoured to remain in treatment. Their disparaging descriptions of street life embodied a narrative structure that could be invoked to reconcile these seemingly contradictory propositions to one another. Through use of an ecological contrast between life in the programme and life 'out there', programme members cast themselves as accountably invested in, and capable of, recovery through participation in the programme but, nonetheless, chronically vulnerable to their addictions, which they claimed were enflamed and made stronger by the temptations and frustrations of living 'out there'. With recourse to this construct, people could describe themselves as 'trying to change', but eminently susceptible to the challenges this dysfunctional ecological space posed to their recoveries. And they could do so such that the environmental enticements to return to drug use would not be construed as incentives to use, but as overwhelming pressures to do so. This was indispensable to the programmes' work insofar as it was necessary to consider clients as amenable to the restorative influence of the programme and, *simultaneously*, afflicted by the disease that, alone, justified their need for, and entitlement to, therapeutic assistance in the first place.

Insofar as it was precisely the therapeutic communities that were held to possess medicinal force, simple logic dictates that whatever forces were held to possess the potential for rekindling addiction (and that alone warranted ongoing participation in the programme) had to be located, as it were, ecologically elsewhere. There were, then, strong organisational incentives for linking people's addictions with an ecological space 'out there', or beyond the confines of the programmes. These incentives, combined with both the empirical evidence of how descriptions of the street drug scene were used in my programmes, and the abundant ethnographic testimony to the richly nuanced social organization of street life and street drug use, strongly suggest the following analytic conclusion: the recurrent descriptions in my settings of a savage space 'out there' flowed less from participants native familiarity with such a uniformly desolate space than from their subjective investment in the practical logic of contemporary drug abuse treatment discourse itself.[6]

Conclusion

In this chapter I have briefly traced the history of ethnography as an academic discipline, noting its movement from what I have called an analytic approach to research to a more reflexive and dialogical approach. I have suggested that this movement has entailed a greater appreciation for social dynamism and diversity and a movement away from more static and structural conceptions of not only language itself, but science, and the social world more generally. This has, in turn, entailed further movement away from the 'scientism' and 'positivism' that qualitative social scientists have so often insisted is misplaced in social research. While many have suggested this intellectual movement must result in a collapse of methodological rigor into a self-indulgent relativism, I have argued this is far from the case. Rather than depriving us of the tools necessary for assessing ethnographic objectivity, reflexive regard for the specific social conditions that give meaning and value to our labours in fact provides us with those very tools (Bourdieu and Wacquant 1992).

Ethnographic objectivity cannot be judged with respect to a fixed set of criteria for scientific excellence, nor can it be assessed with respect to the myth of 'brute social facts'. Instead, it must be assessed with simultaneous regard for the available evidence pertaining to the scientific question at hand and the specific set of analytic outlooks that might be held to provide competing answers. By these lights, ethnographic objectivity is not a matter of achieving correspondence between our analytic propositions and the things they are said to describe. It is, instead, simply a matter of answering questions in ways that account for the available evidence pertaining to those questions more effectively than anyone else. This does not preclude the later discovery of still more effective analyses, nor of disconfirming evidence. Hence, ethnographic objectivity must be viewed as provisional and thoroughly nested in the historically and culturally specific dispute domains within which it is achieved. But, to reiterate, this is not, in any baneful sense, a relativist position. The bane of relativism only arises if and when we find ourselves incapable of assessing the comparative objectivity of genuinely incompatible answers to specific scientific questions. It emphatically does not arise simply by virtue of the fact that the same data can be described in different but equally valid ways. If our descriptions are responsive to different scientific questions, then there are no grounds for judging them incompatible and no bases for judging their comparative objectivity. Hence, the bane of relativism simply does not arise.

The scientific question animating the research I have reported here stemmed from an incongruity I observed between the descriptions of street life and street drug users I was reading in the ethnographic literature and the descriptions I was hearing in the field. In this preliminary sense, my analysis is thoroughly nested in a particular dispute domain consisting in the received ethnographic wisdom regarding street life and street drug users. Once I noted this incongruity, I was faced with a set of analytic choices including: (1) explaining how either the received ethnographic wisdom or my own research subjects might have come to be mistaken; (2) reconciling the validity of both sets of descriptions; or, alternatively, (3) bypassing the issue of comparative validity by showing how these descriptions embody different types of social action. After finding empirical reasons to suspect that the descriptions I was hearing in the field did not just reflect differences between the experiences had by my own research subjects and those reported on by other ethnographers, I began to investigate the work this kind of talk might be doing for programme members. The view that talk can be productively analysed as a form of social action was one I had already encountered in the literature and was one with which I was already sympathetic. Hence, this decision was also informed by the scientific dispute domain within which my analysis was nested.

Insofar as disparaging descriptions of the street were common to the three different treatment settings in which I had done fieldwork, I had empirical grounds to suspect that whatever work these descriptions were doing was probably common to the three settings. However, my analytic effort was confined to working out what it was about these sorts of setting that inclined people to talk of the street as my research subjects did. In this sense my analysis was very much an ethnographic, rather than conversation or discourse analytic, one. I was concerned to work out how these kinds of description figured in the work that characterized these settings as specific types of 'going concerns'. I was not focused on how such descriptions might figure in any other sorts of social action,' although I am certain they do. Hence, my claim is only that these descriptions did a certain type of work that was indispensable within the organizational settings I observed. I have not claimed that this work was never done in other ways, nor that the narrative construct I have called 'the ecology of addiction' is only ever used in this kind of work.

Though it is, perhaps, a modest analysis, I do claim it is objective. But it is objective only because it answers a particular scientific question more effectively than any other prospective analysis I have seen or can imagine. Scientistic and positivistic tendencies towards representationalism notwithstanding, scientific questions just don't always take the form: 'What is the nature of x?' Sometimes, as above, they take the form: 'Why don't some descriptions of x correspond with other descriptions of x?' And, of course, there are many other forms that scientific questions might take and to which objective answers might be given. Hence, ethnographic objectivity cannot be measured with exclusive respect to the putative essence of the things ethnographers presume to describe. It must instead be measured with simultaneous respect to the available evidence and to the other candidate analyses that might be held to provide answers to the specific question at hand. Those who would take issue with my analysis can easily do so. There is no relativist impasse. But they must do so with due regard for the specific question I have sought to answer. This is not to say the value of that question itself cannot be questioned, only that the adjective 'objective' is one we use to evaluate answers to questions, not the correspondence between disinterested descriptions and an unquestioned world.

Notes

1. I will be using the concept 'thing' in this chapter in the non-technical sense of 'discrete object'. By this definition, things are objective entities of some sort but they are not necessarily materially embodied.
2. Some might suggest that I am overplaying my hand here. After all, it might be argued, the complaint against reification is not a complaint against the idea that social life takes objectively identifiable empirical forms. It is only a complaint against abstracting the nature of those forms from the ecological, and intrinsically relational, spaces within which they are sustained. By this logic, social processes may be discussed objectively – that is, as things – without fear of reification insofar as they are not given an ontological status independent of the actually existing practical domains within which they are observed to occur. I would reply with three points. First, this ecological argument doesn't distinguish social processes from the social structures (i.e. states, markets, etc.) we are told must be conceptualized as epiphenomena of organizational and interactional practices. Indeed, it would seem to undermine the

argument that social structures must be treated as epiphenomenal to social processes insofar as they are seen on an ecological par with one another. Second, social processes are often conceptualized with next to no effort to link their reality to the particular ecological spaces within which they are said to occur. Think, for example, of our habitual tendency to assume the concept 'interaction' refers exclusively to the immediate mutual influences exerted by particular people on one another rather than, say, the interaction of nation-states. Third, the ecological solution to the problem of reification begs the questions of *who* is entitled to speak authoritatively to the nature of this ecological context, and *why* they are so entitled. These questions and ambiguities indicate the reification of social processes is by no means a distant threat.

3. This point deserves a bit of elaboration. I do not mean by this that analysis entails interacting with empirical materials in the superficial sense that data must be manipulated somehow in the course of analysis. The point I wish to make is more radical. It is that the very *things* we discover through analysis ought not to be dissociated from the worldly activities that constitute our own embodied practices of discovery (Goodwin 1994). The various things discovered in the course of ethnographic research *interact* with the ongoing conduct of ethnographic research itself.

4. The following two paragraphs are adapted from Weinberg (2002).

5. All names are pseudonyms.

6. See Weinberg (2000) for a more detailed argument in favour of this thesis.

PART TWO
Talk-in-Interaction in the Context of Research in Fields of Substantive Sociological Research

CHAPTER EIGHT **Questions at Work:**
• • • • • • • • •
Yes/No Type Interrogatives
in Institutional Contexts

Geoffrey Raymond

Though it may not be obvious at first, the daily work of many people is accomplished through talk-in-interaction. This is especially true of professionals, organizational representatives and the laypersons who engage them (Drew and Heritage 1992a: 3). The ability to record interactions in such institutional environments has proven extremely useful in refining our understanding of how such work is organized and what we can learn from the patterns of behaviour that characterize it. One main goal of analysts who study talk (and other conduct) in institutional environments has been to uncover basic patterns of action that are related to the participants' role-based identities in a setting. As part of this research, analysts have examined how the participants' talk reflects their efforts to achieve (institutionally) specific goals while managing normative pressures and other systematic contingencies posed by their work.

One very common finding of this research has been that speakers across a range of settings exploit a very basic, and familiar, form of social action: the asking and answering of questions. For example, research on (broadcast) journalism has described a range of practices that journalists use to question public figures – and how those figures respond to them – as a method for understanding how journalists sustain a variety of normative standards critical to their work (Clayman 1992). By always asking questions, journalists can maintain a neutralistic posture even as they vary the 'hostility' of the questions they pose to public figures (Clayman and Heritage 2002b). Questions and answers are also critical to many other types of work. Callers requesting emergency services (e.g. by dialing 911, 999, etc.) will find that their interactions are organized through a series of questions (asked by dispatchers) and that compliance with the terms of those questions is critical to decisions regarding whether to dispatch police, fire or medical personnel (Whalen and Zimmerman 1987, 1990; Zimmerman 1992). Similarly, lawyers' conduct in courtroom interactions (Atkinson and Drew 1979) and police interrogations of suspects (Komter 2003) are organized primarily through questions and answers. And in both cases, when parties can ask questions, how they can ask them, and even whether and how recipients should respond, are subject to legal constraints that can have dramatic consequences for everyone involved. Even much of the talk between doctors and patients is conducted through questions and answers. Researchers have found that more than 90 per cent of doctors' utterances are questions and that patients' talk primarily consists of answers, even though it is patients who are seeking help, and who may need information (Frankel 1990; Roter and Hall 1992). And of course the asking and answering of questions is vital to a range of other types of institutionalized conduct that we don't think of as work; for example, questions and answers figure centrally in the management of sexual relations and charges of date rape (Kitzinger and Frith 1999), the socialization of children (Wootton 1997), and even the maintenance of personhood and identities (Goffman 1971; Heritage and Raymond 2005). Given the centrality of questioning and answering to so many activities of daily life, the analysis of their use in different contexts can provide a great deal of insight into how institutions work, what routine contingencies arise in them, what norms shape them and how they are enforced.

So, how can one begin to uncover patterns of action in institutional interactions? What are the main methodological orientations of research in this area and how do they apply to research on data recorded in institutional settings? In the following, I address these issues and illustrate one method for managing them by examining one of the most common forms that questions and answers take: yes/no type interrogatives (hereafter, YNIs) and their responses. I then consider how this form is used in three distinct settings: courtroom interactions, doctor–patient interactions and survey research.

Interaction in institutions

Explicating the institutional roles and activities that one finds in a setting may appear straightforward. For example, it may be easy to identify the role-based identities of actors in a setting. Indeed, almost any competent person can very quickly figure out 'who is who' in the settings he/she enters and navigates. However, for analysts of talk-in-interaction the challenge has been to identify exactly how this is possible: how do members embody the roles they occupy so that others can immediately recognize them? Specifically, analysts have sought to describe the range of practices through which (participants' role-based) identities – and whatever forms of power and inequality may be associated with them – are linked to specific actions in interaction. To address these issues Schegloff (1991, 1992) argues that analyses should meet two basic criteria: first, an analysis should establish *that* a role-based identity role is relevant for the conduct being analysed; and second, it should establish *how* that identity matters, or is consequential, for that conduct. Thus, although it may be tempting simply to rely on the 'fact' that the subjects involved are, actually, a journalist and public figure, a doctor and patient, or a lawyer and witness, the aim of this sort of analysis is to explicate how those participants are oriented to these facts, and how that orientation matters for what they do. In this respect, a basic aim of such analyses should be to move beyond our common-sense understandings of institutions so that we may learn something new about the settings, people and activities that comprise them.

The 'institutional talk' programme (Drew and Heritage 1992b) represents a highly generative approach to these issues. It addresses them by examining task-oriented conduct that is identifiably distinct from ordinary conversation in an attempt to locate and ground participants' orientations to institutional realities. As research in this area has demonstrated, analysts of institutional settings can begin to establish the relevance of a speaker's role-based identity, or any other aspect of the institutional setting, by focusing on the range of ways in which institutional interactions may be specialized.

As Drew and Heritage (1992b) note, in contrast to ordinary conversation, where the range of actions participants can pursue, and the means they use to pursue them, is relatively unconstrained, interactions in institutional environments typically involve a narrow range of explicitly pursued goals, special constraints on how conduct should be organized, and specialized inferential frameworks and procedures that are particular to an institution. Together, these special features create a unique fingerprint for each type of institutional interaction (Drew and Heritage 1992b). This fingerprint is made up of the ways in which the participants' interactional conduct displays their orientation to the specific tasks, identities, and the like that are distinctive to the setting. In this respect institutionally oriented interaction generally involves a reduction in the range of interactional practices deployed by the participants and a specialization and re-specification of the practices that remain.

As the focus on specialization and reduction suggests, the institutional talk programme is a fundamentally comparative enterprise: analyses of conduct in institutional settings are (typically) grounded by comparison to practices or activities that can also be found in ordinary conversation. Not surprisingly, these comparisons have clustered around a range of organizational matters that can scarcely be avoided in conducting interactions of any sort (Drew and Heritage 1992b: 29–53). These include:

- *How participants manage the distribution of opportunities to speak (turn-taking).* In conversation, who talks, when a speaker talks, and what he/she says or does is managed locally, typically on a turn-by-turn basis. However, in some institutional environments, such as courtrooms, news interviews, debates or ceremonies, any or all of these features can be pre-allocated using specialized turn-taking systems. Unlike less formal environments, when such specialized turn-taking systems are in use, departures from them can be explicitly sanctioned. For example, on news interview programmes where journalists are supposed to ask questions for interviewees to answer, interviewees sometimes complain that interviewers are making assertions rather than asking questions (Heritage and Greatbatch 1991; Schegloff 1991); similarly in business meetings, participants can be sanctioned for speaking out of order.
- *The organization of action through sequences of turns (sequence organization).* In most institutional settings, the specific work conducted in them will be organized through sequences of actions, and expansions of those sequences. For example, when calling

911 (USA) or 999 (UK) a speaker's formulation of a problem functions as a request for emergency assistance. After a series of questions and answers that defer responding to this request, operators will respond to it by saying, for example, 'we'll get someone out there' (in cases where the request is granted). In these calls, then, the entire interaction is organized around a single sequence of actions – a request and its granting or denial – that is expanded to manage routine contingencies like collecting information necessary to make decisions regarding whether to dispatch help, which service(s) should respond, and where they should go (Zimmerman 1992).

- *How participants design their actions (turn design).* Often the actions that speakers select, and how they design those actions, will reflect their management of institutionally specific exigencies. For example, in calling to enquire about a child absent from school, a school representative asks: 'Was Martin home from school ill today?' By posing her question in this way the speaker 'offers as an account for the child's presupposed absence the most commonplace and most legitimate reason for the child to be away from school – sickness' (Heritage 1997: 18). Thus, the school representative builds her question so as to invite a 'yes' response, thereby making a 'best-case scenario' (under the circumstances) the easiest one to confirm. Moreover, this method of informing avoids any implication that the child may be truant (which is a real possibility since no parent has called in to report the child's absence) as well as any implication that the parent has failed to call in if the child *is* sick. In short, the formulation that this school counsellor uses to probe a child's absence from school embodies a very cautious stance towards the circumstances that she is enquiring into and their potential implications for all of the parties involved (Heritage 1997; see also Chapter 5 in this volume).
- *How speakers choose their words (lexical choice).* For example, when the same school representative discusses absences with other parents she routinely uses the formulation 'reported absent' as a method for establishing the official capacity in which she is calling, and to avoid taking a stand on the actual status (or even reality) of the absences.
- *The overall structure of a conversation (or interaction).* For example, in doctor–patient interactions the request for help that patients enact when they present their problems to a physician sets in motion an interactional structure aimed at resolving those complaints. This overarching structure can dramatically shape what gets said in these interactions and how participants manage the possibility of raising other issues (Robinson 2003).

In what follows I will be primarily concerned with the second of these issues: how the organization of sequences of action are specialized in institutional environments. In keeping with the comparative approach described above, I will compare a basic form that sequences initiated by YNIs can take with the use of YNIs in three institutional contexts: cross-examination in courtroom interactions, doctor–patient interactions and survey interviews.

The basic organization of YNIs

YNIs set in motion a sequence of actions that is normatively organized. One can review the basic sorts of practices that figure in these sequences by dividing them into resources for initiating actions (or first-position actions) and resources for responding (or second-position actions). In this section I will briefly review the basic forms that practices in each of these positions can take, the basic framework that their normative organization provides for co-ordinating action, and describe the consequences the availability of these practices have for courses of action organized through them.

YNIs are designed to constrain responses

When speakers pose YNIs for recipients, they rely on a regular grammatical construction,[1] as in the following excerpts.

```
(1)   [MDE-MTRAC 60–1/5 Erma]
1     Erma:   Dj'ear from Joe:?

(2)   [SF 2]
1     BOB:    Mark,hh (0.3) will you come to a party Fridee
```

By initiating a sequence of actions with a YNI, speakers place recipients in a highly defined situation of choice: the grammatical form of these turns make relevant a 'yes' or a 'no'. Indeed, no other standard (or unmarked) grammatical form proposes such a limited choice for responding. In this respect YNIs maximally exploit the agenda-setting and subsequent conduct constraining potential of initiating a course of action.

Recipients of such grammatically formed YNIs face a basic choice in formulating their responses: Will they conform to the constraints set in motion by a YNI, or not?

Responses can conform or not

Most frequently speakers produce responses that conform to the constraints embodied in YNIs. For example, in excerpt (3), line 4, Vera poses a YNI to Mathew:

```
(3)   [Rahmen 4; Interrogative; R = response]
1            Mathew:   'lo Redcah five o'six one?,
2            Vera:     Hello Mahthew is yer mum the:hr love.
3            Mathew:   Uh no she's, gone (up) t'town,h
4     I-->   Vera:     Al:right uh will yih tell'er Antie Vera rahn:g then.
5     R-->   Mathew:   Yeh.
6            Vera:     Okay.
```

Evidently, Vera uses 'will you' to formulate a request: she asks Mathew to inform his mother that she called. In using a YNI to initiate this action, Vera sets the terms by which Mathew should respond: he can grant her request with a 'yes' or reject it with a 'no'. We can note that Mathew's response in line 5, 'yeh', conforms to the constraints set by Vera's YNI. I will call responses that conform to the constraints embodied in the grammatical form of such queries 'type-conforming responses'. For YNIs, type-conforming responses contain either a 'yes' or a 'no' (or equivalent token: 'mmhmm', 'mmm', 'uh huh', 'yep', 'yup', 'yeah', 'nah hah', 'nuh uh', 'hah eh', 'huh uh', 'nope', etc.).

Alternatively, speakers may depart from the constraints embodied in a YNI. For example, in excerpt (4), line 3, Gerri asks a YNI regarding a woman dying of cancer: 'will the remaining three years see her in pain'.

```
(4)   [Gerri and Shirley]
  1            Shirley:    ... she fee:ls ez though, .hh yihkno:w her mother is
  2                        in: such agony now that w'd only make it worse.=
  3   I-->     Gerri:      =.hh Wul will the remaining three yea:rs uhm see her in pai:n
  4   R-->     Shirley:    .hhh She already is in a great deal of pain.,
  5                        (0.7)
  6            Shirley:    C'she has the chemotherapy the radiation.
```

In her response (line 4), Shirley unequivocally confirms the matter raised by Gerri's question, while also departing from constraints embodied in its grammatical form: her response contains neither a 'yes' nor a 'no'. I will call responses such as this, where speakers design their turns to depart from, disappoint, or avoid the constraints set in motion by the grammatical form of a YNI, 'nonconforming responses'.

The choice between type-conforming and nonconforming responses, and the action accomplished by a speaker's selection of one or the other, is made relevant by a speaker using a grammatically formed YNI to initiate a course of action. Having illustrated this role of grammar in the organization of these sequences of action, we can ask: what does the choice between type-conforming and nonconforming responses involve? What are speakers doing when they produce type-conforming responses, and what do they do differently when they produce nonconforming ones?

Choosing between type-conforming and nonconforming responses

The different stances taken towards a first action by type-conforming and nonconforming responses are clearly evident in excerpts (5) below and (6) opposite. The excerpts are from the Health Visitor (HV) corpus that contains recordings of postnatal visits by a representative of Britain's National Health Service to monitor the health of the new mother and baby. These two excerpts are taken from the first visit to the new mother, and in each the HV enquires into the state of the mothers' breasts. In both sequences the mothers report their breasts are currently fine or comfortable. However, in one instance this response is delivered through a type-conforming turn, in the other through a nonconforming one.

In excerpt (5) the HV enquires into the state of the mother's breasts by asking, 'Have they settled down?'

```
(5)   [HV 5A1]
  1   I-> Health Visitor :    How about your breast(s) have they settled do:wn
  2                           [no:w.
  3   R->        Mother:      [Yeah they 'ave no:w yeah.=
  4         Health Visitor:   =( ) they're not uncomfortable anymo:re.
```

Evidently, this question incorporates (1) an explicit reference to the progress of the mother's breasts (i.e. their change over time) and, by extension, (2) an implicit recognition that her breasts had been, in some way, painful or problematic. As a consequence of this question's design, then, a 'yes' response allows the mother to confirm that her breasts have 'settled down' while also indicating that she had suffered some discomfort prior to the visit. And indeed, the mother's 'yeah' confirms this. She then briefly elaborates her response by describing her breasts' current status as an improvement ('they have now') before completing her turn with a further type-conforming token. Thus, the way the HV designs her question allows the mother to use a simple, type-conforming 'yes' to confirm (1) that her breasts are currently unproblematic and (2) that this is an improvement; her brief elaboration underscores the aptness of this design by emphasizing the recency of this improvement.

Excerpt (6) contrasts with (5) in two ways. First, the HV's question only enquires into the current state of the mother's breasts, not their change over time. Specifically, she asks the mother only to confirm that her breasts are not problematic. Second, in response to this question the mother builds a nonconforming response.

```
(6)   [HV 1C1]
 1   I-->   Health Visitor:   Mm.=Are your breasts alright.
 2                            (0.7)
 3   R-->          Mother:    They're fi:ne no:w I've stopped leaking (.) so:
 4          Health Visitor:   You didn't want to breast feed,
```

Plainly, the mother specifically designs her nonconforming response (line 3) to introduce the fact that her breasts had been problematic, even if they are 'fine now'. By doing so, the mother treats the HV's question as problematic. Specifically, she treats the response options made relevant by the question as inadequate for conveying the status of her breasts since the choice between 'yes' and 'no' would only make reference to their current state. To respond with a 'yes' would be to risk implying that her breasts had never been a problem; to respond with a 'no' would be to claim that they currently are one.

Although in both of these sequences the mothers respond by confirming that their breasts are not currently problematic, they rely on alternative resources for conveying these actions. The difference between the type-conforming response produced by the mother in excerpt (5) and the nonconforming one in excerpt (6), can be directly linked to the adequacy of the questions to which they are responding and the actions (that would be) conveyed by the response options made relevant by their grammatical form. In excerpt (5), the mother confirms the adequacy of the HV's question by producing a type-conforming response that accepts the constraints embodied in its grammatical form; in excerpt (6), the mother treats the HV's question as problematic by departing from its constraints to produce a nonconforming response.

As these excerpts illustrate, nonconforming responses are the most overt, sequence-specific method for managing trouble with or misalignments between speakers regarding the particular choice posed by a YNI in its sequential context.

Conversely, type-conforming responses accept the terms and presuppositions embodied in a YNI. In this respect, one can appreciate the import of the choice between type-conforming and nonconforming responses by noting that the availability of nonconforming responses provides a counter-balance to the ways that YNIs maximally exploit the agenda-setting potential of initiating a course of action. To pursue this issue further, we can consider how these response types are consequential for subsequent actions premised on them.

Type-conforming and nonconforming responses have different consequences

By departing from the expectations embodied in YNIs, nonconforming responses are typically designed to constrain the subsequent actions of the participants differently from type-conforming responses. Most commonly, nonconforming responses expand and complicate the sequences in which they participate. For example, in excerpt (7), Leslie asks her friend and fellow teacher, Robyn, about a book Leslie had asked her to retrieve.

```
(7)   [Holt 5/88-1-5]
 1   I-->   Leslie :   =.hhhh Did um (.) .tch (.) Did uh you get that
 2                      book back
 3   R-->   Robyn :    I've got two books f'you:,
 4          Leslie :   Have YOU:[goohhd
 5          Robyn :            [And
 6          Robyn :    An' I 've got th'm in my basket 'n they are ho:me. I
 7                     didn't leave th'm at school in case you wanted them.
 8          Leslie :   Oh:. right.
 9          Robyn :    That alri:ght,
10          Leslie :   Yes fine what are they.
```

By checking the status of a prior request (e.g. as reflected in Leslie's use of the past tense in 'did you' and her use of 'that' to refer to the book), this query initiates a course of action aimed at its resolution. In this respect, Leslie's YNI functions as a possible preliminary to a request (or pre-request, e.g. for Robyn to return the book) or a possible preliminary to an offer (or pre-offer, e.g. to visit Robyn and pick up the book). If Robyn responds positively (confirming that she has the book), she invites the projected action (i.e. the request or offer) by indicating that she will likely grant the request or accept the offer; by contrast, if Robyn responds with a 'no', she blocks this next action. As previous research (Schegloff 1980, forthcoming) has demonstrated, responses that invite the action projected by a pre-request make those projected actions immediately relevant, unless the responding speaker pre-empts the necessity for producing it (as would be the case if Robyn both confirmed she had the book and offered to return it.) Given the trajectory such sequences are designed to make relevant, the consequences of Robyn's preferred, nonconforming response are especially clear in this case.

Although (in line 3) Robyn unequivocally confirms she has the book Leslie has enquired about, she delivers her response as a nonconforming one by reporting that she has '*two* books for' her. Evidently, Robyn's response required a departure from the constraints set by Leslie's use of a YNI because its design did not anticipate what Robyn reports. Indeed, it is precisely by introducing this departure that Robyn invites Leslie to treat her response as news, and 'good news' in particular (see Maynard 1998b for a discussion of this excerpt).

As it happens, the introduction of news complicates this sequence: while Robyn's turn makes relevant the request projected by Leslie, it also makes relevant some pursuit of the names of the books she has recovered, and some appreciation of the good news she has just conveyed. Instead of producing the request made relevant by her own YNI and Robyn's confirmation, Leslie first registers Robyn's nonconforming response as news (using the news-marker 'have you' [Jefferson 1981]) and then assesses its type, 'good'. In turn, this momentary displacement of the action projected by Leslie's query provides an opportunity for Robyn to elaborate on her efforts (lines 6 and 7). While it appears that Robyn may be further encouraging a request/offer from Leslie by conveying where she has stored the books for easy retrieval, Leslie's uptake of this addition (line 8) indicates an abrupt shift from her previously upbeat stance. First, her terminally intoned 'oh' treats Robyn's elaboration as unexpected – and so possibly as bad news (Heritage 1984a). Second, Leslie's use of 'right' (the neutrality of which markedly contrasts with her unequivocally positive reception of Robyn's prior turn) registers its action import for the sequence. Robyn immediately picks up on Leslie's evident disappointment by asking whether these arrangements are 'alright,' thereby inviting her to explicate the problems adumbrated by this uptake. Leslie, however, declines to register any such trouble directly (line 10). Instead she promptly pursues the names of the books Robyn has retrieved (but not yet named) and in talk not shown here, celebrates her good fortune in getting her books back.

In this case, the expansion of the sequence initially prompted by Robyn's non-conforming response sets in motion a chain of events that eventuates in Leslie temporarily setting aside the course of action initially projected by her questions (in lines 1 and 2). As the participants manage each of the multiple relevancies introduced by Robyn's nonconforming response, a new sequence is initiated which is itself subject to further expansion. As a consequence, the matter is only resolved some ten minutes later when Robyn reintroduces it. Thus, despite the apparently benign character of Robyn's nonconforming response, the complications introduced by it have dramatic consequences for the course of actions Leslie initiated in line 1. While the disruption prompted by Robyn's nonconforming response may have been inadvertent, as illustrated elsewhere (Raymond 2003) speakers can *design* their responses to disrupt or alter the course of action initiated by a YNI. More generally, in sequences where speakers produce type-conforming responses, actions premised on them are produced without hesitation (see, for example, the discussion of excerpt (8) below). By contrast, even in cases where speakers produce apparently benign nonconforming responses, such departures result in an expansion and complication of the sequence initiated by a YNI, a disruption of the course of action pursued through it, or some modification of the manner in which it is pursued.

As it happens, speakers who deploy YNIs may anticipate these potential consequences when they initiate courses of action. That is, speakers can design YNIs so that they take their recipients' circumstances into account and thereby promote type-conforming responses. Given the centrality of this observation for our consideration on YNIs in institutional contexts, some elaboration of it here will be useful.

Alignment in YNI sequences

One can begin to appreciate the balance between the resources for initiating courses of action with YNIs and those for responding to them by considering the relative frequency of type-conforming and nonconforming responses. Type-conforming responses are far more common than nonconforming ones (by a ratio of approximately 3:1, see Raymond 2003). This distribution must be understood as an interactional product: it is produced both by speakers who pose YNI *as well as* those who respond to them. And for the most part, the interactional character of this distribution is predicated on the distribution of interactional resources available to speakers within the sequence.

In first position, the variety of constraints set by the grammatical form of YNIs (as well as the preferences and presuppositions embodied in them) shape the choices a responding speaker must confront. In second position, speakers have a variety of resources, including nonconforming responses, to shape their turns and to resist the constraints set by the first speaker. Precisely because responding speakers can resist a YNI by producing nonconforming responses, first speakers typically take the circumstances of their recipients into account when designing their YNIs. That is, the potential consequences of a nonconforming response promote a focus on the design of YNIs. When first speakers do not adequately form their interrogatives, the course of action they initiate can be disrupted, delayed, or otherwise troubled by even a 'positive' nonconforming response. Thus, the fact that most YNIs get type-conforming responses suggests that first speakers design their interrogatives to permit the alignment such responses embody, and that responding speakers accept those designs when possible (perhaps even when they might have chosen differently).

While prima facie evidence for this claim can be found in the gross disparity between each response type, we can also find ancillary evidence in cases in which a first speaker pursues a type-conforming response following a nonconforming one. Excerpt (8), which is taken from a doctor's consultation with a patient complaining of a sore shoulder, provides a clear example of such an effort. In this excerpt, the doctor initiates his physical examination of the patient by asking a YNI (line 1) while manipulating her arm/shoulder.

```
(8)  [CMC Shoulder Pain [11166–106/2]
 1   I-->  Doctor :   Does that hurt right there,
 2                    (0.5)
 3   R-->  Patient:   Mm:, It doesn't uhm I can feel it. [But it's not real=
 4         Doctor :                                      [An-
```

```
 5   R-->   Patient:   =painful
 6    -->   Doctor:    right. W'll what I'm a:sking you is can I reproduce
 7                     your pain by pushing.
 8                     (0.5)
 9          Doctor:    Is there any spot here that when I: push on it bo:y
10                     that just rea:lly kills ya.
11          Patient:   No.
12                     (0.2)
13          Doctor:    Deeper?
```

In line 3, the patient replaces a turn that projected rejection delivered via a noncon-forming response ('It doesn't uhm') with a hedged one in which she reports she can 'feel' the manipulation but says its not 'painful'. Evidently, the design of this response avoids the choice posed by the doctor's YNI on the grounds that his physi-cal manipulation did not permit her to differentiate between the choices posed by the question. Instead of simply accepting this response (or inferring its upshot), the doctor pursues a type-conforming one via two reformulations of his query. First, the doctor states the purpose of his question (line 6 and 7) and, following this, he resets its parameters at a more extreme level (lines 9 and 10). Evidently, these features of his pursuit are designed to make a choice by the patient virtually unavoidable.

Given the terms set by this pursuit, if the patient is to respond without indicating some other trouble with the sequence, she must choose one of the type-conforming tokens made relevant by the doctor's YNI. With little room to manoeuvre, the patient produces a 'no' (line 11), thereby satisfying the doctor's pursuit of a choice. And hav-ing solicited such a choice from the patient, the doctor directly moves on to probe the possibilities the response suggests. In this stretch of talk, the doctor's reformula-tion of his initial query provides an especially clear illustration of the role that *first* speakers play in promoting type-conforming responses. While responding speakers may be constrained in terms of the response options from which they can choose, speakers who initiate actions must design their YNIs to permit the alignment a type-conforming response embodies. The relative frequency of type-conforming and non-conforming responses (which reflects the different stances these alternative forms of responding take and their consequences) suggests that the normative organization embodied in its grammatical form is systematically biased in favour of promoting alignment in courses of action. As we shall see, however, this bias, and the balance of resources on which it is predicated, may be altered in specific institutional environments.

YNIs in institutional settings

In this section I will examine how speakers use YNIs in institutional settings, con-centrating on two sorts of issue. First, I will establish the relevance and procedural consequentiality of the participants' institutional orientations by focusing on how YNIs are systematically manipulated in institutional settings. Second, I will explicate how these transformations can reveal the ways in which these institutions are situated relative to social life more generally.

Each element of the system of practices we have described so far can be reshaped or simplified to accomplish specific institutional outcomes. For example, institutions can be 'talked into being' (Drew and Heritage 1992b) by manipulating three basic features of the sequences set in motion by YNIs. Specific tasks and goals can be accomplished in institutional settings by:

1   systematically shaping how YNIs are designed (e.g. by limiting the presuppositions and expectations embodied in them);
2   re-specifying the range and types of choice made relevant by the YNI (e.g. by constraining speakers to produce only type-conforming responses);
3   constraining how speakers take up responses to YNIs in subsequent actions.

To begin illustrating these observations, I will consider how YNIs are deployed in courtroom cross-examinations.

YNIs in court

In courtroom cross-examinations, participants operate within a specialized turn-taking system where the order of speakers and the types of action they can produce are pre-allocated: lawyers ask questions and witnesses respond to them (Atkinson and Drew 1979). As has been well established, the types of question that lawyers overwhelmingly ask in this environment are YNIs, and the manner in which witnesses respond to them can be legally constrained (Atkinson and Drew 1979). Limiting our focus to the conduct of witnesses, we can note that there are two constraints on their responses. First, witnesses can be compelled to produce type-conforming responses to YNIs. Second, lawyers can request that any talk beyond a 'yes' or a 'no' 'be stricken from the record'. These rules pose (at least) two questions for researchers: (1) what are their consequences and (2) how are they applied?

In the first place, the sheer availability of rules constraining witnesses' responses has consequences for sequences of action initiated by YNIs because they enable cross-examining attorneys to engage in hostile or aggressive questioning. Since witnesses can be compelled to produce type-conforming responses (thus removing the reciprocal constraint posed by the availability of nonconforming responses), attorneys are largely free to compose questions that embody whatever presuppositions or views will support their version of events, and their argument more generally (so long as a proper legal foundation has been supplied for them in prior testimony, which involves a constraint on *question* design that we will not consider here). To fully appreciate the consequences of this transformation of YNI sequences, however, it may be useful to consider variations in the way participants manage this rule.

As with any rules, the rules governing courtroom conduct must be applied and the actual application of constraints on witnesses' responses varies considerably. That is, although these rules 'officially' apply to every response to a cross-examining attorney's

YNI, it is not enforced in every sequence. As a result, requests to the judge to enforce rules regarding witnesses' responses often indicate which questions (and their responses) are particularly significant for attorneys' arguments. The role of such constraints in developing attorney's arguments is particularly evident if we compare the variety of methods lawyers deploy to manage nonconforming responses. For example, in the following exchanges the witness (the alleged victim in a rape trial) produces a series of nonconforming responses:

```
(9)    [Oulette 45/2B:2 Cross exam] [D = Defense Attorney; W = Witness]
  1              D:    An you went to a: uh (0.9) uh you went to a ba:r? (in) Boston
  2                    (0.6)
  3    l-->            Is that correct?
  4                    (1.0)
  5    R-->    W:      It's a club
  6                    (0.3)
  7              D:    A clu:b?
((9 lines ommitted))
 16              D:    It's a uh singles club. Isn't that what it is=
 17                    =((sound of striking mallet))
 18              P:    (      )
 19                    (0.9)
 20              J:    No you may have it,
 21                    (1.1)
 22    l-->            It's where uh (.) uh (0.3) girls and fellas meet.
 23                    Isn't it?
 24                    (0.9)
 25    R-->    W:      People go there.
 26                    (4.9)
 29              D:    (An') when you went down there
```

Although the lawyer has posed a series of YNIs to the witness (in lines 1–3, 16, 22–3), when she produces nonconforming responses (in lines 5 and 25) the defense attorney declines to protest this feature of her responses. For example, although the attorney *does* challenge the *substance* of the first nonconforming response by repeating it (line 7), 'a *club*?', he simply follows up the witness's transparently evasive nonconforming response in line 25 with a next question (line 29). It should be clear, however, that the lawyer has not missed an opportunity to impugn this witness. Although he lets the witness's responses stand as a matter of record, his use of follow-up questions (in lines 7, 16, 22, and 29) promotes two distinct outcomes. First, his questions portray the witness as unwilling to co-operate in confirming even relatively uncontroversial formulations (e.g. that she went to a 'bar', line 1). Second, he uses her resistance to repackage elements of her response (in line 5) as part of a claim that the bar was, in fact, a 'singles club' (lines 16 and 22). In light of these pursuits, then, the witness's nonconforming response in line 25 ('people go there') does little to actually challenge the lawyer's line of questioning (since it offers little more than token resistance), and the lawyer simply moves on. As this stretch of talk illustrates, attorneys have various resources for managing witnesses' (nonconforming) responses (beyond appealing to the judge). Given these alternatives, the deployment of any one of them, including requests to enforce the legal constraints on witnesses' responses, must be understood as selection from among those alternatives (and can therefore be understood to reflect elements of the attorney's strategy).

This can be most clearly illustrated by comparing the attorney's conduct in excerpt (9) with his management of the same witness's response in the following exchange. In (10) the lawyer asks the witness whether she told the police the defendant had been drinking using a YNI that anticipates a 'yes'. Although the witness initially produces a 'negative' type-conforming response, the talk she adds to her 'no' (apparently in response to the attorney's challenge in line 7) modifies the action it would otherwise deliver.

```
(10)    [Oulette 45/2B:2 Cross exam]
1       D:      now: miss dussette (1.2) when you were in'erviewed by
2               (.) the poli:ce (.) some times later, (.) –some time
3               later that evening, (1.0) didn't- you tell the
4               police (.) that >the defendant had been drinking?<
5               (0.2)
6       W:      no[::
7       D:        [>didn't you tell em that?<=
8       W:      =I told them there was a cooler in the ca:r
9               an I never opened it.
10              (.)
11      D:      the answer:uh (.) may the balance be uh stricken y'r honor:,
12              an the answer is no:?
13      J:      the answer is no:
```

Evidently, this addition – 'I told them there was a cooler and I never opened it' – modifies her response in a manner that might undermine any subsequent contrasting claim by the defense attorney. Rather than redesigning his question so that the witness could produce an unmitigated 'yes' or a 'no' (as the doctor did in excerpt (8) above) or challenging the substance of her response (as the attorney did in the previous excerpt), however, he appeals to the judge, asking that the rules governing witness responses be enforced so that only her 'no' is 'officially' registered (lines 11–12). Thus, in this case, the defense attorney specifically designs his question so that the facts most salient for his argument are highlighted and confirmed by the witness, while appealing to institutionally specific rules governing witnesses responses to exclude any aspects of her response that might mitigate subsequent claims by him (see Drew 1992 for a more extensive analysis of this sequence; see also Atkinson and Drew 1979).

In this stretch of talk the participants' orientations to their role-based identities are evidently consequential for practices they use to organize their talk. In the most basic sense, the attorney's appeal to a third party (the judge) to enforce rules on responses reflects an interactional dynamic that is simply not available in ordinary conversation. More subtle, and perhaps more pervasively consequential, however, is the sheer availability of these rules. Whereas the resources available to responding speakers in ordinary conversation may prompt speakers to design their YNIs so that they permit type-conforming responses, the constraints placed on responses in courtroom cross-examinations significantly shift the balance of power. Since, in each sequence, the (potential) constraints on witnesses' responses permits lawyers to produce partisan questions, cross-examining lawyers can build lines of questioning designed to impeach their witnesses (instead of aligning with them) that would be considerably more difficult if those witnesses could not be compelled to produce type-conforming responses. Thus, the transformation of these sequences in courtroom interaction provides some insight into the interactional mechanisms upon which lawyers' work is premised and the outcomes it aims for. The constraints on witnesses' responses in courtroom cross-examinations provides for the achievement of an essentially hostile, asymmetrical relationship between questioners and answerers that is directly fitted to exigencies of deposing witnesses from the opposing side (who may be reluctant to co-operate).

YNIs in medical consultations

Unlike courtroom interactions, interactions between doctors and patients are not subject to constraints that pre-allocate turns and the types of action that either party can legitimately pursue. Nevertheless, the conduct of doctors and patients, exhibit highly regular patterns. For example, when doctors talk with patients, approximately 90 per cent of their utterances are questions and, of these, YNIs are two to three times more common than other types of question (Roter and Hall 1992: 83). While a discussion of what makes YNIs so common in this environment is beyond the scope of this chapter (see Boyd and Heritage forthcoming), we can note that the design of these YNIs reflects systematic constraints related to the tasks doctors must accomplish. When doctors talk to patients, they must gather a range of information regarding the patient's background, history and living circumstances. Indeed, they must gather virtually the same information from every patient. Despite the routine character of the questions they pose to patients, however, no physician can afford to sacrifice rapport with patients, by producing 'survey-like' questions (Boyd and Heritage forthcoming). As a consequence, in the course of questioning patients during an office visit, the presuppositions and preferences embodied in the design of doctors' questions – features of question design that cannot be avoided without sacrificing rapport – typically reflect their efforts to convey concern for, and an understanding of, a patient's circumstances. For example, in questioning a middle-aged woman whose daughter was born around 1960 a doctor asks: 'Are you married'?

(11)   [Midwest 3.4:6] (from Boyd and Heritage forthcoming)
1   Doc: Are you m<u>a</u>rried?
2   (.)
3   Pat: No.
4   (.)
5   Doc: You're divorced (cur[rently)
6   Pat: [Mm hm,

The doctor formulates his query to anticipate a 'yes', thereby revealing his understanding that, for this recipient (given her age and child), being married is preferred over other options (he could have indicated a different stance by asking, 'are you divorced?', 'are you widowed?', or 'are you single?'). Thus, while I offer no moral judgement regarding which arrangements are valued, insofar as this doctor must choose one way of asking the question over others, the choice he makes reveals what he considers to be the 'best-case scenario'. In light of this YNIs design, we can note that the patient's unelaborated, type-conforming rejection, 'no' (e.g. instead of 'no, divorced') can be heard to unfavourably comment on either her marriage (Boyd and Heritage forthcoming) or the expectations revealed in the question. Because doctors cannot deploy questions that treat patients anonymously, they cannot avoid communicating preference and presuppositions regarding their recipients and the states of affairs they enquire into. But these preferences and presuppositions are by no means random.

The pattern of preferences and presuppositions embodied in doctors' questions reflect their efforts to manage exigencies specific to the institutional tasks in which they are engaged, such as promoting the health of patients and establishing rapport with them. As Boyd and Heritage (forthcoming) note, the questions doctors ask typically reflect two principles: (1) the principle of optimization; and (2) the principle of recipient design. The principle of optimization reflects doctors concern with the well-being of their patients. For example, doctors tend to ask whether parents are alive rather than dead (e.g. 'Is your mother alive?'), or about the *absence* of serious symptoms rather than their presence. Such questions, in preferring 'no problem' responses simultaneously promote the quick movement through a series of questions while making visible any potential troubles indicated by a response (Boyd and Heritage, forthcoming). Further, the principle of recipient design is critical to the achievement of rapport since it reflects doctors' efforts to fit a series of questions asked of nearly every patient (much like a survey) to the particular life circumstances of the singular patient before them, as revealed through their responses to previous questions, and/or their conduct in prior interactions. As Boyd and Heritage (forthcoming) note:

> these principles cannot easily be departed from. The more that physicians design their questions so as to exclude presuppositions and preferences, the more their questioning will become drained of the concern for and understanding of the patient that medical questioning should properly convey, and come to embody the 'essentially anonymous' relationship of the social survey and other forms of bureaucratic questioning.

Finally, while there is no explicit injunction against nonconforming responses in doctor–patient interaction, as we noted in analysing excerpt (8), doctors may pursue type-conforming responses where nonconforming ones undermine the activity in which they are engaged.

YNIs in survey research

While courtrooms and doctors' offices provide familiar examples of contexts in which YNI sequences figure prominently, perhaps the most systematic manipulation of this form can be found in survey research. In survey research the design of both the interrogative and the responses it makes relevant are subject to extensive, institutionally specific constraints. Most generally, the conduct of interviewers and interviewees in survey research reflect their management of a specialized turn-taking system that pre-allocates turns and types of action between the participants: interviewers ask questions and interviewees respond to them. Within this turn-taking system, however, we can further note that the design and production of survey questions reflect multiple constraints designed to promote the survey's status as scientific instrument. And for the same reason, nonconforming responses by respondents are to be avoided. However, since there is no third-party to which a questioner can appeal (such as a judge in the courtroom), the mechanism for enforcing this latter constraint is markedly different in survey research.

As with the patterns of questioning and answering in courtrooms and doctors' offices, the constraints on questions and answers in survey research reflect the relatively unique concerns and values they are built to embody. In contrast to their use in these environments, however, questions in surveys are designed to *avoid* shaping which of the response options a recipient selects. Recall how the doctor enquired into the marital status of his patient in excerpt (11) – he asked: 'are you married'. As we noted above, in asking such a question the speaker reveals expectations about the recipient's marital status by anticipating a 'yes' response. In fact, in most interactional environments (including ordinary conversation and most institutional settings) speakers cannot avoid communicating assumptions and expectations about themselves, their recipients and the relationship between them, and as a consequence, cannot avoid shaping the response options made relevant by their enquiries (Boyd and Heritage forthcoming). By contrast, surveys questions are typically designed so as to *avoid* any such presuppositions or expectations. For example, a similar question in a survey might be posed as: 'what is your marital status: are you single, married, divorced, separated or widowed?' Such distinctively designed questions specifically 'minimiz[e] the communicated presuppositions and preferences' embodied in them (Heritage 2002a), thereby allowing surveys to be administered as 'fixed measuring instruments' (Schuman and Presser 1981; see also Suchman and Jordan 1990 and Schegloff 1990 for a contrasting view) since any person will stand in essentially the same relationship to the design of the question. In this respect, one aspect of the scientific character of surveys as standardized devices is predicated on the systematic manipulation of the basic grammatical form of YNIs and the constraints set by them.

Though sequences initiated by such modified YNIs are critical to the scientific status of surveys, they cannot guarantee it; to be sustained as fixed measuring instruments interviewees must respond to survey questions by selecting one of the response options enumerated in them, and interviewers must be careful to manage the responses interviewees actually produce. Although interviewees typically conform to the survey question's design, occasionally they produce nonconforming responses. While such responses may simply indicate that respondents are still learning how to produce adequate responses, in some cases survey respondents find trouble with the design of a question in light of their personal circumstances. For example, in the following exchange, a speaker's nonconforming response (line 5) indicates her trouble providing a response to a query regarding whether she worked for pay in the last week (lines 1–2).

```
(12)   AW01 (from Moore forthcoming)
  1      I:     .hhh Did you do any work (.) fer pa:y (0.1)
  2             last wee:k.
  3      R:     .hh We:ll,
  4             (0.5)
  5      R:     I'm still getting paid but school's ou:t (.) so:.
  6             (0.6)
  7      I:     Okay, s:o:,
((8 lines of restarts by I omitted))
 16      I:     it's yer ca[ll
 17      R:                [I got paid (0.3) [fer work
 18      I:                                  [ok(h)ay(h)huh=
 19      R:     but  I   was]n't at work.
 20      I :    huh huh huh]
 21      I :    .hhh Okay? (.) And how many hours did you work last week
```

Evidently, the respondent's, 'I'm still getting paid, but school's out, so' indicates trouble with the question in light of her actual circumstances (e.g. she *was* paid, but she did not 'do any work'). Despite the trouble this response indicates with the question, the interviewer pursues a type-conforming response (first in line 7 and after a number of restarts, again in line 16), treating the initial response as an instance of simple non-compliance. In response, however, the interviewee produces another nonconforming response (lines 17–19), underscoring the manner in which her circumstances do not fit the terms posed by the question. Across this sequence, a struggle emerges between the respondent, who persists in treating her circumstances as beyond the scope of the response options provided by the query, and the interviewer, who attempts to prompt her compliance with them, and thereby to sustain the sequence as part of a fixed measuring instrument.

This stance is further exemplified in the interviewer's subsequent conduct. In asking a follow-up query, the interviewer specifically avoids taking into account the respondent's previous nonconforming response (as would be relevant in ordinary conversation – and most other environments – where speakers are accountable for designing their talk for the particular recipients addressed by it). Directly after the respondent reports that she was not at work *for a second time*, the interviewer asks 'how many hours' she worked. By reading the next question exactly as it was written, the interviewer declines to treat the respondent's prior talk as relevant for her, even though she was its primary recipient, thereby engaging in a practice designed to sustain her identity as an interviewer, and her recipient's as an interviewee.

The consequences of interviewers' orientation to specific constraints of survey interviews can be reflected in both how they ask questions and how they deal with (nonconforming) responses. Unlike ordinary conversation (in which nonconforming responses may be managed in a variety of ways), nonconforming responses in surveys are typically rejected. Specifically, (1) such responses are not treated as 'data' in the survey (in the sense that the 'extraneous' matters introduced by them are not collected as data); (2) interviewers do not revise their questions to permit (or encourage) a type-conforming response (as in excerpt (8) above); and finally, (3) unlike the constraints on recipient design in ordinary conversation, nonconforming responses in surveys are not treated as relevant for the design of subsequent items in the administration of the survey. In these respects, the effort to produce standardized measurement results in the participants enacting an essentially anonymous relationship with one another. By reading questions exactly as they are worded and by encouraging respondents to produce responses in a formatted fashion, the variations detected by the survey instrument can be taken to reflect the 'real' variations in the phenomenon being investigated rather than different ways of asking questions, or the different expectations inadvertently communicated by interviewers' attempts to design such queries for the actual recipient to whom they are addressed (Maynard and Schaeffer 2002b). Thus, in contrast to courtrooms (where attorneys specifically build their questions to maximize bias in the responses they solicit), and doctor–patient interactions (where doctors attempt to establish rapport by specifically designing questions for their recipients) the design (and articulation) of questions and the constraints on responses in surveys aim to avoid the error and bias that might otherwise contaminate their status as a standardized scientific instrument.

Summary

In this chapter I have briefly introduced a well-established method for analysing patterns of conduct in institutional settings. In doing so, I have covered a range of issues. I began by introducing the central methodological challenges posed by this form of analysis. The issues of relevance and procedural consequentiality raised by Schegloff are, in the first place, posed so as to challenge our conventional thinking in an effort to promote novel observations about what social actions and social institutions consist of and how they are organized. These methodological criteria, then, are not barriers to saying what one 'knows' to be true about a setting, category of persons, and the like; they make it possible to actually *discover* something new about those settings, and thereby to potentially transform what is 'known to be true' about people and social reality. This surely must be a basic goal of research in the social sciences.

In briefly considering the range of ways in which the issues of relevance and procedural consequentiality have been addressed in the institutional talk programme, I have introduced some analytic tools that suggest where to look, and what to look for, in audio and video records of human interaction. These by no means exhaust how one may address the challenges posed by this form of analysis and there are more to be discovered. However, since all participants in interaction must take turns talking, compose sequences of action, manage the overall trajectory of their interaction, and the like, examining the range of practices through which these (and other) systematic contingencies are organized will likely provide some insight into the affairs being managed in virtually any setting one might choose to analyse.

In providing an extended illustration of this method, I focused on sequence organization, and specifically YNIs and their responses. As I noted in introducing this form of investigation, analysts typically proceed by comparing interactional practices found in both mundane and institutional occasions. To establish a basis for comparison I began by describing the constraints on speakers who produce and respond to YNIs in their most basic form – and the consequences of these resources for the courses of action organized through them. While the constraints set by YNIs promotes accepting the definition-of-the-situation formulated by the YNI speaker, the possibility of a nonconforming response may also constrain how the YNI speaker 'defines' a situation in the first place.

In considering how YNIs are used in courtrooms, doctor–patient interactions and survey research I noted that the resources available to speakers in the basic form of YNIs reflect a variety of constraints – some that are explicitly formulated in rules of conduct (as in courtrooms and survey research) and others that reflect the implicit management of routine contingencies (as in doctor–patient interaction). In this respect, institutions can be 'talked into being' by manipulating one or more aspect of the sequences initiated by YNIs. For example, as we noted, speakers can:

1   systematically shape how YNIs are designed (e.g. by limiting the presuppositions and expectations embodied in it);
2   re-specify the range and types of choice made relevant by the YNI (e.g. by constraining speakers to produce only type-conforming responses);
3   constrain how speakers take up responses to YNIs in subsequent actions.

To illustrate these observations I considered the ways that YNI sequences are shaped in these institutional settings. In briefly sketching how YNIs are deployed in these institutional environments I developed my analysis in two ways. First, I have sought to explicate that, and how, participants in these institutional interactions orient to the specific task, rules and goals that are distinctive to them. Second, by considering these institutions comparatively I have specified how such institutions are situated relative to social life, and how the lives and experiences of people moving through them are shaped into forms usable for institutionally specific tasks. In pursuing both of these goals, this analysis promotes our understanding of the activity of questioning, which must stand as one of the most basic and ubiquitous activities engaged in by our social species.

Note

1.   Speakers can form a YNI 'by placing the operator before the subject' (Quirk et al. 1985: 807), that is, by placing the copula/auxiliary verb before the subject.

CHAPTER NINE ●●●●●●●● Understanding News Media: The Relevance of Interaction

Steven E. Clayman

Perhaps no area of social scientific research is more saturated with varieties of discourse than the news media. In the prototypical media moment, public affairs information is conveyed to the audience primarily through the vehicle of some form of discourse: a written story, a spoken comment, an exchange of interaction. Such discursive forms are utterly familiar and taken for granted by consumers of media culture, so it is not surprising that they tend to be overlooked by media scholars. Researchers often use the 'content' of media discourse as a resource for exploring other matters – the organizational pressures bearing on journalists, the social psychological effects on audiences, and the broader socio-political context in which mass communication is embedded. It is much less common to examine media discourse itself as a topic in its own right – the elementary forms in which it appears, and the practices of which each is comprised.

This emphasis is consistent with the dominant metaphor that has guided news media studies. Researchers from otherwise diverse perspectives tend to treat the news as analogous to a 'mirror', to be investigated for the degree to which it accurately reflects, or alternatively distorts, the world at large. Like any metaphor, the news-as-mirror analogy both illuminates and obscures its target. A focus on the *representational function* of news comes at the expense of enquiry into the *social practices* that constitute news and make it an intrinsic part of the world in which it is embedded. As Hallin and Mancini (1984: 829) have observed, drawing inspiration from the later writings of Ludwig Wittgenstein:

> ... just as language is not really separate from the 'world' it 'pictures,' the media do not stand apart from the social processes reflected in the content of the news. Just as language is embedded in the 'forms of life' in which we use it, constituted by and helping to constitute those forms, the media are an integral part of political and social life.

Interest in the 'forms of life' that constitute news discourse has flowered only in recent years, although the seeds of this development were planted as far back as the 1970s, when a few seminal studies spawned what would eventually become a variety of distinct approaches. Following Weaver (1975), some researchers focus on the overall design of the news narrative (see Bell 1991), which through comparative analysis becomes a window into the culture of journalism as it is constituted in different national contexts (Hallin and Mancini 1984) and historical eras (Schudson 1982). Following Tuchman (1972, 1973), others focus on the foundations of journalistic objectivity and authority, examining the discursive and televisual practices through which the facticity of news is achieved and dramatized (Clayman and Heritage 2002a: Chapter 5; Raymond 2000; Zelizer 1990). Following Fowler et al. (1979), those in the critical discourse analysis tradition have been concerned with the relationship between media discourse and relations of power and inequality in the wider society (Fairclough 1995; van Dijk 1988).

New analytic challenges are posed by the recent diversification of media discourse. For many years, most news and public affairs information was presented to audiences in the form of a narrative or story, and most academic studies of the news media – including studies of production processes, thematic content, and audience effects – quite naturally used the traditional story form of news as data. However, at least within broadcasting, the story form has steadily declined in prominence since the 1980s with the proliferation of programme formats and media events organized around interaction rather than narration – news interviews and conferences, formal and informal debates, panel discussions, town meetings between politicians and ordinary citizens, and talk shows of various kinds. The reasons for this development are complex (Clayman 2004), but it is abundantly clear that interaction in various forms, and involving various combinations of media professionals, public figures and ordinary people, has become a central means by which news and commentary is now packaged for public consumption. This development plainly requires new modes of analysis suited to capturing the increasingly prevalent interactional dimension of news.

Apart from its current pervasiveness, why is the interactional dimension so important? First and foremost, broadcast interaction now plays a major role in the determination of news content. For the traditional news story, the content of news is in essence scripted, determined 'behind the scenes' through processes of research, writing and editing. Forms of interaction, in contrast, are essentially unscripted and to some extent unpredictable. Of course, each interactional participant may have a preconceived agenda in mind at the outset, a more or less settled idea of what they would like to say and do. However, there are multiple participants, and each is an independent agent in this process. And since every contribution to interaction is an important contingency affecting what happens next – every 'move' forms the context for and to some degree conditions the next 'move' – anyone's capacity to realize an agenda is necessarily contingent on the actions of others. The actual course of a broadcast interaction is thus by no means predetermined; it is an emergent product of how the participants choose to deal with each other then and there, moment by moment, move by move. Given this, explanations of contemporary news content will be incomplete unless the interactional dimension is taken into account.

If broadcast interactions are not scripted in any strong sense of the word, neither are they a disorganized free-for-all in which 'anything goes'. Indeed, the parties to any form of talk observe an elaborate set of social conventions, some generic to interaction *per se*, and others specialized for that particular form of talk in that environment of broadcasting. These conventions are largely tacit and taken for granted, and yet they are very real and very powerful. They define the boundaries of permissible conduct and shape the actions of the participants in singular ways. Adherence to the special-ized conventions is what makes any given genre of broadcast talk recognizably dis-tinct from other genres, and distinct also from the form of talk that is most pervasive and fundamental to social life: ordinary conversation. Moreover, these conventions are meaningful in their own right, and can illuminate both the 'content' of the news and the social world of which it is a part.

This final point bears elaboration. Broadcast interactions are, in the first instance, arenas where journalists and other media professionals, government officials and other elites, and ordinary people engage one another in various permutations on the public stage. The manner in which these encounters unfold is shaped by, and in turn contributes to, diverse segments of society and their interrelations. Correspondingly, their study provides a unique window into these societal arrangements. Just as the conventions that organize news interviews and news conferences can shed light on the institution of journalism and its evolving relationship to government and polit-ical processes, the conventions that organize town meetings and audience-participation talk shows can shed light on constructions of the public and its shifting relationship to elite segments of society.

In short, investigating the 'forms of life' that organize broadcast interaction has the potential to shed new light on both news content and the diverse societal arrange-ments that it sustains. Accordingly, researchers have begun to explore various genres of broadcast talk in these terms. Much of this work draws on conversation analysis as an approach, and uses ordinary conversation as a comparative reference point for illumi-nating what is distinctive about each form of broadcast talk.[1] Thus far, most work has focused on journalistic interviews (e.g. Clayman and Heritage 2002a, 2002b; Corner 1991; Greatbatch 1988, 1992; Harris 1986, 1991; Jucker 1986; Myers 2000; Roth 1998, 2002) and audience-participation talk shows (e.g. Bhimji 2001; Hutchby 1996, 1999; Thornborrow 2001a, 2001b; Tolson 2001; see also Martinez 2003). A related stream of research investigates speaker–audience interactions in a variety of contexts, focusing on collective audience responses such as applause, booing and laughter (Atkinson 1984; Clayman 1993; Heritage and Greatbatch 1986).

Space does not permit a complete review of the literature, nor a comprehensive intro-duction to the methodology of conversation analysis. The objective here is more modest: to explore at least some of the analytic issues involved, and to illustrate what can be gained by examining the interactional foundations of news media discourse.

Basic ground rules

It will be useful, as a point of departure, to think about forms of broadcast talk as analogous to games of various kinds. Like genuine games, an interactional form is a distinct mode of activity that is bounded off from the ordinary run of social life, involves participants with at least partially divergent goals and interests, and is played through a succession of moves and counter-moves.

To understand any such game, an important step is to investigate the basic ground rules that constitute the game as a recognizably distinct mode of activity. While setting-specific interactional conventions can exist at varying levels of scale and with varying degrees of salience (Drew and Heritage 1992b), some operate across occasions of interaction in their entirety and thus inform every contribution. It is these over-arching conventions that qualify as constitutive ground rules for a given form of talk. The existence of such ground rules can often be linked to professional norms, insti-tutional pressures, or practical constraints intrinsic to the context of broadcasting.

Two species of ground rules may be distinguished. The first type governs the *over-all structure* of an encounter. Unlike ordinary conversation, some forms of broadcast talk (like institutional talk more generally: see Chapter 8 in this volume; Drew and Heritage 1992b) have an overall shape to them, a recurrent trajectory in which the parties address a succession of tasks in a more or less standard order. Structured inter-actions of this sort can be either brief or extended. At the brief end of the continuum, the telephone call episodes that comprise many radio call-in shows unfold in a routine and predictable way, with opening and closing phases bracketing phases of position-taking by the caller, response by the host, and subsequent argumentation (Hutchby 1996: 14–16). At the other end of the continuum, most TV talk shows fea-turing ordinary people and studio audience participation (e.g. *Donahue, Oprah* and *Jerry Springer*) have at least a partially routinized trajectory spanning the entire pro-gramme. Such routinization, which can include predetermined phases for dramatic conflict, spectacular revelations, etc., in part reflects an effort by programme pro-ducers to exert control over the encounter in a way that will reliably ensure a suffi-cient number of lively moments with substantial audience appeal (Grindstaff 2002).

The second set of ground rules concern the *system of turn taking* that organizes access to the floor and hence participation in the encounter. Some forms of broad-cast talk, for example late-night celebrity talk shows and radio call-in shows, have turn-taking arrangements that are not significantly different from ordinary conver-sation (Greatbatch 1988; Sacks et al. 1974). In these cases, there is no predetermined plan or format for taking turns, so who gets to speak at any given point, for how long, and what they can do within their turn at talk, are determined for the most part from within the interaction as it unfolds. Thus, the order of speakership, as well as the length and content of turns at talk, varies from interaction to interaction. Such interactions tend to be experienced and understood as relatively 'casual' or 'non-formal' in character (Atkinson 1982).

Other forms of broadcast talk are organized by specialized systems of turn-taking which are distinct from ordinary conversation and hence involve a more or less predetermined format for the exchange of turns. Most campaign debates unfold in this way, as do news interviews (Clayman and Heritage 2002a: Chapter 4; Greatbatch 1988) and news conferences (Clayman 2004). For both of the latter cases, talk is restricted to questions and answers allocated to journalists and public figures respectively, although this generalization encompasses noteworthy variations. In the prototypical news interview, a single journalist assumes the role of questioner. In the news conference, large numbers of journalists share this role, posing the problem of who gets to ask each successive question. In most news conferences, questioners are chosen through a process similar to that found in Prime Minister's question time – journalists bid for the opportunity to ask each question (by raising their hands, calling out the politician's name, etc.), and the politician then selects among the bidders. Notwithstanding such variations in turn-taking, the persistent adherence to a predetermined question–answer format is linked to the journalistic norm of neutrality (discussed below), and endows the interaction with a relatively 'formal' character (Atkinson 1982).

Turn-taking arrangements provide for the management of interactional traffic, but they have a much broader significance that bears on the substance of the discussion. In the news interview, for instance, the turn-taking system empowers the journalist to set the topical agenda for politicians, and to ask follow-up questions that pursue resistant or evasive responses. In the news conference, by contrast, with multiple journalists competing to ask each next question, the opportunity for follow-up is much more restricted and contingent. In effect, the journalistic role is fragmented, making it easier for politicians to resist questions and thus 'stay on message'. Correspondingly, US presidents in their news conferences have periodically experimented with alternative methods for selecting questioners (e.g. requiring written questions submitted in advance, using a lottery, etc.), often in an effort to foster greater decorum and to gain greater control over the discussion agenda (Clayman 2004; Schegloff 1987).

Although many turn-taking systems may be summarized in terms of a simple rule, that is 'questions and answers', such rules are, by themselves, commonsensical and not particularly enlightening. Analysis moves beyond the obvious by explicating how the rule is implemented in practice, that is, for the case of news interviews, how a stretch of talk is designed so as to 'come off' as a series of questions and answers (Clayman and Heritage 2002a: Chapter 4; Greatbatch 1988). The following excerpt, which typifies news interview talk, illustrates some of the many complex and subtle practices implicated in this process. It is the opening exchange in Dan Rather's infamous 1988 interview with Vice President George Bush, and concerns Bush's involvement in the Iran–Contra scandal.

```
(1)   [CBS Evening News: 25 Jan. 1988]
1     DR:    Mister Vice President, thank you for being with us tonigh:t,
2            .hh Donald Gregg still serves as your trusted advisor, he
3            was deeply involved in running arms to the contras, 'n 'e
4            didn't inform you.
5            .hhh Now when President Reagan's (0.3) trusted advisor:
6            Admiral Poindexter: (0.5) failed to inform him::, (0.7)
7            thuh President (0.4) fired 'im.
8            (0.5) Why is Mister Gregg still:: (0.2) inside thuh
9            White House 'n still a trusted advisor.
10    GB:    Because I have confidence in him, .hh 'n because this matter
```

```
11        Dan:, as you well know:, 'n your editors know:, has been looked
12        at by .hh the ten million dollar study by the: (.) Senate 'n
13        thuh Hou:se, .hh it's been looked at by thuh Tower commission ...
```

Here Rather 'asks a question' and then Bush 'answers it', but what underlies this seemingly simple exchange? To say 'the interviewer asks a question' glosses over what he has actually done to produce talk that is recognizable as 'doing questioning', just as it glosses over the more general issue of what is regarded as acceptable 'questioning' in the news interview context. Rather's turn at talk is not a simple question – it begins with various assertions (lines 1–7) before the question proper (lines 8–9) is delivered. Complex statement-prefaced questions are absolutely routine in this context, and it's one of the features that distinguishes the news interview from other forms of talk with superficially similar turn-taking arrangements. Courtroom trial examinations, for example, are also organized around questions and answers, but there the range of acceptable questions is much more narrow and confining.

To say that 'the interviewer asks a question' also obscures the interviewee's role in this process. Rather would not have been able to deliver his complex prefaced question without co-operation from Bush, who withholds speaking until the question is completed. There are at least two points (at lines 5 and 8) where Rather not only completes a sentence but provides a bit of space before launching into the next unit of talk. These are places where, in ordinary conversation, it would have been appropriate for a recipient to begin speaking, but Bush declines to produce either a substantive response or even a brief acknowledgement (e.g. 'uh huh'). This is particularly remarkable given the damaging nature of what Rather has said in his prefatory statements. He has drawn a contrast between Bush and Reagan in terms of how they have handled advisors implicated in the scandal, a contrast that portrays Bush's conduct as ethically suspect. That Bush nonetheless declines to respond to this accusatory contrast or its components reveals an enormous amount of self-control on his part, but Bush is by no means unusual in this respect. Interviewees generally withhold speaking in this way, and this is also part of the work involved in following the question–answer rule.

Correspondingly, to say that 'the interviewee answers the question' glosses over a parallel set of issues and practices – that interviewees must withhold speech until the question is completed in order to have a sequential environment where an 'answer' would be relevant and intelligible, that they must design their talk so that it will be recognizable in context as an 'answer', and that interviewers must collaborate in this process.

Finally, the question–answer rule, by itself, says nothing about how departures from that framework are managed and dealt with.

Clearly, then, turn-taking arrangements, which may at first seem utterly commonsensical when boiled down to a simple rule, rest upon a substrate of underlying practices that are complex and far from obvious. Investigating these arrangements directs attention to, and reveals the organized character of, an enormous amount of interactional conduct.

Playing the game

Playing any game necessarily involves much more than simply following its ground rules, and this is true not only for literal games but also for the metaphorical games of broadcast talk. Participation involves a complex repertoire of practices and actions, deployed with an eye towards the state of play at a given moment, and geared to a variety of tasks and objectives. Three orders of phenomena, of varying levels of concreteness, may be distinguished. These are thoroughly interdependent orders, and most research combines attention to their interrelations, but they will be distinguished here for purposes of exemplification.

Practices

At the most concrete level, analysis may focus on particular ways of talking or interacting with the aim of explicating what each practice 'does' or accomplishes when it is deployed within some game at a particular moment in the state of play. A wide range of practices may be analysed in this way – lexical choices, non-vocal behaviours, and just about any aspect of the design of turns at talk and their placement within larger sequences of turns.

For example, Heritage (2002b) examines a particular practice of questioning found in news interviews and news conferences (as well as ordinary conversation). The focal practice is a type of yes/no question, termed a *negative question*, designed so that the interrogative component is negatively formulated e.g. 'Isn't it', 'Aren't you', 'Don't you think that'. For example:

```
(2)    [Clinton News Conference: 7 March 1997: Simplified]
       IR:          Well Mister President in your zeal for funds
                    during the last campaign
              1->   didn't you put the Vice President and Maggie
                    and all the others in your administration
                    top side in a very vulnerable position,
                    (0.5)
       BC:    2->   I disagree with that. How are we vulnerable because ...
```

The negative component (at arrow 1) is entirely optional, in that it could have been omitted without any loss of propositional content or intelligibility (cf., 'did you put ...'). What, then, are journalists 'doing' by asking questions in this way? Heritage demonstrates that negative questions invite the recipient to respond with a *yes*-type answer to the question, so they are, in effect, 'tilted' in favour of *yes*. Indeed, the preference for an affirmative answer is so strong that recipients often treat such questions as if they were expressing a point of view rather than simply asking a question. In the preceding example, Clinton's response – 'I disagree with that' (arrow 2) – clearly treats the prior turn as embodying a viewpoint to be disagreed with, and not merely a question to be answered.

Here, then, we have a practice of question design that is understood by the participants as falling demonstrably short of absolute neutrality, and hence as strongly opinionated or assertive in character. This way of formulating a question exerts pressure on the interviewee to answer in a particular way. Moreover, when the viewpoint encoded in the question runs contrary to the interviewee's interests (as in the preceding example, which proposes that Clinton's campaign fundraising efforts were problematic and damaging to his associates), the question is demonstrably adversarial.

In the very different context of radio call-in shows, Hutchby (1996: Chapter 4) examines a particular practice that hosts use when responding to the caller's initial statement of opinion. This practice, which takes the form [You say X, but what about Y], involves quoting or paraphrasing some aspect of the caller's opinion statement (arrow 1 below) before proceeding with a substantive response (arrow 2).

(3) [Hutchby 1996: 62]
     Caller: ....women've been fighting for equalitie:s (.) e::r
                      fo::r, u-yihknow many yea:rs, .hhh an:d i-it seems
                      to me that erm, they' want their cake and eat it.
                      (0.5)
     Caller: Er:m,
                      (0.3)
     Host: 1->   m-d- You s- You say you sa:y "the:y"
                2->   but I mean: .hh er your voice seems to give awa:y
                      thee erm, .p fact that you're a woman too.

This practice is used recurrently within hosts' oppositional responses. However, it is by no means necessary to counter or dispute what the caller has said; it represents a choice among alternative modes of opposition. This particular choice enables the host to avoid directly confronting the thrust of the caller's position, and instead focus on particular aspects of it (such as the caller's choice of words, as in the above example) which are singled out as arguable in a way that casts doubt on the encompassing position. Given the impetus for talk show hosts to generate conflict and controversy routinely, and in response to a wide variety of callers and viewpoints that cannot be fully known in advance, this device is a useful and effective resource.[2]

Actions

Interactional practices tend to cluster into groups in terms of the goal-directed actions that they accomplish (Schegloff 1997). When analysis focuses on encompassing actions as the primary object of interest, the objective is to survey a range of practices that can be deployed in the service of that action.

For instance, Heritage and Roth (1995) have explored the range of practices that stand as acceptable 'questions' in a news interview context. Such practices include not only the prototypical grammatical interrogatives (e.g. yes/no interrogatives, wh- interrogatives, etc.), but also various other practices that can render even declarative statements recognizable as doing the work of 'questioning' (e.g. rising intonation, b-event statements, etc.). Concerning the same news interview context, Clayman and Heritage (2002a: Chapter 7) have explored a range of practices for 'doing answering', as well as practices that facilitate resistant or 'evasive' responses with a minimum of friction.

Interview questions can themselves be deployed in the service of a variety of other journalistic activities. Interviewers can use their questions not only to elicit opinions from interviewees, but also to accuse them of wrongdoing (as in examples (1) and (2) above), to manage disagreements between interviewees, and so on. Consider example (1) above, where Dan Rather uses his question to mount an accusation against Vice President Bush, proposing that Bush failed to fire or distance himself from a morally tainted advisor who was centrally implicated in the Iran–Contra scandal. Bush's ethical failure is portrayed (in lines 1–7) by means of an explicit contrast with President Reagan, who dutifully fired his own advisor under similar circumstances. Correspondingly, Bush uses his answer (lines 10–13) to defend himself, justifying his retention of the advisor and suggesting more generally that he remains untainted by the Iran–Contra scandal. Questions are thus a vehicle for diverse journalistic activities, each of which can be analysed in terms of the specific practices through which it is realized.

A focus on actions can move beyond standard vernacular categories of action to examine aspects of action that are less familiar. Thus, Clayman and Heritage (2002a: Chapter 6) have explored how yes/no questions can be 'tilted' in favour of a particular answer, thereby encoding a point of view into the question as it is asked. The negative question practice discussed above is just one of a family of allied practices that have the effect of treating a particular answer as correct or preferable. Some of these practices are embodied in the linguistic form of the question itself (e.g. negative questions, statement + tag questions, the inclusion of negative polarity items like 'really' or 'seriously'), while others involve statements produced as prefaces to the question. Much like 'asking a question', the act of 'asking a question while favouring a particular answer' can be accomplished in a variety of describable ways.

Tasks, norms, and constraints

At yet another level, research may be geared to explicating the broader concerns towards which the participants are oriented in and through their practices and actions. Such concerns frequently arise from the institutional environment in which the interaction is embedded, and may take the form of professional norms, organizational tasks and pressures, practical contingencies, and so on.

In news interviews and news conferences, for example, journalists' questions are informed by two deeply engrained professional norms which are often in conflict. On the one hand, consistent with the norm of objectivity, journalists are supposed to remain formally *neutral* in their questions. Absolute neutrality is, of course, an unattainable ideal, but journalists strive for it through various forms of conduct that have a formally neutral or 'neutralistic' character: restricting themselves to the activity of questioning, avoiding assertions except as prefaces to a question or as attributed to a third party, and avoiding acknowledgement tokens and other forms of receipt that can be taken as supportive of the interviewee's remarks (Clayman and Heritage 2002a: Chapters 4 and 5).

At the same time, consistent with the ideal of political independence and the 'watchdog' role of the press, journalists are also supposed to be *adversarial* in their questioning, and should not allow their guests unfettered access to the airwaves to say whatever suits their interests. Adversarialness is achieved by raising topics that run contrary to the politician's interests (as in example (1) above), by embedding unflattering presuppositions that are difficult to counter or refute, and by 'tilting' questions in favour of answers that the politician would rather not give (as in example (2) above) (Clayman and Heritage 2002a: Chapter 6).

The convergence of, and tension between, neutralism and adversarialness is strikingly apparent in this excerpt from an interview with a 'dog psychiatrist' who works with emotionally troubled canines.

```
(4)   [NBC Dateline 16 December 1997]
1     IR:    A lotta people would hear: (.) about your profession.
2     IE:    Ye:s.=
3     IR:    and say that's a bunch o'poppycock.
4     IE:    Ye:s,
5            (0.2)
6     IR:    And you say:?
7            (.)
8     IE:    I say they're entitled to their opinion. .hh And I would
9            also say to those people...
```

Here the interviewer (IR) pointedly dismisses the interviewee's profession as 'a bunch o'poppycock' (lines 1–3), and in so doing he assumes a plainly adversarial posture. However, this attack is not done as an unvarnished action in its own right. By attributing it to 'a lotta people', the interviewer deflects responsibility onto an anonymous collectivity of sceptics, thereby distancing himself from the attack. He also goes on to solicit the interviewee's response (line 6), thereby retroactively packaging the attack as leading up to a 'question'. In all of these ways, he manages to be both substantively adversarial and formally neutral. Correspondingly, this complex stance is affirmed and validated by the interviewee. Although he defends his profession (in lines 8–9), he first waits for a question to be delivered (lines 4–5), and he treats the agent of the prior attack as anonymous skeptics rather than the interviewer ('I say they are entitled to their opinion'). Various aspects of question design can thus be understood in terms of how they bear on, and strike a balance between, the divergent professional ideals of neutrality and adversarialness.

While balancing neutrality and adversarialness is relevant mainly for journalistic forms of talk, other concerns cut across a variety of programming contexts. Consider, for instance, the import of the audience. Although broadcast interactions are in the first instance encounters between programme participants, they have a 'performance' dimension in that they are enacted for the benefit of a third party – the audience who is watching or listening in. This fact is not an inconsequential feature of the context; the participants orient to the audience through the design of their conduct (Clayman and Heritage 2002a: Chapters 3 and 4; Heritage 1985; Hutchby 1996: 14), although the extent and manner in which they do this varies dramatically across different forms of broadcast talk. Thus, in many talk shows involving a studio audience, the on-stage participants directly address their remarks to the audience intermittently throughout the programme. In news interviews, by contrast, the audience is addressed directly only in and around the opening and closing phases (Clayman and Heritage 2002a: Chapter 3), while elsewhere they are acknowledged only in indirect and extremely subtle ways (Clayman and Heritage 2002a: Chapter 4).

Varying styles of play

Thus far, the focus has been on the most fundamental features of broadcast talk, features that are broadly characteristic of specific genres. To return to our game metaphor, we've touched on the basic ground rules that are constitutive of each interactional game, and the elementary practices and actions through which the game is played. But the analysis remains at a fairly elemental level, couched mainly in terms of the basic building blocks of interaction. How do these building blocks combine into more complex patterns or styles of play, and how do these styles in turn vary in relation to features of the social context in which the game is embedded? In addressing such questions, the analytic focus begins to shift away from the inner workings of broadcast talk itself, and towards the social identities, relationships, and institutions that converge on the playing field of interaction to then shape, and be shaped by, courses of conduct.

In principle, styles of play can vary along any number of contextual dimensions. At the level of individual participants, those involved can have varying occupational, professional and organizational backgrounds, as well as varying demographic characteristics and levels of status or prestige. At the level of the broadcasting environment, interactions unfold on different programmes, for different networks, and under different ownership and financing regimes. At the societal level, interactions unfold under different political-economic conditions, national contexts, and historical eras. To what extent do these contextual dimensions matter for the conduct of broadcast talk, and what can the study of broadcast talk in turn reveal about its social environment?

Answering such questions requires systematic comparative analysis, the specific nature of which will depend on the order of phenomena to be investigated. When variations in conduct are substantial enough to involve a fundamental transformation of the normative order of interaction (i.e. the different turn-taking arrangements characteristic of news interviews and ordinary conversation), then they can be investigated by the established methods of conversation analysis involving the detailed case-by-case analysis of both 'normal' and 'deviant' instances (ten Have 1999: 39–40; Heritage 1984b: Chapter 8). But when the differences are less dramatic than this, involving only differences in the relative frequency of specific forms of conduct, then formal quantification is in order.

The quantitative analysis of interactional conduct is not without pitfalls (Schegloff 1993). It cannot proceed in a defensible way without a thorough grasp of the basic sequential structures and forms of conduct operative within a given domain of talk, as these are understood by the participants themselves. But once this foundation is in place, quantification becomes viable and the payoffs can be substantial.

Consider the case of the presidential news conference, and what comparative analysis can reveal about the White House press corps and its evolving relationship to the president. The tenor of president–press relations has been of interest to scholars from a variety of disciplines, who have suggested that the White House press corps – and US journalists more generally – has become less deferential and more aggressive in recent decades. The domain of the presidential news conference is in many respects an ideal environment in which to test the hypothesis of an increasingly aggressive news media, since it is a locus of direct encounters between journalists and the highest official in the land. But until recently systematic comparative/historical studies of news conferences were rare and underdeveloped. Indeed, the consensus among researchers was that this domain eludes measurement and quantification. As Kernell (1986: 76) observed, 'the adversarial aspect of presidential–press relations is an elusive quality, difficult to quantify'. The difficulty arises from the fact that quantification requires a basic understanding of how aggressiveness is instantiated at the ground level, in actual practices of questioning. It requires, in other words, a grasp of the fundamentals of question design.

Building on previous research on questioning in broadcast news interviews, Clayman and Heritage (2002b) developed a framework for measuring the level of vigor or aggressiveness in questions. The framework decomposes the general concept of aggressiveness into four component dimensions: (1) *initiative*, the extent to which the question is enterprising rather than passive in its aims; (2) *directness*, the extent to which the question is delivered bluntly rather than cautiously or indirectly; (3) *assertiveness*, the extent to which the question displays a preference for a particular answer and is in that sense opinionated rather than neutral; and (4) *adversarialness*, the extent to which the question pursues an agenda in opposition to the president or his administration. Each dimension has multiple indicators encompassing both the 'content' of the talk as well as formal features of question design that previous research has shown embodies salient forms of aggressiveness.

This framework can be likened to a 'thermometer' for measuring the 'heat' in journalistic questions. To illustrate its potential for comparative analysis, consider how the issue of the federal budget was put before two presidents spanning almost three decades – Dwight Eisenhower and Ronald Reagan.

```
(5)  [Eisenhower 27 Oct 1954: 9]
1     JRN:   Mr. President, you spoke in a speech the other night of
2            the continued reduction of government spending and tax cuts
```

```
3          to the limit that the national security will permit.
4          Can you say anything more definite at this time about
5          the prospects of future tax cuts?
```

(6)   [Reagan 16 June 1981: 14]
```
1    JRN:  Mr. President, for months you said you wouldn't modify
2          your tax cut plan, and then you did. And when the
3          business community vociferously complained, you changed
4          your plan again. I just wondered whether Congress and
5          other special interest groups might get the message that
6          if they yelled and screamed loud enough, you might modify
7          your tax cut plan again?
```

Although both questions concern budgetary matters and tax cuts, the question to Eisenhower is much more deferential. Its agenda is non-adversarial: indeed, it is framed as having been occasioned by Eisenhower's own previous remarks, and it contains nothing that disagrees with, challenges, or opposes his views. It is non-assertive: it displays minimal expectations about what type of answer would be correct or preferable, and is formally neutral in that respect. It is also cautiously indirect: it exerts relatively little pressure on the president to provide an answer, and even allows for the possibility ('*Can you* say anything...' in line 4) that the president may be unable to answer.

Reagan's question, by contrast, is in various ways more aggressive. This question is similarly occasioned by the president's previous remarks, but here the journalist details damaging contradictions between the president's words and his actual deeds, making the agenda of the question fundamentally adversarial. And far from being neutral, the question's preface (lines 1–4) assertively favours a *yes* answer, which would in turn require the president to admit to being weak and subservient to special interests.

As it turns out, these questions are fairly typical of the Eisenhower and Reagan eras (Clayman and Heritage 2002b). Analysis of a systematic sample of Eisenhower and Reagan news conferences revealed substantial and statistically significant differences for all indicators, all in the direction of greater aggressiveness for Reagan than Eisenhower. But how typical are these particular presidents? Subsequent research currently in progress on all postwar presidents from Eisenhower to Clinton (1953–2000) demonstrates that there has indeed been a significant long-term decline in deference towards the president, as White House journalists have grown more vigorous on every dimension over time.

This generalization, while broadly accurate, glosses over some important complexities (Clayman et al. 2006). The trend for directness stands out as more gradual, continuous and unidirectional than the other dimensions. Thus, while journalists in the 1950s were exceedingly cautious and indirect in their questioning (e.g. 'Would you care to tell us ...', 'Can I ask whether ...'), they have steadily become much more straightforward in putting issues before the president. Since this trend has steadily advanced across three decades, increasing directness is unrelated to local historical events or socio-political conditions; it appears to be a general secular trend. Indeed, it may not be a journalistic trend *per se*, so much as one manifestation of a broader societal change involving the decline of formality in American life and the coarsening of public discourse.

By contrast, initiative, assertiveness and adversarialness are more contextually sensitive, rising in a more concentrated manner in certain historical periods and falling in others. These dimensions remained at a relatively low level from Eisenhower to Johnson, rose moderately from Nixon to Reagan's first term, declined from Reagan's second term to George Bush, and then rose again during Clinton's time in office. These patterns suggest that a series of historical events and conditions – (i.e. the deceptions of Vietnam and Watergate, the decline of political consensus, economic hard times) prompted journalists to exercise their watchdog role with increasing vigor from the late 1960s to the mid 1980s.

Quantitative research need not be limited to long-term historical trends. Once a valid and reliable framework for measuring deference/aggressiveness is in place, it becomes possible to conduct multivariate analyses addressed to a range of research questions about the specific factors affecting journalistic conduct. Do economic conditions have an impact? It turns out that at least some of them do – the unemployment rate is a broad and consistent predictor of question design. When the unemployment rate is rising, journalists become significantly more aggressive in a variety of ways. Journalists thus exercise their watchdog role more vigorously during economic hard times.

What about foreign affairs? Consistent with the 'rally 'round the flag' syndrome and the maxim that 'politics stops at the water's edge', journalists are significantly less aggressive when raising foreign policy and military matters than when raising domestic matters. Presidents are to some extent shielded from vigorous questioning on foreign affairs, although the shield is not invincible. Such questions have grown more aggressive over time, closely mirroring the trend for questions generally, but foreign/military questions are, on average, consistently more deferential or 'tame' than their domestic counterparts.

What about individual journalists? Questions also differ depending on who is asking them. Contrary to stereotypical notions of masculinity and femininity, female journalists have generally been more aggressive than their male counterparts. Correspondingly, broadcasters have been more aggressive than those working in print. In both instances, it is the 'new kids on the block' of the White House press corps who have taken the more aggressive posture.

―――――― **News content revisited: illuminating specific media messages** ――――――

The final payoff of the approach outlined here is that it facilitates the illumination of specific media messages and their 'contents'. All of the findings generated through previous research on broadcast talk and on interaction more generally, together with the sensitivity to detail that this approach fosters, can be mobilized to explicate particular utterances and segments of interaction. This can in turn reveal subtle and nuanced levels of meaning that tend to elude less fine-grained modes of analysis, whether offered by social scientists or popular commentators.

How to do things with 'compliments'

During an interview with Bob Dole when he was majority leader of the Senate, the journalist at one point characterized Dole as 'a very candid man'. This might at first glance appear to be a straightforward compliment – favourable treatment that could be taken as an index of the interviewer's biased attitude in support of his guest. However, upon closer examination of how the remark was used in context, it becomes apparent that it was far from friendly in its import. Consider, first, how the remark (arrowed below) figures in the larger turn at talk in which it is embedded (lines 12–15).

```
(7)     [Meet the Press: 8 Dec. 1985: Dole]
1    IR :   =If you don't do that Senator tell me wh:at
2            'r the o:dds next year (.) for a tax increase.
3            (0.8)
4    BD:    Well I think it's a very complicated uh::: area
5            because you've got thuh tax reform bill 'at may or
6            may not come over from thuh Hou:se, .hhh you've got
7            uh:: thuh reconciliation process 'at'll be in place
8            next year: .hhh an' then you've got th'so called
9            Gramm Rudman.=So outta that (.) I assume you're gonna
10           have some revenue changes.
11           (.)
12   IR :   You're a very candid man. I think you're
13           [du]cking that question.=[What]'re the odds. Will there=
14   BD:    [ya ]                    [(no) ]
15   IR :   =be tax increase next year d'you think.
16           (0.7)
17   BD:    Well there's a tax increase in thuh bill that's uh being
18           uh sen' over f'm thuh House Ways 'n Means Committee ... .
```

The praise of Dole's character ('You're a very candid man') is followed without pause by a sharply contrasting remark attacking his previous response ('I think you're ducking that question'). The juxtaposition exposes a contradiction between Dole's general tendency towards 'candidness' and his current evasiveness, which in turn casts the latter as deficient by Dole's own standards. It is clear in retrospect that the compliment was merely the first phase of a larger and essentially aggressive course of action.

If we cast the net a bit wider and consider how this turn at talk operates as an action within the larger sequence of actions to which it contributes, its full adversarial import becomes apparent. The topic is the federal budget and the likelihood of a tax increase. The contrastive portrait of Dole is prefatory to a follow-up question (lines 13–15) that treats Dole's prior response as inadequate. The preface looks backward and sanctions Dole for not fully answering the previous question about the prospects of a tax increase, while the ensuing question looks forward and presses him again for a fully-fledged answer.

Contrasts of this kind are recurrent in the more adversarial questions found in news interviews and press conferences (Clayman and Heritage 2002a: 231–4); indeed, we saw another prefatory/adversarial contrast above in example (1). In general, such contrasts function to portray the interviewees' conduct as problematic in some way – self-contradictory, or incompatible with 'reality', or falling short of some normative ideal. In this discursive environment, words of praise routinely help to cast the interviewee as failing to live up to his or her own standards of conduct (Roth 1998: 94–6). Interviewees themselves may recognize that superficial flattery can be merely prefatory to something that is on balance unflattering. For example (analysed in Roth 1998), returning to Dan Rather's interview with Vice President George Bush about the Iran–Contra scandal, at one point he characterizes Bush as 'an anti-terrorism expert' (arrowed).

```
(8)   [CBS Evening News: 25 Jan. 1988: Bush and Iran/Contra]
1     IR :    =.hhh Can you explain how- (.) you were supposed tuh be the-
2              ->eh- you are:. You're an anti terrorist expert. .hhh
3              We- (0.2) Iran was officially a terrorist state.
4              .hh You went a[round telling eh::- eh- ehr-        ]
5     GB:                    [I've already explained that Dan, I] wanted
6              those hostages- I wanted Mister Buckley outta there.
```

This ostensibly favourable characterization treats Bush as an authority on terrorism, but only as a preface to counter-information (begun in lines 3–4 but not completed) outlining his willingness to sell arms to the 'terrorist state' of Iran. That Rather is moving to develop a damaging contrast is projected by his initial formulation in line 1 ('you were supposed to be the...'), which is epistemically downgraded and thus begins to cast doubt on Bush's true expertise. The developing contrast proposes, in effect, that Bush should have known better. Or it would have; it is not brought to completion. Rather had only asserted that 'Iran was officially a terrorist state' (line 3) and had begun to point out something about Bush's conduct (line 4), when Bush interjects (line 5) to forestall the contrast and defend himself. Here, then, the interviewee himself recognizes that what appears complimentary can be adversarial in its import.

Controversial remarks as co-constructions

As we have seen, detailed interactional analysis can illuminate 'the content' of broadcast talk, but the potential for such analysis goes beyond merely understanding the friendly/hostile valence of talk. Analysis can also shed light on what has been termed the *co-construction* of talk – the extent to which it is a product not of isolated individuals but of the joint efforts of multiple participants. Since popular commentaries tend to allocate praise and blame to individual journalists and public figures, the insight regarding co-construction is often counter-intuitive, and its ramifications can be of some significance.

Consider a case involving Bob Dole during the 1996 presidential campaign.[3] Dole faced a major setback when he publicly downplayed the addictiveness of tobacco, and suggested that Surgeon General C. Everett Koop may have been 'brainwashed' by 'the liberal media' on this issue. While he can indeed be construed as having said these things in an interview conducted by Katie Couric on *The Today Show*, commentaries on the event tended to overlook the extent to which Couric's questioning played a role in what transpired, particularly with respect to the key Surgeon-General-as-brainwashed remark.

The relevant excerpt appears below. Prior to the excerpt, Dole sought to defuse public criticisms of his seemingly pro-tobacco statements by blaming 'the liberal media' for biased coverage of the tobacco issue. This prompted Couric to point out (lines 1 and 3 below) that even 'Dr. Koop' – the Surgeon General and a Reagan appointee – 'had a real problem with your comments'.

```
(9)   [NBC Today Show: 3 July 1996: Dole Interview: official transcript]
1      IR:    But I'm saying, you know, you're saying it's the liberal media.
2      BD:    But again, you read something that-
3      IR:    But even Dr. Koop had a real problem with your comments.
4      BD:    Dr. Koop, you know, he watches the liberal media and he
5             probably got carried away.
6      IR:    He's brainwashed?
7      BD:    Probably a little bit.
8      IR:    I'm not here to nail you in any way ....
```

Dole deflects this (lines 4–5) by observing that Dr. Koop also 'watches the liberal media and he probably got carried away'. This remark plainly suggests that the Surgeon General was unduly influenced by the media, but that influence is characterized in comparatively mild and 'innocent' terms ('got carried away'). It is Couric, in the next question (line 6), who formulates the import of Dole's remark in more extreme terms (see Heritage 1985), offering 'brainwashed' as a way of characterizing Dole's view of the Surgeon General. Dole in turn confirms this (line 7), albeit with marked caution ('Probably a little bit'), such that his confirmation is both qualified and rendered as less than certain.

So while Dole does come to endorse the contentious proposition that generated so much commentary and criticism, he does so only when prompted by the interviewer and in terms offered by her. Neither the action itself nor the terms in which it is expressed are of his own choosing. Moreover, Couric herself tacitly acknowledges that by nudging Dole to this point she is co-implicated in what has transpired. Notice that her very next contribution (line 8) is a disclaimer, disavowing any attempt 'to nail you in any way'.

In other cases involving highly controversial remarks, interviewers may take steps to minimize their own agency in the process. Consider a fateful interview with Al Campanis, then general manager of the Los Angeles Dodgers. In this interview, Campanis made racially insensitive remarks that were so inflammatory he was fired the next day. The issue emerged when another guest on the programme raised the question of why 'there are no blacks running ball clubs' (lines 1–2). The interviewer, Ted Koppel, takes up this issue and asks Campanis to reflect on the absence of blacks at the managerial level in baseball, and more generally to address the existence of prejudice (lines 3–10).

```
(10)   [ABC Nightline: Best of Nightline: Al Campanis]
  1   RK:   I think if Jack were alive today Jack would say: uh:.hhh (0.1)
  2         how come there are no blacks running ball clubs.=
  3   IR :  =Mister Campanis it's a: (.) it's a legitimate question you're
  4         an old friend of Jackie Robinson's but it's a: it's a tough
  5         question for you you're still in baseball:, (0.3) Why why is it
  6         that there are no black managers, no black general managers, no
  7         black owners, (0.3) And I guess what I'm really asking you is to
  8         eh eh you know peel it away: a little bit just tell me (.) why do
  9         you think it is is there still that much prejudice in baseball
 10         today?
 11   AC:   No I don't believe it's prejudice I: I: I truly believe that .hh
 12         (0.2) they may not have some of the: uh: (.) necessities (0.3) to
 13         uh: (0.5) be: uh f- (0.1) let's say a field manager, or a puh
 14         perhaps uh (0.3) a general manager.
 15   IR :  ->You really believe that.
 16   AC:   (0.5) Well (0.3) I don't say that the: they're all of them but
 17         ther:e they certainly are short ih. (0.5) H:ow many quarterbacks
 18         do you have how many pitchers do you have that are black.
```

Campanis rejects prejudice as an explanation and suggests instead that blacks 'may not have some of the necessities' to serve in management (lines 11–14). This remark, while as yet somewhat vague and unexplicated, *may* be construed as having racist implications and thus marks the beginning of Campanis's troubles.

Koppel, prompted by the unsavory implications of Campanis's remark, probes for further elaboration (line 15, arrowed), but in a way that is strikingly different from the approach taken by Couric in the example analysed previously. Rather than reformulate Campanis's remark in less vague and more extreme terms (cf. 'Are you saying that blacks are less intelligent?'), Koppel merely invites Campanis to reaffirm or retract what he already said: 'You really believe that?' Furthermore, the alternative possible responses (yes/reaffirm versus no/retract) are not equally weighted in Koppel's probe; the probe is built so as to invite a *no* answer (via the inclusion of 'really') and thus, in effect, urges Campanis to back away from what he has said.

When Campanis declines to back down (lines 16–18 above), after further talk and a commercial break Koppel gives Campanis yet another opportunity to recast his remarks and thus minimize the anticipated fallout (lines 2–8 in except (11) below). He goes out of his way to characterize Campanis as 'a decent man and a highly respected man in baseball' (line 3), while also downplaying his own expertise in this area (lines 4–5), and he then explicitly formulates his intention to give Campanis 'another chance to dig yourself out because I think you need it' (lines 5–8).

```
(11)   [Nightline: Best of Nightline: Al Campanis]
  1           ((Intervening talk; commercial break))
  2   IR:   Al Campanis I want to I'd I'd uh from everything I understand
```

```
 3            you're a very decent ma:n an:d and and a highly respected man in
 4            baseball I confessed to you before we began this program .hhh
 5            baseball is not one of my areas of expertise and I'd like to
 6            give you another chance to dig yourself out.
 7    RK:     Dyuh hah hah.
 8    IR :    Uh:[: cause I think you need it.
 9    RK:        [ha ha.
10    AC:     I:: (0.1) have never said that that blacks are not intelligent I
11            think (0.2) s- many of them are highly intelligent .hh but they
12            may not ha:ve (0.3) the desire (0.2) to be in the front office.
13            They're (0.1) fleet of foot (0.2) a:nd uh this is why there are a
14            lot of black (0.1) major league ball players. (0.2) [Now: (.) as
15    IR :                                                         [eh eh
16    AC:     far as (0.3) h:aving the (.) background to become a (0.3) club
17            presidents, (0.5) uh presidents of the bank I: don't know.
```

But while Campanis modulates his position, he declines to do a complete 'about face'. Although he claims to believe in the intelligence of black people as a group (lines 10–11), he goes on to cast doubt on their 'desire to be in the front office' (line 12), and to question whether they have 'the background to become club presidents' (lines 16–17).

In both cases where an interviewee comes to make inflammatory remarks, the interviewer is co-implicated in the outcome, although the extent to which this is so varies markedly from case to case. In the Dole case, the interviewer is rather centrally implicated. After an initial objectionable remark is made, the interviewer exerts pressure on Dole to adopt a more extreme stance, to the point of supplying the specific terms that will eventually be his undoing. In the Campanis case, the interviewer's role is relatively minimal, limited to broaching the subject that causes so much trouble. Once the initial objectionable remark is made, the interviewer twice invites Campanis to back away from the stance he seems to have taken. The interviewer thereby conducts himself so that the key remarks can be attributed exclusively to Campanis, although the basis for such an attribution is itself jointly produced. While both interviewees undoubtedly said the things for which they were criticized, the interviewers were to varying degrees co-implicated in the process by which these remarks came to be articulated.

Conclusion

This chapter has argued that recent research on news discourse amounts to a fresh approach to the study of the news media. It is an approach that puts aside the mirror metaphor and the preoccupation with the representational function of news, and focuses instead on the social practices or 'forms of life' that constitute news and make it an intrinsic part of the social world in which it is embedded. Moreover, it moves beyond the confines of the traditional story form of news to encompass various forms of interaction that generate and constitute so much contemporary news and commentary, and that serve as a public arena for encounters between representatives of diverse segments of society.

This approach has the potential to yield insight into both the content of the news and the evolving societal relationships and institutions that it sustains. However, it stands at a very early stage of development, and much remains to be done. Numerous genres of broadcast talk are as yet largely unexamined. Those that have been studied can be enriched by further attention to their complex inner workings, as well as their outer connections to aspects of the social world of which they form a part.

Notes

1. For general introductions to the methodology of conversation analysis, see Heritage (1984b: Chapter 8) and ten Have (1999). For the study of institutional talk in partic-ular, see Boden and Zimmerman (1991), Drew and Heritage (1992a), and Heritage (1997).
2. For the more general practice of radio hosts quoting/paraphrasing callers' talk, Bhimji (2001) finds even finer levels of detail – the tense of the attributive verb – that do systematic work.
3. I'm grateful to Tim Halkowski for bringing this case to my attention.

CHAPTER TEN **Talking Sex and Gender**

Celia Kitzinger

Research on sex and gender[1] has very often involved collecting talk – talk produced in interviews or (more recently) focus groups in which people talk about their experience. For example, the most famous studies in the history of sexology, carried out by the sex researcher Alfred Kinsey and his associates (Kinsey et al. 1948, 1953) in the USA in the 1940s and 1950s, involved collecting talk via nearly 18,000 interviews, organized around questions about how the interviewees masturbated, their sexual fantasies, the kinds of sexual position they preferred, and their experiences of oral sex, anal sex, sex with same-sex partners, with children and with animals. Publication of their findings caused a sensation ('perhaps the largest public event in science since the atomic bomb', Gagnon 1977: 37) because they exposed how common it was for people to have sexual experiences that were socially disapproved of at the time, including pre-marital sex (around 50 per cent of women had coitus before marriage), extra-marital sex (around 50 per cent of married men and 26 per cent of married women had engaged in extra-marital coitus) and homosexuality (37 per cent of men had an experience of same-sex sexual activity to orgasm). Although they illustrated their statistical findings with some quotations from the interviews, these researchers were not interested in talk about sex on its own terms. Instead, they wanted to know about the sexual practice that was being reported through the talk – to see through the talk to the underlying reality behind it. For many researchers, then, interviews offer only 'second-hand' data: that is, the data they can see and hear at first hand is the person talking in interview, and this is used as a second-hand substitute for the 'ideal' data, which would be direct observation of the person doing sex/gender in 'real life'.

The problem, for researchers, with interview talk as 'second-hand' data is that what people say in interviews may not accurately reflect the reality of their lives. People may deliberately lie or exaggerate, they may forget information that the researcher thinks important or they may try to give the sorts of answer they think the person asking the question wants to hear. According to one prominent sex researcher:

People are, in general, rather poor reporters of their own sexual conduct. The ways in which most of them have learned to talk about sex will distort what they think is desirable and what they will remember. Men often want to brag, women to dissemble; therefore, men may exaggerate their premarital sex experience, women may not want to tell about one-night stands. (Gagnon 1977: 53)

All the major sex/gender researchers have recognized this problem and tried various ways of solving it. For example, Kinsey's (1948, 1953) interviews included checks for consistency such as asking the same question twice in different ways during a single interview; asking both a husband and a wife the same questions about their joint sex life; and re-interviewing some of the respondents months or years later to see whether they gave the same answers.

It is common practice to treat interviews as 'second-hand' data in this way. Researchers interested in sex and gender from a whole range of different theoretical perspectives have employed interviews to elicit information that they treat as offering access to some objective features of their informants' lives and experiences. Informants are asked questions like: 'How do you define your gender?', 'How do you express this gender identity to others' and 'What have been the most significant events that helped you to develop your sense of gender and sexual identity?' (in interviews with intersex people, Preves 2003), or 'How do you tell other people that you are gay' (with lesbians and gay men about how they reveal their homosexuality to others, Seidman et al. 2002). Such researchers are usually aware of the problems of treating the talk that people provide in interview as offering an accurate and 'transparent' window into the facts of their lives but it simply seems more realistic to collect *talk about* events they are interested in, rather than to try to observe (for example) intersex people expressing their gender identities in the course of their ordinary lives, or lesbians and gay men actually doing 'coming out' instead of talking about doing it.

An important alternative to *asking* people about their sex/gender lives (and basing analysis on self-report data) is to *observe* people doing sex and doing gender. Observing people 'doing sex' and 'doing gender' doesn't necessarily mean watching people engaged in actions like masturbation, cunnilingus or sexual intercourse – although it can. In one of the most famous studies of human sexuality, William Masters and Virginia Johnson (1966) watched more than 700 people engaged in various sexual acts in the laboratory, and filmed many of them often with elaborate equipment such as a miniature camera that was inserted into the vagina. Instead of asking them what they did sexually, they watched them doing it, and bypassed the need to collect talk data altogether. But many ways in which sex and gender are performed in everyday life involve talk, and sometimes are accomplished exclusively through talk, for example: obscene phone calls and sex phone services, sexual harassment, flirting and sexual innuendo in conversation; sex talk and fights between lovers; courtroom and tribunal hearings about rape, sexual harassment, or discrimination on the basis of gender or sexual orientation; television talk shows and parliamentary debates focusing on topics relating to sex or gender.

Although a great deal of research has focused on people whose sex/gender is considered deviant or unusual in some way, it is important to notice that people talk about and engage in sex/gender behaviours in very routine ways in daily life. Some researchers have studied sex/gender talk in ordinary settings in part because they offer the opportunity to observe, at first hand, how people do sex and gender in 'real life' (instead of how they answer questions about sex/gender in research interviews). As we move out of the research interview and into people's lives, we can also begin to see how ideas about sex/gender underpin a great deal of ordinary interaction that is not 'about sex/gender' at all, but that relies on common-sense notions about sex and gender in the course of some other activities in which people are engaged.

In this chapter, then, I will first show how talk 'about sex/gender' produced in research settings can be usefully studied not only for what it reveals about the informants' behaviour *outside* the interview (as second-hand data), but also for the ways in which sex/gender is being produced right there and then, between interviewer and interviewee, or between focus group moderators and participants (as first-hand data). In the second section I will describe some studies focusing on sex/gender-related talk outside research interviews, in which people produce themselves or others as sexed/ gendered. In particular, I will show how even in talk that is not 'about sex' at all (conversations in which people are making doctors' and dentists' appointments) people display an orientation to, and thereby construct, a normative kind of sexuality.

Talking sex and gender in research settings

Around a decade after Kinsey's research was published, another major contribution to sex/gender research was launched, based on 35 hours of intensive interviewing with just one person, a 19-year-old typist called 'Agnes'. Her interviews with sociologist Harold Garfinkel led her to become one of the world's most famous research subjects and it was on the basis of these interviews that Garfinkel constructed a major part of his theory of ethnomethodology – the study of the methods people use to construct an ordinary social world through everyday talk and action (Garfinkel 1967b). Garfinkel believed that we can learn about what is taken for granted in a culture by studying what happens when there are 'violations', and Agnes was interesting to him because, by her very existence, she seemed to violate the belief that there are 'naturally' two sexes – men (who have penises) and women (who have vaginas). Although she was 'tall, slim, with a very female shape ... long, fine dark-blonde hair, a young face with pretty features, a peaches-and-cream complexion, no facial hair, subtly plucked eyebrows, and no makeup except for lipstick' (Garfinkel 1967b: 119), she had lived for the first 17 years of her life as a male, and had a normal man's penis and testes, as well as a female body shape including well-developed female breasts which she claimed had grown naturally. She was diagnosed as having a 'rare disorder: testicular feminization syndrome' (Stoller, in Garfinkel 1967b: 285).

Most researchers at the time were interested in transsexuals and intersex people as 'deviants' and their work focused on questions like 'what causes it?' and 'can it be cured?' Garfinkel, by contrast, was interested in how Agnes's experience illuminated the day-to-day social construction of gender by everyone, including people who think of themselves as 'naturally' male or female. Instead of taking for granted the ordinary (Western) belief in the objective reality of two sexes, Garfinkel explored, with Agnes's help, how the sense of two objectively 'real' sexes is produced in everyday interaction. Garfinkel was trying to distance himself from the familiar view that people are either 'male' or 'female' and to treat sex as 'anthropologically strange'. On the basis of Agnes's description of what she had to do to create the sense of being a 'real' woman, Garfinkel assembled a list of properties of 'natural, normally sexed persons' as cultural objects. Cultural beliefs about sex, he said, include: the idea that everyone has one; that there are only two (female and male), and that whichever you are now, you always were, and always will be; that genitals are the essential sign of sex; and that the male/female dichotomy is a 'natural' one that exists independently of biologists' or anyone else's criteria. He showed how, in the course of her everyday life, Agnes's accomplishment was to contribute to producing the sense of these 'objectively real facts' about sex, even though she was an example of how those facts are not always true. For example, because she wanted others to treat her as a 'natural woman' in a culture in which 'natural women' were implicitly defined as women who were born female and who have always been female, she avoided talking about her past as a boy (and became 'an interesting conversationalist by encouraging her male partners to talk about themselves', Garfinkel, 1967b: 148); because she lived in a culture in which only men have penises, she concealed hers ('an accidental appendage stuck on by a cruel trick of fate', p. 129) by never undressing in public, pleading modesty on dates and in medical examinations, and by wearing tight-fitting underpants and a bathing suit with a skirt for trips to the beach. Garfinkel considers at some length how Agnes differentiates herself from a male homosexual – by claiming that her boyfriend, Bill, had fallen in love with her before he knew about her condition, that he had previously been sexually involved with other women, and that he was not 'abnormal' in any way. She wanted her penis removed and a vagina constructed in large part, according to Garfinkel, for Bill (he quotes her as saying: 'that's what it's for; it's for intercourse', p. 162). Unlike many people, who take their 'femaleness' (or 'maleness') and (hetero)sexuality for granted and are not consciously aware of the work they do to accomplish it – how they 'do being female/male' or 'do being heterosexual' – Agnes was acutely conscious of the construction of her female heterosexuality as an abiding practical preoccupation. Garfinkel, like the Agnes of his report, seems to take for granted that establishing Agnes's 'heterosexuality' also establishes her credentials as a *woman*: the emphasis placed on her heterosexuality suggests that Agnes's chances of being seen as a 'real woman' in a *lesbian* relationship would surely (as other transsexuals have discovered: Prosser 1998) be severely diminished. Although this is one area in which I find Garfinkel's account unsatisfactory (because it takes too much for granted about the role of heterosexuality in the construction of gender), his major contribution overall was to use what Agnes told him as a basis for describing how (what are treated as) the 'natural facts' of sex were socially produced through ordinary activities of everyday life.

However, like many researchers who are dependent on informants' talk to get access to facts about their lives, Garfinkel found Agnes an unsatisfactory interviewee.

Much of the problem was due to the fact that Agnes was talking to Garfinkel about her gender and sexuality only because she desperately wanted the surgeon with whom he was collaborating to remove her penis and testicles and to construct an artificial vagina. From her point of view, the interviews were about proving to Garfinkel that she deserved the operation because she was really, and had been all along, a 'natural woman'. Instead of telling Garfinkel, as he would have liked, the whole truth about all aspects of her life, she gave him only those answers that she thought would convince the experts that she should have the operation. She was, as Garfinkel puts it, 'a highly accomplished liar' (1967b: 174) and Garfinkel reports her deficiencies as an informant at some length. Listening to the tapes of his interviews with her, he is 'appalled by the number of occasions on which [he] was unable to decide whether Agnes was answering [his] questions or whether she had learned from [his] questions, and more importantly from more subtle cues both prior to and after the questions, what answers would do' (p. 147). He complains about her 'remarkably idealized biography in which evidences of her original femininity were exaggerated' (p. 128) and points out that there were times when she was 'evasive' (pp. 152, 168) and would speak only in generalities (p. 167) and others when 'she changed her story' (p. 151): 'another favorite device was to pretend that she did not know what was being talked about, or to deny that something that had previously been talked about had ever really been mentioned' (p. 168). She refused altogether to answer questions about 'what her penis had been used for besides urination' and 'how she sexually satisfied herself and others and most particularly her boyfriend' (p. 163). (She also refused to allow the researchers to talk to her mother or her boyfriend.) Finally, eight years after Garfinkel had first interviewed Agnes (and long after her sex-reassignment operation and subsequent marriage), she revealed to one of his colleagues that her breasts and feminine body shape had not, as she had at first claimed, developed naturally. The feminization of her body, that was so remarkable in a male her age, was not due to 'testicular feminization syndrome' but had come about because, from the age of 12, she had been stealing hormones – the oestrogen pills her mother had been prescribed following a hysterectomy. Clearly, and understandably, Agnes's talk to Garfinkel was motivated by her own desire to present herself as a 'natural woman' deserving of surgery, and not (as he might have wished) by any commitment to an accurate and faithful representation of her life.

Some subsequent commentators have seen the fact that Agnes deceived Garfinkel as discrediting his whole theory (Armitage 2001; Denzin 1990). But as Hilbert (1991), in defence of Garfinkel, suggests, Garfinkel's interest was not the 'real' Agnes but the methods of her femininity, and there is no reason to suppose that she lied about everyday issues such as how she managed either the lack of an appropriate female autobiography or the presence of a penis. More important for our concerns, however, is that Agnes's methods of producing herself as female were made available to Garfinkel not just as 'second-hand' reports but through her talk and behaviour during those 35 hours of interaction between them. She was self-consciously presenting herself as 'the natural normal female' to him. As he puts it: 'at times in her conversations with me, Agnes was the coy, sexually innocent, fun-loving, passive, receptive "young thing"' (Garfinkel

1967b: 129), and her behaviour elicited from Garfinkel such 'masculine' behaviours as 'holding her arm while I guided her across the street … offering to hang up her coat … holding the automobile door for her while she entered; being solicitous for her comfort' (Garfinkel 1967b: 133), all ways of 'doing masculinity in interactional tandem with her doing femininity' (Rogers 1992: 185). And even though Garfinkel knew that Agnes had been brought up as a male and had a penis, Agnes successfully demanded of him that he should 'talk of Agnes as the natural female' (Garfinkel 1967b: 135) so that 'when I employed the usage that she had been "acting like a female" I would get one variation or another on the essential theme: I *am* a female … ' (p. 170). In sum, gender was being produced between the man Garfinkel and the woman Agnes right there in the research context, and can be analysed as such.

Most research interviewers, of course, do not hold the kind of power (of granting or withholding surgery) that Agnes apparently believed Garfinkel to have over her, but interviews are always interactional events, with researcher and research participant(s) engaged in an exchange that may mobilize far more than simply their identities as 'interviewer' and 'interviewee', and that may include their gender/sexual identities. As with Garfinkel and Agnes, so too in other studies: at the same time as (or instead of) answering questions about sex/gender, interviewees may be 'doing sex/gender' in interaction with their interviewer, and sometimes to the interviewer's considerable discomfort. For example, four young women researchers working on four different projects that involved interviewing men about HIV/AIDS found that their sexually explicit questions were treated as 'come ons' by male interviewees, who asked for their phone numbers or suggested that they should provide sexual services in return for participants' co-operation in the research. On one occasion, a male focus group participant removed the microphone from the centre of the table, placed it between his legs and displayed it as a symbolic erect penis. In response, other 'chivalrous' male participants apologized for other men's rudeness in ways that produced the researcher as an innocent, vulnerable female ('stop that, she's blushing', 'don't say that in front of the lady' and offers to 'walk me home' (Green et al. 1993: 631). The participants' behaviour led these researchers to alter their own gender displays: they 'made attempts to minimise features of [their] appearance which traditionally signal "femininity" or "sexual availability", by keeping hair short or tied back, wearing anodyne clothing, preferring trousers to short skirts, baggy jumpers to low-cut blouses' (Green et al. 1993: 632–3). Sex and gender intrude even into research interviews dealing with topics entirely unrelated to them. In the following extract, a young female researcher is trying to interview a morgue attendant about his job (from Easterday et al. 1977: 339):

(1)

1	Int :	How long have you worked here?
2	Atd:	Three years. Do you have a steady boyfriend?
3	Int :	No. Do you find this work difficult?
4	Atd:	No. Do you date?
5	Int :	Yes. Why isn't this work difficult for you?
6	Atd:	You get used to it. What do you do in your
7		spare time?

Although (some) researchers hope the interview can be an objective 'information-gathering' exercise, in which one person conveys the facts about their life, beliefs, attitudes and experiences to a neutral recipient, interviewees bring with them into the research situation their own interests and preoccupations, including their own sexuality/gender and their perception of that of the researcher. For researchers who are trying to get at the facts about men's attitudes and practices in relation to HIV/AIDS or about the job of a morgue attendant, these kinds of interaction are a source of frustration, anger or dismay; they disrupt the data collection process, and can involve the researcher in concerns about her professional competence and/or personal safety.

Increasingly, researchers using interviews and focus groups are investigating not just what is said *about* sex/gender but also how sex/gender are being done in the context of the research interaction itself. Research participants like Agnes, the men in the HIV/AIDS studies, and the morgue attendant are not (just) talking *about* sex/gender: they are actively *doing* sex/gender through their talk – 'doing being' the coy female, the sexually demanding or chivalrous male, and interacting in specifically gendered (and heterosexualized) ways with their interviewers. Research participants may come to the interview with particular investments in how the researchers (or focus group participants) see them as gendered/sexual beings and often with well-rehearsed stories to tell. When researchers ask participants questions like 'do you see yourselves as masculine men?' (Wetherell and Edley 1999: 345); 'do you think the fact you're male affects your leisure in any way?' (Speer 2001: 121); or 'would you consider yourselves to be new men?' (Gough 1998: 41), they are not likely to get 'truthful' or 'accurate' answers, but answers which produce them as particular kinds of 'men'. All of these researchers treat what men say to them as occasioned in interaction (although they differ in the extent to which they analyse their data with reference to pre-existing cultural ideologies of 'masculinity'). Careful attention to what people are doing through talk in interviews and focus groups can begin to show us how particular versions of sex/gender are constructed during the course of the interview itself.

As someone who has been involved in research on lesbian issues for many years, I am particularly interested in exploring how heterosexuality is produced as the normal, ordinary, taken-for-granted way to be. When researchers ask people questions in interviews (such as 'do you know any lesbians or gay men?' or 'what are your views about gay rights'), people often attend quite carefully to the possibility of being heard as prejudiced or heterosexist. But when talking about some other issue entirely, universal heterosexuality is often assumed, and lesbians and gay men are treated as non-existent. As part of her doctoral research on 'the vagina', one of my students was running focus groups with women about their experience of and attitudes to their vaginas (see Braun and Kitzinger 2001a, 2001b, 2001c). This included questions about their experience of medical examinations, intercourse, menstrual practices, cervical smears, and so on, none of which she was in a position to observe during the course of the focus groups. In that sense, her data were all 'second hand' compared with the first-hand data she would have obtained from observing (say) gynaecological interactions as they happened. But there was a different issue relating to sexuality that came up as a 'first-hand' event in her focus groups – the heterosexist presumption that everyone is heterosexual. Here are two examples from her focus groups. In the first, it is the researcher herself ('Ginny') as focus group moderator, who makes what she subsequently (as researcher) analyses as 'a heterosexist assumption': she is asking the focus group members about making comparisons between their own, and other women's, genitals:

(2)
```
 1   Gin:   Like guys can compare with each other
 2          if they you know so choose.
 3   ( ):   ((laughs))
 4   Gin:   when they're at the urinal or when
 5          they're you know in a communal shower
 6          or something I know they're not supposed
 7          to look but you know
 8   ( ):   mm
 9   Gin:   I think they probably do.
10   Tar:   They do
11   Grp:   ((laughter))
12   Tar:   Of course they do.
13   Jul:   Of course they do.
14   Gin:   I mean I bet they do, exactly. But
15          you know for women, women don't have
16          that kind of- any kind of comparison.
```

She says of this interaction:

> I am assuming that women do not get to see other women's genitals – a het-erosexist assumption. While this maps on to the common-sense view that women's genitals are 'hidden' and men's are 'visible', it also assumes that the only way women would see other women's genitals (and indeed men would see other men's) would be in a non-sexual context such as a communal shower. This formulation does not include the possibility that women might be having sex with other women. (Braun 2000: 135)

In the second fragment it is one of the focus group participants, Mia, who makes what Braun analyses as a heterosexist presumption during the course of a discussion about internal examinations and pap smears:

(3)
```
1    Mia:   When I was pregnant um the consultant
2           did an internal examination and I really
3           f- afterwards just felt like saying
4           'don't you ever have sex don't you know
5           the shape of the vagina y'know d'you
6           real- 'cause he just kind of goes 'oh
7           this is gonna be a bit uncomfortable'
```

Here, as Braun (2000: 136) points out, 'having sex' refers specifically – but without naming it – to heterosexual sex, to 'knowing' what a vagina is like inside. Mia does not consider the possibility that the doctor might be gay. As with notions about the existence of two and only two sexes, the idea that everyone is heterosexual until proved otherwise is (still) a common taken-for-granted assumption in many cultures. Braun (2000: 136) says her examples 'might not immediately be heard as heterosexist to the heterosexual researcher. They map on to common-sense ideas about what is: "normal" and "natural". ... Heterosexuality is revealed as a core assumption in talk by heterosexuals in these groups' (see also C. Kitzinger (2004) for an instance of a heterosexist presumption that is not challenged by a lesbian focus group moderator, analysed as an instance of 'not coming out').

Talking sex and gender outside research settings

Whereas 'doing sex/gender' may arise only incidentally – and sometimes, intrusively – in research interviews, which are rarely set up explicitly so as to occasion them, sex and gender are very often done through talk outside the research context. Instead of eliciting talk in the artificial context of an interview or a focus group, many researchers have collected and analysed talk about sex/gender that is already out there in the culture: on television talk shows discussing lesbian and gay issues (Gamson 1998), or date rape (Crawford 1995: 108–23) or sexual 'confessions' (Lupton 1998); on television panel discussions about the 'promotion' of homosexuality in schools (Speer and Potter 2002); or in parliamentary debates about equalizing the age of consent for heterosexual and gay male sexual acts (Ellis and Kitzinger 2002).

Sometimes 'private' conversations are made publicly available: when a member of parliament in Finland was found guilty of an attempt to sexually abuse a child, his taped conversation with a 15-year-old girl – a key piece of evidence against him at the trial – was released to the media, and subsequently analysed (Tainio 2003). In the early 1990s British newspapers published the full transcript of a private conversation (illegally recorded by a radio enthusiast listening in to a cell phone network) between a man believed to be the Prince of Wales and a woman believed to be his lover, which included sexually explicit talk (most famously, the man's expressed wish to be a Tampax). As one analyst comments, this is not 'talk *about* sex' but 'talk which *does* sex' (Channell 1997). Sociologists Liz Stanley and Sue Wise (1979) collected the obscene phone calls made when their home phone number was advertised on posters and in newspapers as the contact number for a local lesbian group. They recorded 105 obscene calls during a seven-week period and analysed the calls for what they revealed about the experience of sexism.

Sex and gender are also constructed in specialized contexts to which some researchers have gained access, such as lesbian and gay affirmativeness training (Kitzinger and Peel 2005), rape cases in court and tribunal hearings (Drew 1992; Ehrlich 2003), HIV counselling (Peräkylä 1995), group therapy sessions held for rapists in a large state prison in Britain (Lea and Auburn 2001), academic tutorials (Stokoe 1998) and neighbourhood disputes (Stokoe 1999). In many of these settings, sex/gender is produced through talk that is not 'about' sex/gender at all. For example, in extract (4), drawn from a research project in which health visitors were recorded in interaction with new mothers in their homes, the researchers remark on the way in which gender is produced as a result of an apparently casual observation by the health visitor ('He's enjoying that, isn't he', presumably referring to some sucking behaviour by the baby), which is treated very differently by the baby's father and mother. Whereas the father takes the remark at face value and responds with an agreement, the mother's response is, as Heritage and Lindström (1998: 403) say, 'notably defensive':

```
(4)
1     HVt:     He's enjoying that [isn't he.
2     Fth:                        [°Yes he certainly is° =
3     Mth:     =He's not hungry 'cuz(h)he's ju(h)st
4              (h)had 'iz bo:ttle .hhh
```

The researchers comment on this episode that 'the mother's initial response treats the [health visitor's] observation as implying that the baby may be hungry and, by extension, as possibly implicative of some failure on her part. She denies that the baby is hungry and goes on to produce an account that justifies her claim' (Heritage and Lindström 1998: 403). Competence as a parent is something with which the mother, but not the father, shows concern, and it is not hard to see how this might be a gendered phenomenon.

Of course people do also talk explicitly about their relationships (dates, marriages, romantic entanglements, divorces, etc.) as part of ordinary conversation and a number of researchers have collected data in which people are 'just chatting', but in which issues of sex and gender are talked about in ways that function to produce them as gendered/sexed speakers. A casual conversation between five young men at a college in the USA was analysed by Deborah Cameron (1997) for the way in which heterosexual masculinity is produced in the talk. She quotes their shared puzzlement about why the college they are attending should need a 'Gay Ball' ('it's hilarious') and they then gossip about individual men who are said to be gay: 'the most effeminate guy I've ever met', 'a fat, queer, goofy guy', a 'blond hair, snide little queer weird shit', and so on. Finally, one of the men remarks that 'four homos' in one class are continually 'hitting on' (making sexual overtures to) one of the women, described as 'the ugliest-ass bitch in the history of the world'. As Cameron points out, one might have thought that a defining feature of a 'homo' would be his lack of interest in 'hitting on' women, but none of the participants seems aware of any problem or contradiction in this exchange. Her analysis is that the term 'gay' means, for these men, not so much *sexual* deviance as *gender* deviance – failing to measure up to the group's standards of masculinity (Cameron 1997: 53). She makes the important point that talk like this: '… is not only *about* masculinity, it is a sustained performance *of* masculinity. What is important in gendering talk is the "performative gender work" the talk is doing; its role in constituting people as gendered subjects' (Cameron 1997: 59).

As we have seen from Braun's focus group data and Cameron's conversational data, heterosexuals frequently display their own heterosexuality, either by simply assuming that everyone is heterosexual, or by talking about non-heterosexual people in ways that make it very clear that they themselves are heterosexual. In other conversational data, too, heterosexuals are very explicit in displaying their sexual preference: they report on their own heterosexual activities and interests, engage in heterosexual joking and innuendo, tease each other about heterosexual behaviour, and talk about heterosexual engagements, weddings and marriages (see C. Kitzinger 2005). But even when they are not talking *about* their own (or other people's) heterosexuality, heterosexuals frequently talk in ways that make their heterosexuality available as an inference. A major way in which they do this is by using terms that display heterosexual relationships: whether or not someone is 'really' heterosexual, when they mention a different-sexed 'husband' or 'wife' (or 'boyfriend' or 'girlfriend') they are likely to be heard as such.

Heterosexuals frequently make their heterosexuality apparent to complete strangers early on in interactions with no thought that they are doing anything special. Look, for example, at the interactions in extracts (5)/(7), in each of which someone is calling an unknown doctor. It is a weekend and a locum doctor is taking calls on behalf of the regular doctors in the practice, and displaying themselves as having a heterosexual relationship with the person they are calling about (see Kitzinger 2005b).

(5)
[DEC: 2-1-4]
```
1    Doc:    hello:?
2            (0.4)
3    Clr :   u::h hello.
4            (.)
5    Clr :   This is Misses W((deleted))
6            (0.9)
7    Doc:    mm hm?
8    Clr :   Um::. (.) My husban::d, (0.2) isn't very
9            we:ll.
```

(6)
[DEC: 1-2-12]
```
1    Doc:    Hel:lo:,
2    Clr :   Hel:lo, is that' th' doctor¿
3    Doc:    <Yes, Doctor ((deleted)) speaki::ng,
4    Clr :   i:i: Yeah couldja's come an' see my wife
5            please, .h[h
6    Doc:              [Yes:.
7    Clr :   She's breathless.<She can't .hh get 'er
8            breath.hh! .h[hhh
9    Doc:                 [What's: her ↑name.
```

(7)
[DEC: 2-1-16]
```
1   Doc:    Hello:, 'octor ((deleted)) speaking¿
2           ((sniff))
3   Clr :   Hello:, I'm: tu- I was wonderin' if you
4           could help me, ((some deleted material here).)
5   Clr :   Um my boyfriend's uhm: really ill at the moment.
6           <'E's got really bad stomach pains. An' fever.
```

In each of these extracts callers display their heterosexuality: a woman self-identifies both as female and as married by using the courtesy title 'Mrs', as well as by referring to her 'husband' (extract (5)); a man refers to his 'wife' (extract (6)); and a woman refers to her 'boyfriend' (extract (7)). By producing themselves as members of one sex and their spouse/partner as members of a different sex, these people make available an understanding that they are heterosexual. They are not, of course, 'coming out' as heterosexual in the sense that they are explicitly oriented to conveying information about their sexuality. Their primary goal is to get the doctor to come out to see a sick person. But in pursuing this goal, they are able to draw on heteronormativity as a resource. A woman calling on behalf of her husband or boyfriend or a man calling on behalf of his wife is engaged in a culturally-understood-as-normal activity: nothing special is happening in terms of the relationships displayed. Whatever other interactional hurdles the caller has to negotiate (conveying the nature of the medical problem, describing the symptoms as sufficiently severe to merit a home visit, and so on: Drew 2005) these calls do *not* have to deal with the issue of why *they*, in particular, are calling on behalf of the patient, or what their relationship with the patient might be. These casual displays of heterosexual relationships in the service of local interactional goals constitute a mundane instance of heterosexual privilege. Such terms are not available – in any unproblematic way – to lesbian or gay couples in most countries of the world where same-sex couples are denied equal marriage rights under law (Wilkinson and Kitzinger 2005). Without any orientation to doing so, heterosexual speakers 'give off' their heterosexuality in the course of getting on with the business of their lives, treating their own and others' heterosexuality as entirely unremarkable, ordinary, taken-for-granted, and displaying it incidentally in the course of some other action in which they are engaged.

One of my graduate students, Victoria Land, has collected a data set of around 150 calls to and from lesbian households. In not one of these calls does a lesbian speaker display the gender of her partner, and hence her lesbianism, to a stranger within the opening moments of a call. When the lesbians in the Land corpus make institutional calls to unknown persons on behalf of their same-sex partners, or when they find it necessary to refer to such persons during the course of their interactions, they routinely select gender-neutral terms ('partner', 'spouse') rather than the gender-specific ones ('wife', 'husband', 'boyfriend', 'girlfriend') selected by heterosexuals. This is hardly surprising given lesbians' (and gay men's) reported experiences and expectations of heterosexism. For example, asked to state their 'expectations' when 'interacting with an unfamiliar person who has just found out that you are lesbian/gay/bisexual', 36 per cent of respondents mentioned fear of physical or verbal abuse

(Conley et al. 2002). On the whole, then, the lesbians do *not* make their lesbianism available in institutional contexts with people who do not already know of it: in calls to telephone and water companies, plumber, banks, employment agencies, veterinarians' and doctors' receptionists, interactants who do not already know that they are talking with lesbians, never find out.

When lesbians *do* make their lesbianism available to people who do not already know of it, they almost always do so in order to correct their co-conversationalists' displayed presumption that they are heterosexual. It is a routine experience in most lesbians' lives to confront what Sedgwick (1993: 46) calls 'the deadly elasticity of heterosexist presumption': it means simply that parties to any interaction in straight settings are presumed to be heterosexual unless otherwise demonstrated.

We can see how the heterosexist presumption works, and how a lesbian caller deals with it, in extract (8). Nicola is talking with a receptionist at a dentist's surgery whose contact details she has just obtained from the NHS Direct helpline. She uses the gender-neutral term 'partner' (line 13) to refer to the person she wants to register as a new patient. The heterosexist presumption is displayed through the receptionist's use of the masculine pronoun to refer to this person – first in the recycled question at line 23 ('what was his name') and then through her repair initiation at line 46 ('is it for him or for you').

```
(8)   [Land OC04]
 1              ((ring-ring ring-ring))
 2    Rec:      Good afternoon Johnson Olivier and
 3              Tilsley?
 4    Nic:      Hello. >uhm< I was wondering if it would
 5              be possible to find out if I could r-uhm
 6              register as a new patie:nt.
 7    Rec:      Yes certainly.= Miss Boon's thee (.) only
 8              patient taking NHS: .hh any- only dentist
 9              taking N-H-S patient[s.
10    Nic:                          [Mm hm¿
11    Rec:      mcht U:hm: I'll just take some
12              detail [s from you.          ]
13    Nic:             [Well it's for my part]ner actually.
14    Rec:      Ri:ght.
15              (0.5)
16    Rec:      'Scuse me a moment.
17    Nic:      Okay than[k you
18    Rec:               [Mr Leggett¿ ((off phone))
19              (.)
20    Rec:      Would you like to go: up. hh ((off phone))
19              (0.8)
20    Rec:      An' what was the na:me¿
21              (0.8)
22    Nic:      >Sorry my name.<
23    Rec:      What was his name.
24    Nic:      Oh uhm it's S:andra Ferry
```

```
25              (0.5)
26              (( [another phone] [ringing))]
27    Rec:       [ Ferry¿     ]
28    Nic:                    [ Yes::.   ]
29              (3.5)
30    Rec:     Ye- Just hold the line a second.
31    Nic:     >Okay< Thank you.
30              (10.5)
32    Rec:     Sorry about that.= We've got (.) dentists
33             swapped surgeries 'n' .hh one's come
34             downstairs and one's gone upstairs an' the
35             patients don't know whether they're
36             co(h)ming [or go(h)ing.
37    Nic:               [Huhuh huh huh
38             [No](h) prob(h)lem don't [worry about it
39    Rec:     [So]                     [Ferry did you
40             say¿
41    Nic:     .hh Yes. F double R Y.
42              (.)
43    Rec:     A:n' the Christian n:ame¿
44    Nic:     It's: Sandra. hh
45              (0.5)
46    Rec:     F- Is it for him or for you:.
47    Nic:     It's for her.
48              (.)
49    Rec:     Oh for her- O:h °sor(h)ry° .hh[h     ]
50    Nic:                                   [.hh £I]t's
51             oka:y£
52    Rec:     Uh huh huh huh huh Sandra.
53    Nic:     Yes:.
54    Rec:     .hh Right. An::d date of birth¿
```

When she answers the receptionist's question about her (presumed male) partner's name, Nicola does not explicitly correct the presumption, but in giving a culturally-known-as-exclusively-female name for her partner (at line 24), Nicola is making available to the receptionist that her partner is female. The half-second gap that follows may indicate some problem with this, but it is the surname (both at line 27 and, again after an apology sequence following an interruption to the call while the receptionist deals with a patient, at line 39) that the receptionist repeats for confirmation. Having apparently entered the surname into the computer, she returns to the problematic first name and, unlike the surname, which she repeated for confirmation, her question (at line 43) is not designed to display any prior grasp of it. After Nicola repeats her partner's name (at line 44) this common English name pronounced – on both occasions – clearly and audibly, with no interference on the line, or overlapping talk, is unequivocally treated as problematic. After half a second of silence, the receptionist's next question displays her orientation to solving the puzzle of why she has been given a female name rather than the male one she showed herself to expect. Instead of inferring that Nicola has a female partner (a possibility interdicted by the heterosexist presumption she has already displayed, and one that would violate the 'nothing unusual is happening' stance) she checks out the possibility that she has misunderstood which of the two presumed heterosexual different-sex members of the couple is being registered. Although Nicola has already made clear at line 13 ('well it's for my partner actually') that she is registering her partner, and although the receptionist has already shown herself to have understood this (through the design of her question at line 23 which asks for the partner's name), she is apparently searching for some explanation other than the lesbianism of her co-conversationalist. In response, Nicola produces an embedded correction, answering the question (about which of them is registering) but using an alternative pro-term ('her', line 47, instead of 'him', line 46). After a short delay (line 48) the female pronoun is adopted as a replacement by the receptionist (line 49) and she accepts and apologizes for what she thereby treats as having been a correctable offence. (See Land and Kitzinger, 2005, for a more detailed analysis of this data extract, and others like it; for an examples of a lesbian *not* coming out, see Wilkinson and Kitzinger 2003.)

Summary

In this chapter, then, I have suggested that if we want to know how people do sex/gender, instead of *asking* people about sex/gender (and treating what they say as 'second-hand' data), it may be more useful to *observe* people doing sex/gender at first-hand. I have shown that sex/gender is often done through talk and I have suggested that the most interesting features of sex/gender – even in studies which might be considered quite 'exotic', such as like research on transsexuals or vaginas – are often the most 'ordinary' mundane features that people simply take for granted in their everyday lives. In particular, drawing on my own conversation analytic research that pays detailed attention to talk (see also Kitzinger 2000), I have shown how both interviews and ordinary social settings in which people are going about their daily lives enable us to see the ways in which one particular form of sex/gender, hetero-sexuality, is 'routinized' and 'normalized'. Heterosexuality (meaning sex between Agnes and a man) was taken for granted by Garfinkel and his co-researchers (and apparently by Agnes too) in considering her claim to be a 'natural' woman; hetero-sexuality was a way of doing gender for the male research participants in the studies of AIDS (and the morgue); heterosexuality was presumed universal by young women in the 'vagina' study, and deployed as symbolizing proper gender conformity by the male students in Cameron's study. Finally, in the calls to the doctor and dentist, het-erosexuality was produced as the 'normal', 'ordinary', 'taken-for-granted' way to be, so that a lesbian caller found herself correcting the presumption that her partner must be male. Through talk-in-interaction, then, an ordinary everyday world of properly gendered/sexed social members is produced and reproduced without any-one necessarily meaning to be prejudiced or to discriminate against non-heterosexuals or people who don't fit into the dichotomous gender categories. Through the study of talk-in-interaction, we can begin to uncover some of the ways in which sex/gender categories are made real, and reproduced, in our social world.

Note

1. In this chapter, I use 'sex' to mean sexual activity (however that is constructed by the participants, including non-heterosexual sex, oral and aural sex, fantasy, etc.) and 'gender' to refer to categories such as 'female', 'intersex', 'male', 'transgender', etc. I deliberately avoid the distinction, introduced in the 1970s and now conventional in many social science textbooks, between 'gender' (treated as the socialized production of 'masculinity' and 'femininity') and 'sex' (treated as the biological substrate of 'maleness' and 'femaleness'). As the research discussed in this chapter shows, this separation is untenable, not least because it treats biology as outside 'culture', rather than as a product of it. Moreover, I have tried not to treat 'doing sex' (i.e. sexual behaviours) and 'doing gender' as distinctive activities, since, as the research presented here also shows, sexual behaviours are profoundly gendered, and gender is in part constructed through sexual behaviour (e.g. the deployment of heterosexuality to constitute oneself as a 'real' man or woman). In describing particular studies I have generally used the author's own terminology.

CHAPTER ELEVEN

Anomalies and Ambiguities: Finding and Discounting the Relevance of Race in Interracial Relationships

Byron Burkhalter

Social scientists regularly confront the problem of how to find the phenomena in which they are interested. Whether they are interested in gender pay inequities, dating rituals in college or economic globalization, social scientists must find some 'data' to collect and analyse. My own interests are in 'racial interactions', that is, how do people use race – and more generally how does race matter – when people talk with one another in everyday life? Among the first issues I confronted was how to collect such interactions. This may strike some as a paradox, given the apparent ubiquity of racial phenomena in contemporary America.

Indeed, most social researchers have had little trouble finding and collecting data related to racial phenomena. This can be partly explained by examining the ways these researchers have looked for racial phenomena, and the types of explanation they have sought for them. Perhaps the most common method for collecting racial phenomena involves isolating a single variable, such as income, wealth, or voting patterns, that can be used as the basis for comparing the aggregated populations of different racial groups. For example, Oliver and Shapiro (1995) compare household income and wealth of black and white Americans. They found that even when black and white households earn similar incomes, these two groups accumulate wealth at vastly different rates. Thus, a racial phenomenon – racial wealth inequality – has been uncovered by comparing the aggregated outcomes of two racial populations. Racial groups, which are based on researchers' efforts to compose racially homogeneous aggregates, have been compared on a vast set of variables, including occupation and occupational status (Lieberson 1981; Ong and Valenzuela 1996), education (Kozol 1991), marriage (Tucker and Mitchell-Kernan 1990), housing and neighbourhood location (Clark 1996; Massey and Denton 1993) and the like. Through these comparisons, sociologists can describe the effects of racial phenomena (and in some cases, aspects of the social mechanisms that produce them) on larger populations.

A second method for collecting racial phenomena operates at what might be called the individual level of analysis. This method involves comparing analytic observations drawn from a set of individuals who can be claimed (unproblematically) to represent a racial group by reference to their racial identities. For example, in his study of white racist discourse Teun van Dijk (1993) talked to a group of individual whites about racial issues and then analysed those statements as evidence of 'elite white racial discourse'. Using this method, researchers have shown that racial identities can be correlated to differences in language use, values, customs, beliefs and other cultural markers (as represented in the thoughts and actions of particular individuals). Through these racial representatives, sociologists demonstrate a variety of racial phenomena at the individual level.

The fruitfulness of these methods speaks to the massive ubiquity of racial phenomena in the social world. These studies clearly demonstrate that one's racial identity impacts on one's life in substantial and sundry ways; racial identity shapes one's position in the social structure, including one's income, life expectancy, education, occupation and neighbourhood; and racial identity can also be linked to one's religious beliefs, trust in banking institutions, attitudes towards education and premarital sex, and the like.

Perhaps not surprisingly given their very different methodologies, these two approaches employ different theoretical concepts to explain the availability and ubiquity of their data. For example, in the first method – where racial aggregates are compared – the prevalence of racial phenomena is explained using the concept of 'institutional racism'. This concept treats social structures themselves as the source of racial phenomena (and specifically racial inequality); the concept of institutional racism treats racial phenomena as arising from a racist social structure which was originally designed as a social control mechanism, but which now operates without regard to the specific intentions of individual actors (Feagin and Vera 1995).[1] Since institutional racism is ingrained in virtually every social institution from marriage to education to mass media and the legal system, these institutions continue to produce racially disparate access to social resources at a structural level across generations, across social and political contexts, and without regard to any particular situation. Even without knowing that we are doing its bidding, we continue to turn the wheel of racism's mighty engine.

The second method – comparing the conduct of individuals identified as members of a racial category – relies on a very different set of concepts to explain racial phenomena. In this method, the ubiquity of racial phenomena is explained by reference to Herbert Gans' assumption that race is a 'master identity' (Gans 1979). Gans argued that racial identity is a salient and relevant feature of human conduct in every situation, and thus constitutes one of our 'master identities'. The phrase 'master identity' was chosen to capture the myriad and disparate ways in which racial identities are thought to matter for conduct: for example, being African American presumably affects the way one speaks, thinks, sees and feels. Similarly, if a European American and an Asian American are talking about race relations, we might reasonably expect them to disagree because their racial identities have afforded each a different perspective on the topic. Even if the European American and the Asian American claimed that race was not relevant to their beliefs, we might still assume that their differing identities had to matter in ways of which they were not aware. In this approach, one assumes these differences in behaviour and attitude without knowledge of the particular individual or the situation in which the individuals operate.

Despite these differences, however, these approaches share the assumption that racial identity is omnirelevant, that is, both approaches assume that racial phenomena are largely beyond the control of individual actors, and that these phenomena shape outcomes irrespective of the particulars of any situation. Given this underlying assumption, collecting racial phenomena is fairly straightforward: once researchers have noted the racial identity of each participant, they need only tabulate the relevant variable measurements, or compare the statements within and across racial groups, and one can infer racial phenomena from any differences (or commonalities) one has discovered.[2] Thus when van Dijk collected white discourse, he could use any white person speaking on race as 'representative' of white racist discourse in general.[3] Because racial identity is always salient, any 'raced' person will necessarily be speaking from their racial identity. In this respect, both institutional racism and master identity are useful for the collection of racial phenomena because each allows the social analyst to assume the relevance of race for the structural and cultural position of any individual. As a consequence of the assumption that racial identity is omnirelevant, virtually anywhere we look for racial phenomena we should be able to find ample data.

Two methods and interracial couples

For the most part, research on interracial couples has exemplified the assumption that race is omnirelevant. However, interracial couples also seem to cause trouble for scholars using the first two collection methods. If all social institutions are designed to create and maintain a racial social structure, how does the social analyst explain interracial couples who seemingly operate across the racial divide? On the other hand, if race is a master identity, how do interracial relationships begin and, often enough, thrive?

Perhaps with points such as these in mind, social researchers using the two methods described above have treated interracial couples as a phenomenon that requires additional explanation. In line with the concepts of master identity and institutionalized racism, these researchers explain interracial couples either by reference to the psychological motivations of the individuals involved in them or by reference to external demographic correlates that are thought to lie beyond their control.[4] For examples, researchers have attributed the choice of an interracial relationship to rebellion, sexual curiosity, psychological needs, or a quid pro quo exchange of wealth for status. Evidence for these explanations typically rely on racial history, racial demographics, or racial psychologies, and thereby tacitly (and in some cases explicitly) assume the omnirelevance of racial identity *for those in the relationship*, thereby sustaining the researchers' assumptions regarding racial phenomena.[5]

Perhaps the most prominent and influential work involves explanations of individuals' 'real' reasons for entering into and continuing interracial relationships. The Hypergamy theory, often attributed to Merton (1941), suggests that men of racial and ethnic groups with less status (e.g. Blacks, Jews, Filipinos, etc.) who have gained some socio-economic status marry women from racial groups with higher status who lack talent, wealth, beauty or intellect. Essentially, this theory holds that the partners in such relationships are engaged in a kind of exchange: wealth, talent or beauty is traded for the status attributed to members of different racial categories. Although this theory is dated and has never had any direct corroborating evidence, it has survived intact and continues to influence researchers in this area (Fu 2001; Washington 1970). In cases where what is being exchanged is not self-evident, less rational motivations are attributed to the partners. As Davidson (1991: 15) summarized, members of different races may form a partnership because:

> (1) the black person is seeking social and/or economic mobility; (2) the white person has a desire to rebel against his or her family or the greater social order; (3) the white person is mentally pathological; (4) the black person is hostilely preoccupied with the white race; (5) both parties are exhibitionists; (6) both parties are overwhelmed by sexual curiosity.

In sum, studies of interracial couples commonly imply that the complex array of factors involving love and mutual attraction, which are thought to supply the taken-for-granted rationale of most modern couplings, cannot explain why interracial couples come together.[6] Saxton, for example, suggests that awareness of additional problems forces interracial couples to consider more than romantic attraction (Brown 1987: 26). Staples advises counsellors that one must always look for ulterior motives in interracial marriages (Brown 1987: 26). By focusing on the 'complicating forces' and ulterior motives, researchers suggest that interracial couples become involved 'in order to' achieve some purpose other than the relationship itself – specifically a race-based purpose. In this respect, these studies claim that each partner in an interracial relationship views the other as a racial object from the outset, much as the social researcher assumes the same thing in using the two methods sketched above. And further, given the specificity of racial experiences, researchers argue that each race is motivated by factors that are unique to the experiences and social position of its members. Thus, distinct motives for engaging in interracial relationships are attributed to Asians, Latinos and Whites and African Americans. According to this view, then, race is a significant and continuously relevant context for such interracial relationships.

The two methods described above evidently simplify collecting evidence regarding racial phenomena; both methods also illuminate certain racial phenomena.

However, each also conceals certain racial phenomena. In using the concepts of institutional racism and master identity, the social researcher approaches race as an already relevant feature of social structures and an individual's beliefs and orientations. Assuming the omnirelevance of race, however, makes the analysis of interactional data more difficult since a focus on aggregated populations or individual characteristics draws attention away from the events and actions that comprise interactional conduct in everyday life. Viewed through the lens of interaction, race is not a state of being but a state of doing. Indeed, ethnomethodologically informed research has shown that social relations that have (traditionally) been treated as a/the context for interactions can be usefully analysed as a product of the very practices people use in those interactions.

For example, instead of searching for a single, one-dimensional explanation for why Japanese-American women and Anglo-American men get married – an explanation that may be at odds with those offered by the couples themselves – we might ask when, and how, the racial identities of such a couple become relevant, and when and how the potential relevance of race is actually suppressed. As we shall see, participants in interracial relationships manage the relevance of race in a variety of ways when they interact with each other, their children, family, friends and the odd interviewer: at times they highlight it, at times they hide it or dismiss it; for some purposes they may positively affirm their racial identities while in other cases they may distance themselves from them. Since my aim is to understand how racial phenomena are managed in interaction, I do not assume that racial identities are *necessarily* relevant for every aspect of people's behaviour. By treating race as potentially relevant, but not omnirelevant, researchers gain access to the ways in which people manage race in their interactions with one another, and thus to many of the ways in which racial phenomena are actually sustained in everyday life.[7]

In what follows I invoke, and examine, the racial identities (and other racial phenomena) of this study's participants on those occasions in which it is observably relevant for them. Further, once I establish the relevance of race in some bit of talk or other conduct, my aim has not been to connect the phenomena they indicate to taken-for-granted notions of culture and social structure; rather, I have sought to understand what the interviewees might have been doing by managing race on that occasion, and in this way I have attempted to understand how race matters for them.

Anomalies and ambiguity in managing the relevance of race

In examining how race matters for individuals in everyday interaction we must turn from the characterization of race in professional research literature and turn towards the non-professional, everyday racial analytics that interracial couples are more likely to encounter. In everyday racial talk conceptions such as institutional racism and master identity have less public penetration than the psychological concepts of unconscious behaviour and intentional action. When discussing whether an event is a racial or racist event, unconscious and intentional categorizations of action become more important. For example, consider the following quote from a talk show on interracial couples:

> Well my basic standpoint, the standpoint of the organization basically is that inter-racial dating, as a whole there is nothing wrong with it. The only time it becomes a problem is when a person has a preference for another race because whether unconsciously or even subconsciously they feel this other race has some type of special superior quality to their own race; something sexual, something social, something emotional. And by saying that they're saying that their own race is inferior to the other race. (Kimathi Innis, Congress of Racial Equality)[8]

The idea of a racial preference is particularly powerful when it is cast as present in the unconscious mind. How can a person deny that a racial preference is in their unconscious? By definition, it is exactly the kind of preference of which they would remain unaware. On the other hand, the choice of a differently raced partner can be seen as a conscious, intentional act of not choosing a partner from one's own race. In either case the person in an interracial couple is put in an unenviable position.

One defence to the charge of racism was captured by a common T-shirt slogan of the 1980s that proclaimed 'love sees no colour'. This slogan suggests that interracial love was true love because skin colour was overlooked. For many, it would seem log-ical to defend one's choice of a differently raced partner as an indication that race was not important or even visible. However, overlooking race can also be seen as lending support to the racial social structure (Frankenburg 1991/2). If we overlook the effect of racism in society, if we pretend that race and racism do not exist, then racism is not a problem to be fought, allowing it to persist and flourish. The interra-cial couple defending itself is on a thin line. The couple is left with the choice of denying the importance of race, and thereby associating themselves with reactionary social rhetoric or exhorting the importance of race and thus casting their own rela-tionship as founded on something other than love.

However, these couples are not defenceless against these assessments. In the fol-lowing pages I describe two ways that interviewees account for their interracial relationships. In both sorts of account, the interviewees specifically downplay the relevance of race in selecting their partner even as they convey their awareness of a racial phenomenon. I call the first practice 'anomalizing': in these accounts people describe themselves or others as atypical members of a racial group. In par-ticular I discuss how and when one partner casts another as either physically anomalous or anomalous in terms of their socialization. I call the second practice, 'strategic ambiguity': in these accounts interviewees find that race may or may not have been part of some social situation. While both of these methods deny or at least diminish the claim that race was intentional or unconsciously relied on in the search for a partner, each of them also confirms a basic awareness of race and an agreement with the assumption of its general importance in social life. That is how the thin line is tread.

Racial anomalies

The line between a racially motivated interracial coupling and one that is not racist was described in one interview as the difference between 'searching for' and 'finding' someone of another race:

(1) [I-6: Kevin]
K: I do feel very strongly, especially in the African American male, needs to evaluate why it is he is searching for an interracial relationship if he in fact is- searching for it. And there is sort of a difference between finding it and searching for it ...
X: So when you won't go after a relationship because of race or other factors ...
K: I think at that point you are searching for a particular type of relationship ... now searching for someone within one's own race- now this is where it gets tricky- but uh I think in our society for one to be non-white it is a natural search for them to search for someone of their same color, or that is at least a non-white person as well.
X: You mean that's an in-born thing?
K: um-hmm. NO I don't know about necessarily in-born it's just convenience. Given in our society it's more convenient to be in that relationship.

In this stretch of talk Kevin is not issuing a blanket denial of the importance of race – far from it. He acknowledges that 'especially in the African American males' it is important for those in interracial relationship to examine their motivations. And he acknowledges the importance of racial identities in understanding the motives for these relationships. For example, he notes that non-whites 'naturally' search for other non-whites because *de facto* racial segregation in the USA makes monoracial coupling more convenient. Indeed, by focusing his attention on interracial couples, Kevin's distinction implies that intraracial couples need not account for their choices. Thus, in making the distinction between 'finding' and 'searching' Kevin indicates that what really matters in choosing a partner is the stance (or attitude) that one takes towards potential partners, and not just their racial identities. Assuming the couple has not intentionally searched for a differently raced partner, Kevin's distinction makes space for a legitimate and morally acceptable interracial coupling. As it happens, Kevin was not alone in viewing interracial couples in these ways.

In each interview I conducted, the participants reported having 'found' their partner. The possibility of their having searched for a differently raced partner was variously discounted, transcended, thought mistaken, impossible, or unlikely. In this way, race was treated as anything but the source of attraction in the relationship. As evidence for these claims the participants emphasized the ways in which they, or their partners, were anomalous members of their racial group – they just weren't like other members of their racial group. The accounts used to support such claims drew on a variety of resources, including physical appearances, life experiences, and 'culture'. The following sections offer examples of variations in these accounts and how interviewees deployed them to support claims that race did not play a role in their pursuit of an interracial partner, even though they were aware of the importance of race generally.

The logic of constructing one's partner as a racial anomaly – as an atypical member of a racial group – is fairly simple. If a person is actively searching for a person of another race, he/she presumably want a stereotypical member of that race. In fact, for a person with a racist motive, we can presume that potential partners will be more attractive the more stereotypical they appear to be. By describing their partners as anomalies, then, interviewees can demonstrate their lack of racial intent. At the same time, however, by displaying their competence in seeing and recognizing race (or racial features) in their accounts, interviewees can simultaneously demonstrate that they are not blind to race. In this respect such 'anomalizing' accounts can be used to sustain the romantic basis for an interracial relationship *and* a commitment to the reality of race as a phenomenon of everyday relevance.

Physical anomalies

Accounting for the physical appearance of a partner is perhaps the trickiest part of anomalizing. Quite aside from the ability (or desirability) to claim that race does not matter, interviewees found it virtually impossible to claim that they did not recognize the racial identities of their partners. And if interviewees did recognize their partner's racial identity, how can they claim that it was not relevant in their decision to purse a relationship? One method of handling this apparent contradiction was for interviewees to find beauty in those aspects of a partner's body that are treated as stereotypical of his/her own race. The interviewees claimed to have been just walking along, doing what any good member of their race would do, having as criteria for attractiveness what any good member of this race would have as criteria when, following that criteria, one 'found' oneself with someone of another race. The following respondent reported initially mistaking his partner's ethnicity:

(2) [I-1: Andy and Bea]
X: I'm curious as to how you would describe her
A: Well she has a very large butt, uncharacteristic for Chinese women. Which is actually one of the first things I noticed about her. When I first met her I thought she was black. Because from behind – she was on the [basketball] court. You don't find too many Asian women, at least I didn't at that time, shooting. Secondly she had krimped hair, kinda like a permed krimp, which a lot of light-skinned black girls have and thirdly she had a big butt. She was very tan and I walked up to her and I thought she was honestly black and she turned around and it wasn't a shock to me, you know I didn't jump back, but at the same time it was a little bit of a surprise. It's big but it's very nice, when I say big I mean. ... When I say 'she got a big ole butt,' That means its a nice butt. ... She has a lot of hair, her hair is very very thick and very very long, very nice shape body, but her facial features are very characteristic of Asian women, and that's not a stereotype that's just an observation, but like I said when you put all the aspects together, she is a very weird Asian girl, I mean she doesn't look characteristically Asian—
B: You mean stereotypically
A: I'm sorry, I mean stereotypically Asian, because I'm not attracted to the stereotypical Asian woman, which is a woman who is generally skinny, ya know skinny and not too large of a butt and that kinda thing- but Bea, when I say weird, I mean very different, I mean from behind you would not know she is an Asian girl at all.

Despite the fact Andy is now dating an Asian woman, he notes that he is not attracted to women who look stereotypically Asian, and has not in any sense stopped using African-American standards of beauty. Indeed, he claims that it is just those African-American characteristics in Bea that he finds beautiful. In this respect, Andy maintains that he was not searching for characteristics typical of other races, and so he could not be 'searching'. Of course Andy does not deny that Bea is Chinese; he simply claims that he was attracted to what he took to be black physiognomic features when he first saw her. As in Kevin's distinction between 'searching' and 'finding', it is Andy's methods and motives for looking that require explanation, not Bea's racial identity.

In the former segment Andy claimed his partner so resembled members of his own race (from a distance) that he was initially surprised to find that she was actually a different race. In the next segment Harriet reports that other members of her race often mistake her husband for being a member.

(3)　[I-4:　George and Harriet]
X:　Can you describe George to me?
H:　He is about 5'8" and he's slim, he's small size, you know. His father is very petite. He looks, a lot of times he is mistaken, he assumed [to be] Cuban. Because he looks more like a Hispanic black.
X:　Why? In what way?
H:　They're not as tall and lanky. So he's not – he's very well proportioned and so his legs are not overly long for his body. The arms are not as long and his hands are not long fingers, none of those- he looks like a Hispanic it's hard to explain. When we're together a lot of people assume, especially it happens with Cubans, they ask him if he is from Cuba, they don't immediately see him as black.
X:　That's really happened in public?
H:　Yes, oh yes, ... like I say he's not overly tall and he's not big, big boned or anything like that and he doesn't have those traits and I don't know- in his family we have just found out in the last 3 or 4 years- he knew that one side of his family were Cherokee descendants and now we find out that the other side of his family the grandfather was Blackfoot – he was a Blackfoot black. We just found out somebody was tracing.
X:　When people mistake him for a Cuban do you correct them?
H:　No we just laugh......

Harriet, in her own terms, is Hispanic. As this excerpt shows, she uses a highly detailed description of George's physical features to support her claim that he is mistakable for Hispanic. In fact, she does not describe any physical aspect of him except for those that suggest he is Hispanic. In this respect Harriet doesn't merely claim that George is an atypical African American, she claims he is typically Hispanic. Notably she reinforces this claim by mentioning occasions where Hispanics have reached the same conclusion. If Harriet had been searching for an African American – consciously using racial criteria in her selection of a partner – then George would have been a poor choice since he actually appears to be a member of her own racial group.

In these two excerpts, then, Andy and Harriet paradoxically use racial criteria as a method for claiming that they select their partners on the basis of simple, romantic attraction. They accomplish this by describing their partners in terms that make them potentially identifiable as members of their own racial group. This is notable since, as Kevin mentioned above, intraracial couples need not explain the role of race when describing how they were attracted to their partner. Thus, through descriptions of the physically anomalous features of one or both partners, a physically intraracial couple is negotiated, for all practical purposes, by these interracial couples. Moreover, in providing specifically racialized accounts of their own coupling, these interviewees actually sustain intraracial relationships as the default form such partnerships should take – even as their own romantic partnerships depart from such expectations.

Anomalous socialization

As the forgoing excerpts suggest, interracial couples can account for their initial attraction to their partners by emphasizing how much they physically resemble a member of their own racial group. Yet the fact that each person is actually a member of a different race, and thus has likely had distinctive experiences related to their racial identity, remains. Race might be overlooked in an initial meeting, but in an ongoing relationship such experiential differences should emerge. How are such differences managed?

Often interracial couples spoke of their partner's unique, or at least different, socialization process. I use the term 'anomalous socialization' to refer to the ways in which members of interracial couples accounted for the values, beliefs and actions of a partner who was claimed to be different from others of their same racial group and was the product of distinct experiences. Put simply, these members claim that due to their partners' unique socialization, racial differences are irrelevant in their relationship. Foremost among the socialization experiences are childhood experiences. These experiences can be particular tricky to rely on when the parents who raised the anomalous child also hold stereotypical views of their child's partner. For example, Nick has grown up around upper-class whites. His parents are not particularly happy with Nick's choice of a black wife. Mary explains Nick's acceptance of other races by differentiating between what his parents told their children and what his parents practice:

(4) [I-7: Mary and Nick]
X :   Well how did Nick come out the way he did?
M: Who the hell knows. I think to be honest with you, I think his parents were both-, they raised all
      their kids the same, I think that sometimes in life a kid hears everything you say and he
      practiced it. I think unfortunately, for the sake of Nick, he practiced what he may have heard ...

In turn, Mary also discounts the possibility that her mother might object to her relationship with Nick:

(5) [I-7: Mary and Nick]
X: Your mom is all right with [interracial relationships]?
M: Oh yeah, I think she is- I mean who knows, she's not gonna, my mom's not the
      type-she's got what she got cause she raised us a cert- If you want, in my opinion, if you
      want your kids to marry someone black raise them in a black environment.

Mary accounts for her own interracial marriage choice by invoking an interracial interactional environment. Earlier in the interview Mary described growing up in a white neighbourhood. In this excerpt she specifically invokes that environment as a reason why her mother cannot criticize her choice of a white partner. Indeed, she is responsible for raising Mary in a racial environment that predisposed her to form an interracial relationship. As in the accounts of physical attraction above, race is not denied, absent or irrelevant in the choice of partner. In fact, just the opposite is true: race is treated as having special relevance. But because this relevance was established in childhood it is now treated as a matter of habit rather than an interviewee's intentional choice. Thus, in such accounts the mere fact of a person's racial identity is not enough to establish it as actively relevant in their choice of a partner.

In the next instance Diane accounts for her own upbringing in much the same way. In the course of her interview, Diane identified herself as both Japanese and a 'third-generation Japanese', which she notes is 'really American'. Beyond indicating the fluidity of Diane's racial identity, Diane uses these identities to establish a racial experience that is similar to that of her husband.

(6)   [I-2: Charles and Diane]
D: ... and then Japanese, which is what I am, is totally different, its not like my household was 'ah-so', it was not like that either because I'm third generation Japanese --> here, and so I'm really an American. I mean mentally the way I visualized myself, I was probably in my thirties before I thought of myself as being Japanese, I always thought of myself as 'media white'
X: Were you around Japanese people
D: Yeah, yeah, basically. But ... I grew up in a Japanese community essentially.

Diane finds that her racial identity is tied to the media interactions she had in childhood. Even though she was raised within a largely Japanese community, the telling factor in her racial identity was the media. By identifying her racial identity as 'media white' Diane does not deny the 'biological' or 'cultural' basis of her Japanese identity, but she does discount their relevance in shaping her self-understanding and, by extension, her interactions with her (white) partner. Interestingly, once Diane establishes her 'media white' identity she then uses it to account for her own lack of intraracial relationships:

(7)   [I-2: Charles and Diane]
X: Was there a reason you weren't dating Asians?
D: I attribute it to the way I-I was a boob tube kid, you know, I was raised on TV. And because the media was- is- was white, the medium was white, I would spend endless hours watching the TV, therefore the only modeling I had was there.

In claiming that the only 'modeling' she had was white, Diane suggests that her habitual understanding of herself was white. In effect, for her to date Asians would have been an interracial experience, and might have required conscious effort on her part. As in the previous cases, Diane treats race as a relevant feature of her identity; unlike those other cases, however, she claims an habituated identity that is at odds with her parent's racial identity to account for her current interracial relationship.

Since she thinks of herself as white, it is quite logical that she married a white person. Much as the accounts of physical anomalies treated intraracial relationships as the default form that such partnerships should take, these accounts of racialized experiences embody a claim that both partners are essentially of the same racial identity, despite their contrary superficial appearances.

As it happens, not everyone can use such accounts. Those who grew up in homogeneous neighbourhoods and whose parents were not particularly progressive did not have the same interactional resources as the previous interviewees. However, they were not without resources of their own. For example, one interviewee claimed that a complicated and contradictory home environment led to a confused identity. In the following, Charles (Diane's partner) describes his parents' different ethnic and religious identities.

(8)   [I-2: Charles and Diane]
C: I was raised with a father who was an agnostic and German- what was he (asking Diane)
D: Belgian
C: See I have a confusion about 'what am I' and my mother was and my mother was Italian
        Catholic and he was Belgian and she was very religious and he was agnostic. So I think
        even to this day, most of fifty years of age, don't know quite what I am or how to relate
        to either or both or you know what I mean, so I never felt a part of anyone. I have a feel-
        ing that's what happens, I wonder even with our children ...

Because of his parents' religious and ethnic differences, Charles claims he developed a confused identity that he has not yet resolved. In light of this observation we can note that Charles appears wholly unconcerned with living up to his racial identity since he has no single ethnic or religious identity to turn against.[9] In this respect, Charles is making a very different statement about his status as a member of a racial category than previous interviewees have. Instead of claiming to be concerned about being a 'good member' of his racial group, he questions whether he is a member of any group at all. It is not incidental that Charles grew up in a homogeneous environment. Since he cannot claim to have had sustained interracial interactions, and does not claim his parents raised him to be especially racially tolerant, his explanation accounts for his interracial relationship in a very different way. Unlike Andy, Charles does not say that Diane looks white. Unlike Diane, Charles does not claim to feel Japanese. Instead, Charles claims not to have any racial identity or racial consciousness at all. And as a consequence, he simply could not be pursuing a member of a different race.

Just as a person may be said to have had an atypical socialization process, in some cases interviewees claimed simply that a person held atypical beliefs for a member of his/her racial group. For example, in the following excerpt, Kevin describes what makes Alice, a white female, special. Kevin has just spoken of the curiosity which (much like searching) causes blacks and whites to find out about each other:

(9)   [I-6: Kevin]
X: Did you see [mere curiosity without real feeling] in your partner
K: ... definitely not with Alice, Alice has dated interracially before and that's probably why
        we get along and we're still best of friends today. She always has known what time it is

and where she's at and where other people are at and take other people for who they are. She's sort of a unique individual I think in terms of her ability to be that way.

In this excerpt Kevin accounts for his relationship with Alice in terms of her past experiences with members of other racial groups and the unique beliefs she has developed as a result. As Kevin notes, these experiences have allowed her to develop a unique ability to know 'what time it is' – that is, to understand her position and the position of black people. In this respect, Kevin's understanding of Alice's identity, and his account of their relationship are both interactionally based. Kevin maintains that without her unique beliefs and experiences, their relationship might not have been possible. Indeed, Kevin accounts for their continuing relationship by describing Alice's views as opposed to those he claims are typically held by whites.

Similarly, in the following excerpt Mary depicts Nick as an atypical white person not only because his parents espoused racial equality (as we noted above), but because he has adopted a set of beliefs that she claims are different from most members of his racial group.

(10)　[I-7: Mary (black, married) and Nick (white)]
X:　　Well how did Nick come out the way he did
M:　　Who the hell knows. I think to be honest with you, I think his parents were both, they raised all their kids the same, I think that sometimes in life a kid hears everything you say and he practiced it. I think unfortunately, for the sake of Nick, he practiced what he may have heard, versus the rest of him, he's in a very difficult situation anyway, not just with racial, that's just one of the elements, but his beliefs are extremely different than I would say upper-class, white, suburban, male ... he stays home, he is the primary care-taker of the kids, his career path, we have allowed my career path to go first, I think also he is extremely diverse in the sense of sensitive to women's issues, gender issues

Nick is upper-class, white, suburban, and male. But Mary describes him as not being what one might expect of such a person. And there is a sense that she could not be with a stereotypical male member of a white, upper-class, suburban community. As her account suggests, it is only because he is so exceptional that the couple remains compatible.

By 'anomalizing' themselves and their partners, members of interracial couples sustain a version of their relationship as one based on romantic attraction. Interracial couples find the anomaly in a person rather than racism in their relationships. Whether the accounts focus on physical appearances, socialization or beliefs, one or another member of the inter-racial couple is treated as an atypical member of her/his racial group, thereby normalizing the relationship. By virtue of such accounts, these members treat their relationships as intraracial relationships for the purposes of inferring racial motivation.

Strategic ambiguity

Anomalizing works by characterizing one's partner as different from others of his/her racial group. The main payoff for such characterizations is that they allow those claiming anomalies to rebut any implication that racial motives played a role in their selection of a partner from a different racial group. As these accounts suggest, for interviewees discussing interracial relationships, motives and intentions constitute important aspects of managing the legitimacy of one's actions. But motives and intentions are psychological phenomena to which others have only indirect access. As it happens, this lack of access can be both useful and troubling for members. Just because one cannot directly observe the intentions and motives of others doesn't mean that people stop making inferences about them. Since we cannot read minds, however, we must rely on observable evidence to make inferences about the motives and intentions of others. For example, having an anomalous partner constitutes an observable form of evidence others can use to infer a lack of racial intent regarding one's choice of a partner. Such inferences (and accounts) are not limited to descriptions of racial partners, however. They can be used in the interpretation of potentially any action where racial motives might be suspected.

In recounting their experiences as interracial couples, many interviewees described situations where others – partners, friends or family members – acted in a potentially racist fashion. Evidently, such potentially racist actions could have important consequences for their relationship with their partners and whomever else might be involved. If the actions in question were intentionally racist, the affected partner might be prompted to terminate their relationship with the partner, friend or family in question. Yet this rarely happened. In most cases, interviewees could find a way of characterizing the actions of others as 'unintentional', or possibly not racist at all. The work of finding that a racial slur was not intentionally racist may sound like wilful blindness. Yet, as with their accounts of falling in love with a partner of a different race, these interviewees had to walk a fine line. The work of strategic ambiguity lies in managing the fine line between pitfalls of being blind to racial motives and the consequences of finding that loved ones might be racist. Interviewees managed this line by casting the motives and intentions behind a potentially racist action as ambiguous and difficult to ascertain.

In casting an action as only potentially racist, the interviewees did not deny race any more than they denied race when characterizing a partner as anomalous. Indeed, in the very ways that they depict their struggles over how an action should be characterized they acknowledge that racial intent can be inferred from the observable features of actions, and thus recognized racism as a potential explanation. However, in the final analysis they conclude that racist motives could not be conclusively determined because of the particular circumstances in question. For example, in discussing situations where race might be relevant, respondents occasionally described the complexity of those circumstances, and the consequent potential for other less dramatic conclusions about the motives of the participants involved. In the following excerpt, Mary discusses an argument Nick had with his father regarding Malcolm X, a black, Muslim activist:

(11)   [I-7: Mary and Nick]
M: We're in a mess right now with Nick's family. Nick and his dad have a love–hate relation-
        ship period. Of course they are going to, if you can imagine his dad is a very successful
        lawyer and Nick has taken a different route so they have a love–hate relationship anyway,

we get in this big ol' argument over Malcolm X which has nothing to do- ends up that starts the argument, it has nothing to do with the root of the problem but there is always this underlying element, this- always frustration of, does Nick's dad not accept him because he is home with the kids or because his wife works or because his wife is black ... but it's hard and when I keep on looking I think is it me, is it this, is it that.

Evidently Mary struggles with the possibility that the tension between her husband and his father could be related to her racial identity: she say 'when I keep on looking, I think its me'. And yet even though Mary relates an argument over Malcolm X, suggesting a potentially racial element to the disagreement, she also invokes other factors as potentially more significant (such as Nicks decision to be a stay-at-home dad). Notably, these other components do not directly relate to Mary's racial identity. And Mary does not confront the father in an effort to ascertain just how race matters in this circumstance. Instead, Mary points to the presence of other ways the fight could be understood by focusing other ways the participants could be categorized (e.g. in terms of contrasting occupations: successful lawyer and stay-at-home dad; or in terms of family roles: father and son). In doing so, Mary's account exemplifies a recurrent feature of finding ambiguity – the presence of other factors that also potentially explain apparently racially motivated actions. And because of this ambiguity, Mary only raises the possibility of racial motives as a question to herself. If her father-in-law was conclusively demonstrating racial intent, then Mary might not be able to just 'think' to herself, she might feel obligated to act. In an ambiguous situation such a response is not yet appropriate. Thus Mary's account also demonstrates an advantage to finding ambiguity: ambiguous circumstances do not require action because there is no straightforward way to act.

The lengths to which interviewees would go to find ambiguity in the actions of others is exemplified in the following account offered by Andy. After Bea has suggested that her father wouldn't attend their upcoming wedding, Andy both entertains, and then discounts, the relevance of racial motivations in his future father-in-law's likely stance towards the wedding.

(12)   [I-1: Andy and Bea (edited)]
X: [Will] Bea's family come to the wedding?
A: I doubt it very seriously
B: Well, I know my brothers and sisters would but, I don't think my dad would come. My mom would be shaky ... she'll be there, but my dad- I don't think so.
A: Funny thing with that is I don't that – her dad isn't really a bad person for what I've gotten to know of him. I don't know that he wouldn't just strictly because I'm black or he wouldn't be- I mean it's slightly because I'm black and slightly because he might not want to go to weddings (laughs).

It seems plausible for Andy to conclude that Bea's father would not come to his wedding because he is black. And yet, however plausible such a conclusion may be, it is apparently not required. Andy treats Bea's father's potential action (or likely attitude) as only partly motivated by considerations of race; he offers the view that Bea's father simply doesn't like weddings as a factor that complicates his decision – and potentially makes it less than racist. Notably, however, in positioning his account largely as a rebuttal to the inference that Bea's father is racist, Andy treats that conclusion as a 'default' explanation for his likely behaviour. In this way, Andy acknowledges that he understands the inference one would typically make about a father's refusal to attend his daughter's marriage to a black man. However, in claiming intimate knowledge of Bea's father, Andy can discount racial motives as the sole source of his action and treat them instead as having been prompted by a more complex set of factors. This de-racing strategy mitigates the relevance of race, allowing the father to be taken as 'not really a bad person'. Thus, as Andy 'gets to know' Bea's father, he moves closer to discounting the relevance of race as a motivating factor in his actions. In this respect, finding ambiguity and complexity in actions can be a method for sustaining long-term relationships where finding racial motives might be disruptive of them.

In some cases, it appears that the finding of ambiguity is not merely a matter of *post hoc* analysis; members can conduct themselves to ensure that some ambiguity can be invoked to counter potentially racist reactions. For example, in the following excerpt Mary explains that people are more oriented to her strong belief than her race in their negative assessments of her.

(13)   [I-7: Mary and Nick]
M: usually 90% of the people that give me a hard time, once they get to know me in two years they are usually the people I am the closest to. If they take the time. Very few people have I met that hate me because I married [a white person], they may hate me more because of my beliefs. See that's one thing I think, my beliefs may put over more than my blackness. And I make a point to tell people in the beginning what my beliefs are. Sometimes I'm not sure if my reaction is because of just race or because of my beliefs.

In this account, Mary does more than find factors other than her race to account for occasions in which people don't accept her. It appears that she conducts herself so as to ensure that other factors can be invoked. Since Mary 'makes a point' of revealing her controversial beliefs 'in the beginning', she can never be certain whether it is those beliefs or her racial identity that accounts for the reactions others have towards her. In this respect, the ambiguity that Mary finds in her relations with others is not a problem to be solved; it is a solution to a problem. Given that Mary anticipates a lack of acceptance by co-workers, she can 'have a say' in the cause of that reaction. By voicing her beliefs early on, she can ensure that any negative assessments of her can be treated as reactions to those beliefs rather than simply reactions to her own racial identity or her interracial marriage.

In some cases, interviewees' accounts suggested that they have ready-made explanations that can be invoked when a situation may call for them. For example, in the following, Andy complicates the finding of racism by noting that potentially offensive behaviour can simply be a product of pettiness or jealousy.

(14)   [I-1: Andy and Bea}
A: ... And actually the funny thing is when girls stare they're usually staring at Bea because she's so pretty. And when they don't approve of the relationship its usually because I'm with a pretty Asian woman rather than I'm with an Asian in general.

Andy does not reveal precisely how he knows the difference between staring-because-Bea-is-Asian and staring-because-Bea-is-beautiful-and-Asian. However, it does seem clear that by invoking Bea's beauty and the pettiness of others, Andy can transform a situation that might be a source of trouble for the couple into one that is actually complimentary to them. Moreover, by always treating Bea's beauty alongside her racial identity, Andy does not deny the relevance of race, but he also works to ensure that it is not a sufficient account for others' behaviour.

The sort of ready-made accounts that Andy provides and the sort of preparatory work that Mary does suggests that the finding of ambiguity is not only (or even mainly) about saving the reputations of others; this ambiguity is invoked as a method for insulating partners in interracial couples from being treated by others as racial objects. And this, in turn, may figure in other matters that can have reputational consequences for them. For example, finding that actions are ambiguous allows these interviewees to avoid the charge that they did nothing in the face of blatantly racist behaviour. If these interviewees had found that their father-in-law, friends, co-workers, or even strangers had acted in ways that were obviously racist, then they would have been virtually required to say or do something about that. However, if one cannot be certain that actions are racially motivated, then one can appear especially tolerant and nuanced in declining to act.

Conclusion

In this chapter I have argued that interviewees find anomalies and ambiguity as interactional methods for managing the racial contexts of their relationships on specific occasions. This is a very different sense of racial context from that which is found through the comparison of racial aggregates or the comparison of racial representatives. Instead of individuals being mastered by an outside racial context which they cannot affect, in this view the racial context of actions, or a relationship itself, is the outcome of techniques deployed by people in actual situations. Of course, we can only find the work of managing racial context if we set aside the assumption that an overarching racial social structure, or an unchanging racial identity, animates people as if they are puppets.

One concern raised by this type of study is that by setting aside (or, if one wants to be less charitable, by ignoring) social structure and racial identity (except where it is made relevant in the interaction) it contributes to a wilful blindness regarding racial inequality and systemic racism. Interview data specifically, and interactional data generally, are not designed to decide questions regarding whether race is or is not present. An interactional study will not find structural racism present or absent because the idea of structural racism, like the idea of a master identity, depends upon the notion that racism exists without regard to the interactional particulars of episodes, or what might be managed through them. For interactional studies, however, the interactional particulars are exactly what are at issue. What interactional studies can accomplish is an understanding of how racial contexts are experienced as everyday phenomena, and how these are managed through interactional devices.

And this brings up a final point. There is a tendency to connect particular actions with the category of the persons who deploy them. In the case of this study one might be tempted to see the practices as 'practices of interracial couples'. That would be convenient, but misleading. It seems likely that homosexual couples may find strategic ambiguities in their families' reactions to them. Its also seems likely that we could find almost every couple deploying the idea that one partner is an atypical 'woman', 'man', 'someone from the south', 'high-school dropout', or any other category. Just as the interactional research should not begin by assuming the relevance of racial identity, it also should not end by tying particular practices to particular racial identities.

Instead, the issue for interactional researchers involves finding what interactional considerations are involved in casting one's partner as an anomaly, or in finding that a particular comment or action is racially ambiguous. In this case the interviews demonstrate that anomalies are useful when one needs to demonstrate, in an observable way, the non-racial motives for coupling. If the analysis is correct, then in situations where racial motivation needs to be dismissed, anomalization may be one of the techniques employed. In this respect, the practices described above are tied to pragmatic situational concerns rather than to the transituational identities of the people who deploy them. Thus, the practices described above are not invented by or reserved for interracial couples. They are available to others in situations yet to be discovered.

Notes

1. For more about the intentional design of a racial social structure, see Theodore Allen (1997).
2. Ashley Montagu (1964) describes this as an omeleting process whereby the individual differences within a race are whisked out of existence as the consistent batter is methodically and methodologically prepared.
3. From van Dijk's study: 'When White majority group members talk about ethnic outgroups, they do not merely express their beliefs and attitudes. In a different sense of the term, they *reproduce* ethnic opinions of their in-group as a whole, such as shared stereotypes or prejudices and information they have heard or read from other sources.' (1993: 23)
4. In terms of aggregate comparisons, there has been some research on the rates and patterns of intermarriage, especially with respect to race, gender and region of the country (Aptheker 1992; Barron 1946; Spickard 1989; Tucker and Mitchell-Kernan 1990). Some research has looked to group size and in-group sex ratio as explanations for variations in outmarriage rates (for several sources, see Crester and Leon 1982; see also Alba and Golden 1986). Others have looked to propinquity in housing, education, employment (Monahan 1976) and region of the USA (Tucker and Mitchell-Kernan 1990) as

explanations for variation in outmarriage rates and patterns. Research has also examined the stability of interracial unions (Monahan 1976).

5. Intraracial couples are the single exception since it is assumed that race does not matter for them in the same way that it does for interracial couples. Though it might seem counterintuitive, some have characterized interracial relationships as *ipso facto* evidence of racism, while few scholars have characterized the choice of a same-raced partner as racist. Thus the racial motivations of interracial couples is inherently suspect while the racial motives of intraracial couples are seen as 'natural' and self-evident (e.g. see Spaights and Dixon 1984).

6. See Maria P.P. Root 1991 for a notable exception.

7. This analytic stance of bracketing racial identity and racial structure may seem innocuous but be aware that it puts this researcher in very unhappy company. There is a thin line between not assuming the relevance of race and being blind to the relevance of race. Looking at the racial history of Europe and the USA, one easily comes upon numerous examples where the very people who were most involved in maintaining a racial, oppressive social structure were also those most blind to its existence (Gossett 1965; Takaki 1979). Concepts such as 'institutional racism' and 'master identities' are present in the academy today in order to combat the self-serving blindness of those who enjoy the privileges of racial oppression. If research wilfully ignores these concepts and blinds itself to a racial social structure, then perhaps we only assist those who wish to enforce this other type of colour blindness. For me, that would not be comfortable. However, this unhappy company is a discomfort that must be endured because there is a hole in our knowledge of race. For example, absent their reliance on Gans' assumption that race is reliably salient in all social interactions, researchers have little to say regarding how race operates in any specific interaction.

8. Broadcast on the *Jerry Springer Show*, December 1992.

9. Charles uses various methods to convey his confusion. Charles has been trying to claim that he is essentially different from other whites, with varying degrees of success. It is notable, then, that he asks for a piece of information that he should know – the background of his father – to actually demonstrate the confusion he will claim in his next breath.

CHAPTER TWELVE Using Talk to Study the Policing of Gangs and its Recordwork

Albert J. Meehan

Throughout the twentieth century, Americans have had a recurring concern with youth street 'gangs' committing disorderly and illegal behaviours (Klein 1995; Short 1996). At one point during a two-year field study I conducted in 'Bigcity', a pseudonym for a large US city, youth gangs were identified as a significant problem and a special 'gang' car programme was created for dealing with it. This youth gang 'problem' occurred during an election year and consequently had political implications: the claimed presence of gangs allowed Bigcity's police to reinforce the mayor's claim he was doing something 'for the neighbourhoods' by bringing youth gangs under control. As I will show, having such a gang car programme facilitated the categorization of many different problems in the community as 'gang' relevant. The 'gang car' programme continued throughout the summer and fall before the election and was terminated within two weeks after the mayor won re-election (Meehan 2000). Such political pressures constitute an important context of accountability for the police, and the police as an organization tends to manage such pressures through manipulation of their records (Chambliss 1994; Manning 1997; McCorkle and Miethe 1998; Meehan 1993; Seidman and Couzens 1973; Zatz 1987).

Using data from citizens' calls for service, the police response in the 'gang car' and corresponding police records, I will illustrate how the category 'gang' became a resource for citizens and police personnel (e.g. police operators and responding officers) to categorize a variety of problems with young people, usually not gangs, as 'gang' problems. Whereas other researchers have used surveys and vignette scenarios (Decker and Kempf-Leonard 1991) or a combination of media reports, statistics and legislative responses to study the social construction of gang problems (Curry et al. 1996; McCorkle and Miethe 1998), I focus on the various stages and practices through which activities are transformed officially into 'gang' activities by the police. In this approach, the study of the 'gang' problems focuses on talk-in-interaction at each level of the organizational career that creates these gang statistics.

The stages in this organizational career involve:

(a) Citizens' formulations of problems to police operators in a call for service and how such formulations are understood by operators as constituting a gang/group problem and subsequently encoded into an organizationally relevant and actionable category;

(b) Dispatchers' formulations of problems to patrol officers assigned to respond to a call;

(c) Patrol officers' understandings of dispatchers' formulations of the problem they are responding to;

(d) Patrol officers' location and assessment of the 'problem';

(e) Patrol officers' responses to the 'problem'; and

(f) The various records produced by patrol officers regarding their responses and the 'gang' statistics derived from those records.

Two different data sets are used in this chapter to explore the interaction between various participants in constructing this organizational career. One set is a collection of 86 calls from Corktown residents to Bigcity's 911 emergency number. Further, these calls all report incidents where the police operator categorized the nature of the problem in department records as a 'gang incident' and the gang car for the Corktown section of the city was dispatched to respond to the call. Subsequently, the official department records of these calls and the officer's response became a part of the official police statistics on the gang problem in Bigcity and for the Corktown district (see Meehan 2000 for a more detailed description).[1]

The analysis of these calls looks at the relationship of the call to the subsequent categorization of the call as a 'gang' problem as reflected in stages (a) and (b) in the organizational career outlined above. Analyzing the talk in these calls affords a view of the citizens' own formulations of their problems and how these formulations are constituted and negotiated by the operator and citizens as a 'gang' problem (see Sasson 1995). In this way, we can see how the police operator organizationally encodes such problems, a process which is sensitive to the interactional organization of the call, the political context to which the operator/dispatcher and the police are accountable, and the organization's current solution: namely, the availability of a 'gang' car to handle such problems.

The second data set I use consists of all available records and recordings for one evening's work in the gang car in the Corktown district.[2] These data provide an examination of stages (c) to (f) in the organizational career. With the officer's permission, a videotape of the evening's work in the gang car was made and the transcripts of the officer's response in the car discussed later in this chapter are from those videotapes. Currently, video cameras in patrol cars with officers wearing wireless microphones, afford similar data for researchers. I also supplemented this videotaping with fieldnotes and I transcribed all of the citizens' calls, the dispatchers' assignment of the call and obtained the corresponding records (i.e. patrol logs) of the police response for that evening. Using these data, we can examine how the officers assess and respond to the 'problem' they have been assigned and create an official record (i.e. patrol logs) of their work with 'gangs' for this evening. In sum, these materials illustrate how the responding officers constitute the activities of persons as a 'gang', to use Garfinkel's term, 'for all practical purposes'.

The routine interactional practices of persons working in organizations are responsive not only to public and media pressure, but are also accountable to internal recordkeeping procedures and legal and political bodies (Bowditch 1993; Emerson 1991; Margolin 1992; Meehan 1986). This means that interactional and recordkeeping practices, in essential ways, create and reproduce reality (Collins 1981; Fine 1991; Garfinkel 1967a; Rawls 1987). Consequently, an understanding of these interactional and recordkeeping practices is indispensable to the study of crime and deviance and social problems generally (Maynard 1988a).

An analysis of an organization's documentary reality (Smith 1974; Wheeler 1969) is particularly relevant to understanding how the police 'solve' a problem; in this case creating, maintaining and controlling the appearance of the street gang problem. I am not suggesting there were no street gangs in Bigcity, or in the 'Corktown' district I studied. Indeed, officers thought there were one or two identifiable street gangs and most 'gang calls' they were assigned that summer and fall were unrelated to 'real' gang activity. By 'real', the police refer to activities *they* believed to be gang activities, as opposed to how the organization expected officers to report them as gang activities. Both are social constructions, but at different levels. When asked what a 'real' gang was, officers used a classic 'social science' definition: an organized group of young people (typically teenagers) with a leadership structure, who wore common identifiable clothing and who commit serious/violent crime. Yet, as I show in this chapter, officers and dispatchers routinely and unproblematically interchanged the term 'gang' and 'group' when referring to young people. The issue is not whether there were 'real' gang problems, but to analyse how increased awareness of a public problem places particular kinds of constraints upon the police and the organization to show itself as accountable, and solving that problem. Such an analysis can show how groups of ordinary young people are constituted as 'gangs' at various points in citizen complaints and police responses to incidents. Let's turn to the first stage in this process – calling the police.

Calling the police

Citizens often invoke the police organization to resolve matters involving no 'legal' issue (e.g. to seek information about local civic events, or request services such as 'carrying Grandma upstairs'). Such reports are more frequent than 'criminal', or at least marginally illegal matters which constitute approximately 20 per cent of all police calls. Most patrol work is reactive (i.e. responding to citizens' calls for service) rather than proactive (officer-initiated work). This reliance upon citizens' input illustrates the collaborative nature of the police and citizens' production of official police statistics. The decision to call and determination of an outcome from the call (i.e. send a car/don't sent a car) begins the organizational career of records from which official statistics are derived.

From this perspective, it makes sense to begin a study of the record-generating activity of the police by examining the talk-in-interaction in the call for service. To do this, we will first examine how both citizens and operators orient their talk in the call towards producing a 'complaint package'. Then, the analysis will turn to discussing some conversational features of gang calls to see if *talk about* gangs can shed some light on the gang problem facing the community and the police as reflected in these calls. Our focus here is not simply about looking at outcomes (i.e. what type of record it produced) or by locating lexical items in the conversation that employ police categories (i.e. 'gang'). Rather, the emphasis is upon the ways police and citizens negotiate and achieve an understanding about the 'gangness' of an incident over the course of the call.

Lastly, the police operators' assessment of the 'police-worthiness' of complaints plays a critical role in generating such records, as does the citizens' accountability for producing a police-worthy complaint (i.e. they formulate descriptions of events in police-worthy form). We will examine operators' formulations to show how, in some calls, citizens' descriptions of reported events are marked for their 'uncertainty' and how this is handled interactionally.

A turn-by-turn analysis is of central methodological importance in the analysis of talk-in-interaction. As Sacks et al. (1974) noted, an important consequence of the turn-taking system is that participants in each turn display their understanding of the prior turn of talk as well as the current turn of talk. Further, this is a central methodological resource for the professional analyst of talk:

> But while understandings of other turn's talk are displayed to co-participants, they are available as well to professional analysts who are thereby afforded a proof criterion (and a search procedure) for the analysis of what a turn's talk is occupied with. Since it is the parties' understandings of prior turn's talk that is relevant to their construction of next turns, it is *their* understandings that are wanted for analysis. The display of those understandings in the talk of subsequent turns affords both a resource for the analysis of prior turns and a proof procedure for professional analyses of prior turns, resources intrinsic to the data themselves. (Sacks et al. 1974: 729, original emphasis)

Thus, the understanding of a turn by participants, as it is produced, over the course of a turn, is an important constraint on the analyst within this perspective.

Complaint packages

Emergency calls to the police reflect an interactional economy which accommodates both the range of reportable problems and maximizes police access to an event with a minimum of interactional work (Meehan 1989). One feature of this interactional economy is how citizen callers and police orient their conversation to achieving a *'police locatable' location* and *police relevant problem* which constitutes a 'complaint package'. Location and problem are *co-topics* in calls, and the achievement of an adequate formulation for each of these, constitutes the topic of, and hence reason for, the call: the 'complaint' and a proposed solution for it.

For example, *reporting only one part of the paired co-topics engenders a solicitation of the other part by police operator.* This is illustrated in call 1 and call 2 below, where the citizen does not initially report a police locatable location (call 39: lines 3–5) and problem (call 3: lines 2–3)

[Call 1: Tape 2]
```
1   D:   Bigcity Police Emergency three five three
2        (1.0)
3   C:   *Yes:s uh kids are playin on (.) The corner there with the
4        football and they just hit my window an_all I'm doin is
5        (.) replacin windows
6        (1.0)
7   D:   *Where is th:s?
8   C:   twenty eight Brighton street Subcity
```

[Call 2: Tape 2]
```
1   D    Bigcity Police
2   C    *yeah could you send someone to one forty-five Bountyhill
3        Street in Subcity please
4        (2.0)
5   D    *whats the problem?
6   C    there's a gang of kids in the (bottom corridor) theyre
7        smokin pon en (.5) drinkin and everything (.) Raisin hell
```

In both examples, the operator solicits information to complete the complaint package after the citizen's first turn. Prior to the operator's solicitation, a pause in the talk occurs between turn transfer (call 39: line 6; Call 3: line 4) which provides an additional opportunity for the citizen to complete the complaint package. *In the absence of the citizen's self-selection to continue his/her turn of talk, wherein the information relevant to completing the 'complaint' could be provided, the operator makes topical the absence of that information in the next turn through a request for that absent information.* Through this contrast, we can begin to observe how the complaint package consists of the formulation of a police locatable location + problem, which is co-topic tied: the selection of utterances used in the formulation of one is a resource for the production and understanding of the other.

While location and problem can be understood as separately describing a 'location' and a 'problem', taken together as co-topics, they are heard for and understood by their relationship to the work of producing a police-relevant complaint, and proposing the police as a solution or remedy. The adequacy of a citizen's complaint is achieved in and through the formulation of location and problem which is 'recipiently designed' (Sacks et al. 1974) for the police. The task of the caller is not only to provide a description of the location and problem, but to select from the available possible descriptions a description which maximizes its relevance for the police.

Some conversational features of 'gang calls'

The analysis of these 'gang' calls, suggests that what constitutes a gang problem is equivocal in a number of ways. The phenomenon, a gang problem, and how it emerges as a problem, is an issue. Increased attention to gangs as a 'problem' (e.g. via media attention) may itself constitute and produce the visibility and problematic character of groups of youths for citizen and police alike. Consequently, any next incident involving young persons can be inspected for its gang-relatedness. The use of a categorization device (Sacks 1972) such as 'gang' can be in vogue given this new found relevance and possible remedy (i.e. a gang car will be sent). The argument is not that citizens use the category 'gang' in a naive or incorrect manner. Rather, the point is that there is a utility to the use of the category. Police operators formulate the caller's problem into categories that reflect organizational utility and priorities. Through this process, callers learn that certain categories are more useful than others in generating a police response.

For example, in call 3, *playing tag football* under the new lights is formulated by the caller, and accepted by the operator, as a gang-related activity. (Note: arrows highlight the features of the call discussed in the text. Timed pauses are in parentheses. Double slashes // indicate overlapped talk. D. represents the police operator, C. represents the citizen caller.)

```
[Call 3: Tape 1]
D:        Bigcity police three eight five
C:        In Corktown
D:        Yes
C:   ->   in front of ninety-eight Bedford Street there's a gang of teenagers playing tag
          football under these new lights (.5) can you get them out of here please?
D:        Yes maam
```

In the following call, the citizen describes no activities whatsoever in his/her turn and nothing is revealed about the nature of the incident except the label 'gang':

```
[Call 4: Tape 2]
PD:       Bigcity Police
CA:       yeah you wanna send a car down to twenty-seven Parton Street in
     ->   Corktown// for the gang of ki-
PD:                   what's the prob–
                      (1.0)
PD:       What's the address again sir?
```

Indeed, the term 'gang', offered by the caller, suffices for a description of the problem. In this call, the operator overlaps the caller at a turn transition relevance point (i.e. after Corktown) to ask what is the problem. However, the caller is continuing his\her turn, providing the problem 'the gang of ki-'. After completing the overlap, the operator requests information about the location again, not information about the problem. The partial production of 'the gang of ki-' in the caller's utterance is sufficient for the operator.

However, using the term 'gang' to describe persons is not a necessary feature of these 'gang' calls. One notable observation about this collection is that the term 'gang' is rarely used. Yet, the calls are encoded as 'gang' calls by the police operator and dispatched to the 'gang car' for the district. The category has organizational accountability for the police operator which enhances its use. Indeed, various types of activity (not necessarily involving legal violations) appear in these calls as categorically tied to 'gangs' and are usable by the caller *and* the operator as a resource for constituting the 'gangness' of the incident.

Such 'gang' associated activities include drinking, fighting, smoking pot, throwing rocks or beer bottles, banging on doors, hanging in the hallways or on street corners, and 'pissing on the rectory steps'. The term 'gang' and those activities associated with it, are clearly interchangeable with 'kids', 'group' and 'youths', and these terms were typically found in these calls. Indeed, descriptions of 'rowdy' behaviour were presumed by police operators to be categorically tied to young kids/groups and officially categorized as 'gang' behaviour.

For example, in call 5, the use of the term 'gang' by the police *operator* indicates that the term 'gang' is not necessarily tied to particular persons or identifiable groups *per se*, but rather, to the types of activity *expected* from groups of kids in general:

```
[Call 5: Tape 2]
  1   D:        Bigcity Police
  2   C:*       Yeah I have a pr-o-hh I'd like to uh:: report a
  3             disturbance on the corner of Shakerhill and Alton
  4             Street in Subcity
  5             ( .5)
  6   D:        Shakerhill and Alton?
  7   C:        that's right
  8   D:*  ->   tch hhh ( ) and whats the problem?
  9             ( .5)
 10   C:*  ->   they're throwing beer bottles and uh//:::
 11   D:*       what's this a gang?
 12   C:        Yeah
 13             ( .5)
 14   D:        right on the corner there
 15   C:        mmhmh
 16   D:        okay we'll send somebody there
 17   C:        thank you
 18   D:        yep
```

The caller's description 'they're throwing beer bottles' is formulated by the operator in the next turn as 'what's this a gang?' which receives an agreement from the caller. Note that the caller's description 'they're throwing beer bottles' lacks a referent (i.e. who is doing this activity), but this is formulated by the operator in line 11 as a 'gang'.

The operator provides a candidate referent for the caller using a police-relevant category ('gang'), inferable from the activities described by the caller. Whereas the activity of 'throwing beer bottles' is implicative of 'gang' behaviour, in the following call, how the operator categorizes the problem as a 'gang' problem is not immediately clear:

[Call 6: Tape 2]

```
 1   C:*        Hi I'd like to report some boys in uh:: right now there
 2               on Masters Street, somebody has to call the cops right?
 3   D:         allright what number Masters?
 4   C:         uh:: its right down from the- ( .5) one twenty nine
 5               Bastille Way
 6               ( .5)
 7   D:         What number are you at now?
 8   C:         one twenny nine
 9               ( .5)
10   D:         ehhh yur at one twenny nine Bastille Way?
11   C:         ye:s
12   D:*   ->   and the gang is out there?
13   C:*   ->   the gang is out there yeah they gotta go home and to
14               bed.
15   D:         allright (.) we'll be down
```

In line 1, the caller reports some 'boys'. The operator formulates and offers a categorization in line 12: 'and the *gang* is out there?' Some 'boys' have now been constituted as a 'gang', to which the caller agrees in the next turn (line 13). Categorizing the problem as a 'gang' problem is done by the operator, not the caller. How some 'boys' become the 'gang' is not inferable from activities described by caller, as in previous examples, because no activities are reported. But, *it doesn't really matter*. The operator's candidate categorization is 'police'-related, whereas exploring the caller's reason for 'reporting some boys' would require more time on the call, which has already been occupied with some difficulties in establishing the location (lines 3–10). The caller concludes by agreeing with the operator's categorization.

Central to the categorization process is how the 'gangness' of incidents is constituted or negotiated by the caller and the police operator. There are some calls where the caller and/or operator use the categorization 'gang' to formulate the problem. In other calls, the designation of a 'gang problem' is an achievement arrived at by the operator and caller *over the course of the call* (sometimes not appearing in the call at all). From a methodological standpoint, it is misleading to search for explicit uses of the term 'gang' by the operator or caller simply because these calls have resulted in the 'gang' statistic. The operator's categorization as an official 'gang' statistic obviously does not depend upon such displays alone, but rather relies on how, for all practical purposes, what is produced by the caller in the complaint can be heard for its 'gangness'.

In calls 5 and 6 above, the operator solicits an agreement for the proposed categorization of the problem. The solicitations 'and the gang is out there?' (call 6) and 'what's this a gang?' (call 5) illustrate the negotiated character of these calls, which are then recorded as *'facts' for all practical purposes* (Garfinkel 1967b). However, this solicitation is occasioned by the citizen's description of the reported problem. That is, in certain calls, callers mark their description as 'problematic' which results in the operator inspecting the reported complaint. One method for accomplishing this inspection is through a 'formulation' of the problem. Formulations are a conversationalist resource that displays a speaker's 'gist' sense, or understanding, to this point in the conversation (Heritage and Watson 1979).

In the context of police calls, operators' formulations are an important interactional place where an understanding of the complaint is displayed and, in a sense, it's 'facticity' for this conversation is negotiated independently of its 'existence' in the world. The problem reported by the citizen has a conversational existence, the facticity of which is only available in and through that interaction. Thus, assessing the facticity of a report is a 'local' (i.e. conversationally local) matter which shapes the subsequent organizational categorization and response.

Operators' formulations

Formulations by the police operator are fairly infrequent. Consequently, as a methodological strategy, examining how they are constructed and when and where they occur sequentially in a call and the interactional work they accomplish is important. Since no explicit inspection of the caller's reported problem occurs in most gang calls, it would be worth considering first how the complaint packages in calls where formulations occur *differ* from other gang calls with no formulations.

As we have seen, a formulation appears to be assessing the police-worthiness of the reported incident or inspecting the grounds for the caller's categorization of the problem. In this context, formulations are an interactional event ripe for misunderstanding or even conflict. So, we will examine the turn construction of operators' formulations and see how they are treated in next turn by the citizen. Since all turns of talk are placed into a sequence with other turns, the issue of sequential placement, or when operators formulate, is an important matter to discuss. Finally, conversational objects, like operators' formulations, are not all alike. So, it is worth examining the similarities *and* differences between the formulations in calls 5 and 6 discussed above and those formulations found in the following calls below (7–10).

In these calls, provided in their entirety, formulations by the operator occur in call 7 on line 13, 'And yuh think they're gonna have a brawl:?'; in call 8 on line 15, 'and they're fighting right now?'; in call 9, on line 19, 'allright (.) and then they're (.) Throwing eggs?'; and in call 10, on line 16 'And the kids are tryin na: h (.) break down the door?' (the first formulation by the operator is recycled again in lines 18 19, 'Whatta yuh say the ki-s are tryin to break down the door?').

[Call 7: Tape 2]

1	P:	(just a minute) Bigcity Police three five seven
2	C:	Yea:h this is just a good neighbor callin up and I'd
3		I'll advise you to send a pa-crowd car over here to the
4		Green Street playground(.) Un Subcity
5		(.5)
6		hh to stop these kids because I think they;re gonna have
7		a big fight over here
8		(.5)
9		thats the //Gre:::
10	P:	Could you give me that address sir?
11	C:	Thats the Green Street Playground at the corner of Green
12		Street and main Street in Subcity
13	P:* ->	And yuh think they're gonna have a braw:l?
14	C:	Yeah I think they're gonna have a little ja:m//(they)
15	P:	Do they have any weapons now sir?=
16	C:	No::: but they come from those foolish projects across the
17		street those Agawam projects
18	P:	Do yuh wanna leave your name with me?
19	C:	No but tha:::ts enough tuh let you know//theres trouble
20		brewin=
21	P:	Okay
22	P:	Okay sir

[Call 8: Tape 2]

1	P:	Bigcity Police three oh eight
2	C:	Yeah at the corner of us::: Walton Way and Beaumont
3		Street theres a kid there Harry O'Donnell(.) (In fact)
4		theres a whole group of kids but this one kid in
5		particular has got a gun
6	P:	He's gotta gu:n?
7	C:	Yeah and they're startin a fight up there and I'm afraid
8		that someone's really gonna get hurt
9	P:	This is on Beaumont Street and wha//:::t?
10	C:	Beaumont and Walton Way
11		(2.5)
12	P:	Walton Way?
13	C:	Yeah ( ) ((Subcity)) I can hear them from my window I
14		live here// ( )
15	P:* ->	and they're fighting right now?
16	C:	yeah they're startin right now and the kid's got a gun
17	P:	didya see the gun?
18	C:	yeah I SAWR it as a matter of fact he's braggin about it
19		(2.0)
22	P:	One Harry O'Donough?
23	C:	O'Donnell O//
24	D:	O'Donnell
25	C:	yeah they know 'im down at ((Subcity headquarters))

```
26              (1.5)
27              he's crazy
28      P:      o::kay we'll send someone over
29      C:      allright thank you
```

[Call 9: Tape 2]

```
 1      P:      ((City)) Police three oh eight
 2      C:      ah:::listen I'm calling from ((Subcity))
 3              (.5)
 4      P:      yeu:p
 5      C:      uh:::( . ) well I don' know ( . ) ya know tricker treatin is
 6              for little kids but there's these big kids thet-uh
 7              hangin around the Clarence Edwards School?
 8      P:      yeup
 9      C:      and they got eggs
10              (1.0)
11      C:      now I don't want them being thrown ay my house
12              (1.0)
13      C:      or the car or anything=so could you have somebody go
14              down ther:e and check it ou:t?
15              (1.0)
16      P:      uh::m what street is th- Brown, Edward School,// or
17              Walker Street
18      C:      At the corner of Edwards sch-yeah on Walke-Street yeah
19      P:*  -> allright ( . ) and then they're ( . ) throwin eggs?
20      C:      Well:: yeah they all got a bunch uh: eggs uh:: about a
21              half a dozen en-some kids went out to buyem( . ) and they
22              gottem in their hands O:K//ay?
23      P:      okay we'll send someone over
24      C:      allri::
```

[Call 10: Tape 2]

```
 1      C:      Will you please come down tuh forty Corey street in
 2              (Subcity) the kids are down in the:re tryin to break
 3              the doors open
 4      P:      Forty ( .5) C-Corey?
 5      C:      Forty Corey Street
 6              ( .5)
 7      C:      Down on the first floor-down there bangin tryin to push
 8              the doors open they're lo::cked
 9      P:      What the kids are tryin tuh (n)
10              (.5)
11      C:      they're lo:cked=they're empty apartments but they're
12              locked up
13              ( .5)
14      P:      O:h ( . ) this=around forty Corey Street?
15      C:      Forty Corey Stre//et (yeah)
16      P:*  -> And the kids are tryin na:h ( . ) break down the door?
17      C:   -> Hu::h?
18      P:*  -> Whatta yuh say the ki-s are tryin to break down the
19           -> door?
```

```
20   C:    Yea:h they're down there tryin nuh (1.0) bang the door
21         open and uh://::(l)
22   P:    Oh they're bangin on the door
23         ( .5)
24   P:    Okay we'll send the police down then
```

A comparison with other complaint packages

In these four calls, the callers' 'complaint package' is different from those in other calls in the larger corpus in the following ways.

1   In the calls reviewed, the police-relevant problem hasn't occurred yet or its relevance as a police problem is *anticipated* by the caller. For example, in call 7 the caller 'thinks' they're going to have a big fight (lines 6–7); in call 8, they're 'starting' a fight (lines 6–7); in call 9 (lines 5–11), the caller reports she does not want eggs 'to be thrown' at her house; and in call 10 (line 2), the kids are 'trying' to break the doors open. By contrast, in the other calls, the complaints are not anticipated problems, but are in fact incidents 'in progress', or have 'happened' (e.g. 'there's a bunch of teenagers breakin bottles and raising hell out here' or 'a group of kids threw beer bottles at everybody').

2   A second feature is an *expression of concern* reported by the caller. In call 7, he's 'a good neighbor callin up to advise the police'. In call 8, the caller is 'really afraid that someone's gonna get hurt'. In call 9, these '*big kids*' are going to throw the eggs at her house. In call 10, the caller's concern is the 'apartments are locked up'. In other calls, citizens' reports are not marked with such 'concern', but rather are descriptions which report some 'state of affairs' without injecting the caller's assessment or evaluation of their occurrence.

3   A third feature is that the reported problem is 'serious' from the caller's standpoint, and in three of the four calls could be 'serious' from a police standpoint. In most calls in the larger collection, callers *minimize* the importance of the reported problem via straightforward reporting of 'facts' (i.e. 'They're drinking and smoking pot', etc.). In these four calls, the callers are reporting potentially life-threatening situations which are prioritized differently by the police. For example, call 7 is a report of a 'big fight', in call 8 'they're startin a fight' in call 10, 'breaking down the door' (at least initially) appears to be a fairly serious matter (e.g. burglary in progress). In call 9, where the kids are throwing eggs, the incident itself doesn't present itself as serious. Rather, the persons who are reportedly involved in the act itself are categorized as 'big' kids as opposed to 'little' kids and the caller produces this contrasting categorization of the type of offender which appears to upgrade the caller's grounds for inviting the police to check them out (i.e. this isn't just 'Halloween fun').

This raises the question of whether this serious/not serious feature distinguishes these from other calls. Is it the case that these incidents *are* life threatening (i.e. more serious)? *Or* is it the case when calling the police about an anticipated problem that callers maximize its importance via these expressive concerns and contrastive structures (e.g. 'they're not little kids they're big kids') to account for the police-worthiness of the problem. A complaint that expresses a citizen's concern marks that report as requiring inspection. Examining the utterance format of the operator's formulation and the sequential placement of it illustrates this inspection practice.

Turn construction and response by the caller

One feature of operator formulations is that they are in question format. Producing the formulation in question format is a strong technique for eliciting either an agreement or disagreement as opposed to providing a summary statement of the problem (i.e. 'and yuh think they're gonna have a brawl?' as opposed to 'a fight in the playground, okay'). The question format marks the operator's formulation as checking out the reported problem rather than a confirmation of it.

Second, the turn initial component in each formulation is (the word) 'and' which seems to do the work of sequentially appending this question-formatted formulation to the operator's prior turn to talk:

Call 7, line 13   And yuh think they're gonna have a brawl?
Call 8, line 15   and they're fighting right now?
Call 9, line 19   allright, and then they're throwin eggs?
Call 10, line 16   And the kids are tryin na:h break down the door?

This issue is discussed below in terms of its sequential placement in the call.

Third, observe how the formulation is treated in the caller's next turn. As Heritage and Watson (1979: 143) note, formulations are designed by speaker to receive an agreement from the other about 'the gist sense of the conversation thus far'. They also report that *where there is disagreement with a formulation, expressed elements of agreement also occur in the disagreement nonetheless.* Thus, one feature of formulations is that elements of agreement and disagreement are hearable in the next turn. In each example, elements of agreement and disagreement with the operator's formulation are present in the citizen's next turn of talk. However, in their turn, *citizens both minimize and modify the reported problem as formulated by the police operator.* (Note: **bold type** indicates the initial formulation, the citizen's agreement component and the subsequent modification.)

[Call 7: Tape 2]
D: And yuh think they're gonna have a brawl?
C: Yeah I think they're gonna have a little jam.

The caller's originally reported problem, a 'big fight', is formulated by the operator as a 'brawl' which is an equivalent categorization. In the citizen's next turn, however, an agreement token 'yeah' plus a modification of the problem from 'brawl' to 'little jam' occurs, downgrading the initial categorization of 'big fight'.

In call 8, the operator's formulation of the reported problem ('and they're fightin right now') is an upgrading of the citizen's initial categorization in line 6 ('they're startin a fight up there') which reduces the anticipatory feature of the original complaint and presents the problem as 'happening' and not a qualified description (i.e. starting a fight).

[Call 8: Tape 2]
D: and they're fightin right now?
C: Yeah they're startin right now and the kid's got a gun.

While there is an agreement token, the citizen's modification, in this case from 'fightin' to 'startin', preserves the original formulation (i.e. 'startin') and focuses concern upon the presence of the gun.

   In call 9, as in the previous example, the operator's modification proffers a legal violation, and reduces the anticipatory character of the original complaint (i.e. throwing eggs versus having them).

[Call 9: Tape 2]
D: and then they're (.) throwin eggs?
C: Well:: yeah they all got a bunch uh:: eggs uh:: about a
     half dozen apiece en– some kids went out to buyem(.) and
     they gottem in their hands O:K//ay?

While the caller provides a tentative agreement with the formulation (as evidenced by 'well:: yeah'), elements of disagreement are evidenced in the retention of the original report ('they have eggs'), and an expansion of the caller's grounds for inferring that the eggs *will* be thrown (i.e. they have 'a half dozen apiece', more are being purchased, 'and they gottem in their hands' ... draw your own conclusion!).

   In call 10, the operator's formulation offers the identical categorization provided by the caller in the initial complaint, but is modified by the caller and its seriousness is minimized, as evidenced by the operator's response 'Oh they're bangin on the door'.

[Call 10: Tape 2]
D: And the kids are tryin tuh break down the door?
C: Huh?
D: Whatta yuh say the kids are tryin to break down the
     door?
C: Yeah they're down there tryin uh (.) bang the door open ...
D: Oh they're bangin on the door

Clearly, the operator's formulation has implications for the categorization of the initially reported problem. The problem, as initially reported by the caller, is inspected by the operator via a formulation which is identical to, or upgrades, the citizen's report. Citizens both agree and disagree with the operator's formulation even where operators modify the citizen's initially reported problem to upgrade its police relevance (i.e. calls 8 and 9). In each case, the citizen modifies the operator's formulation and in doing so either minimizes their initial categorization, or re-orients the operator to their original problem.

When do operators formulate

A striking feature of these formulations is that there is considerable conversational distance between the original turn (complaint package) by the caller and the operator's formulation (i.e. the formulation does not occur in next turn). Instead, there is 'turn distance'. Sequentially, it appears that these formulations are the *second part of the operator's inspection of the complaint package, the first part of which deals with the location of the problem and the second part of which deals with the reported problem itself.* This is quite apparent in the data. The operators do a location check first, then using 'and' append the formulation in their utterance. These location checks occur even in calls where location is not really an issue for the achievement of the complaint package (as illustrated by calls 7–10). Rather, the location check at this point in the call initiates the inspection sequence of the reported problem.

There are, however, three instances in these calls (7, 8, 10) where a direct question concerning specific features of the citizen complaint are produced by the operator in the next turn. In these cases there is no 'turn distance', raising the question of whether the sequential placement of the operator's inspection has consequences for either its interpretation by the caller or its presentation by the operator. How are these 'next turn' inspections treated by the citizen?

First of all, in call 7, line 15, 'Do they have any weapons now sir?' is an inspection of the reported problem. The caller responds: 'No but they come from those foolish project across the street those Agwam projects'. The citizen not only responds to the question (with 'no'), but also appends some additional grounds for his/her inference that 'trouble' is brewing. In call 8, line 17 'didya see the gun?' is an inspection of selected aspects of the reported problem. The citizen's response 'Yeah I saw it as a matter of fact he's braggin about it', provides additional evidence supporting the citizen's inference in the first place that there will be a problem. In call 10, line 9, an inspection of the reported problem occurs in the next turn: 'What the kids are trying tuh-' is cut off by the caller and additional grounds for the reported problem are offered ('they're locked they're empty apartments but they're locked up'). Thus, when next turn inspections do occur, *they are treated by the caller as assessing either the grounds for the call reporting this problem, or perhaps the police-worthiness of the problem itself.* Next turn inspections also occasion callers providing more information to warrant their complaining to the police. When police operators offer formulations with 'turn distance' they are treated as calling for agreement or disagreement.

Maximization of the police-worthiness of citizen's reports

Let us return to the earlier observation made about calls 5 and 6 where the operator categorized the problem as a 'gang' problem *for the caller.* It was observed that the operator used a formulation to solicit the caller's agreement with the 'gang' categorization. In call 5 the designation could be inferred from activities reported by the caller in his/her complaint package ('they're throwing beer bottles'). By contrast, in call 6, a report of 'some boys', no activities were reported. While the operators produce a formulation in these two calls, these formulations differ from the four discussed above because they maximize the police relevance and adequacy which was initially minimized in the caller's version.

In call 5, the caller begins the complaint sequence (line 2) with an interesting repair within his/her turn. The caller begins by saying 'yeah I have a pr-o-hh', which is repaired to 'I'd like to report a disturbance...'. This self-initiated repair does some interesting interactional work regarding the ownership of the problem. By repairing 'I have a pro-' to 'I'd like to report a disturbance' the caller is disengaging his/her personal involvement in the report which follows, and as a consequence, minimizes his/her concern. The operator begins a location check, which the caller confirms (line 7). However, in line 8, the operator asks a direct question 'and what's the problem' before the caller attempts a formulation (i.e. the caller has not reported a categorizable problem). Saying 'I'd like to report a disturbance' leaves open the question 'what is the disturbance the caller is going to report?'. In line 10, through a straightforward description of the activities, the facticity is achieved, and the operator proposes the categorization, maximizing its relevance for the police.

Similarly, in call 6, the operator maximizes the relevance of the report by the citizen, which is also a minimized complaint. It is minimized both through its lack of reference to any activities, and by adding 'somebody has to call the cops right?' While it could be argued this is heard as an expression of concern, I would argue that it is not an expression of *the caller's* concern. In other operator's formulations (calls 7–10), the concerns of the callers were their own concerns, and the callers did not solicit the operator's agreement regarding their concerns. Whereas in call 6, the caller frames the concern as 'anybody's' (e.g. it's a problem for everyone, I'm just the somebody who has to call) and solicits the operator's agreement (e.g. appending 'right?' to the end of his/her turn). The minimized report of 'some boys' receives a maximized hearing for its police relevance by the police operator in line 12 ('the gang'), occurring at some conversational distance from the initial description by the citizen. In line 13, the caller agrees to this formulation, but does not express any element of disagreement. Indeed, there is some humour by the caller suggesting the police are the community babysitter: 'the gang is out there yeah they gotta go home and go to bed'.

To summarize, a turn-by-turn, sequential analysis reveals that assessment of the reported problem by the police operator is a delicate matter. The fact that citizens, by virtue of their access to the situation, 'should' be treated as competent reporters is consequential for the kind of interactional work done by the operators when inspecting the problem 'as presented'. In this sense, holding citizens accountable to some framework for reporting their problem is managed to maximize organizational access to events, for which the police can be made accountable (i.e. 'crime'), while also preserving the callers' (citizens') claims to competency for making such reports.

In most calls in the larger collection, citizens' claims for the police relevance of an incident are not problematic. In one sense, citizens are behavioural diagnosticians, and the problems they are reporting are not for diagnostic consultation *per se*, just a remedy. In fact, by calling the police, the caller is selecting the police as that remedy, as contrasted with (for example) vigilante justice. Thus, the reporting of an incident is preceded by some assessment of its relevance for the police (i.e. 'Is this a matter about which I should call the police?'). However, when such concern is expressed in the citizen's complaint to the police (i.e. in the call itself), that report is marked for its uncertainty, and the adequacy of the complaint's relevance is at stake.

But, it is precisely here that formulations are a resource for negotiating the adequacy of citizens' complaints. Where the police relevance of a call is marked as 'uncertain', it is the operator's work to manage that problem. On the other hand, where the reported problem is maximized (via expressions of concern or claims of seriousness), the operator's work is to test that maximization. In both extremes the operator assesses the police-worthiness of the complaint. Only when callers minimize the degree of assessment in their reported problem, is its 'facticity' for the conversation maximized, and not treated by operators as problematic.

The fine points of reporting 'problems' to the police (minimizing, maximizing, expressing concern, ownership, and sequential placement, etc.) is consequential for the assessment of a problem's police-worthiness, as well as for the operator's formulation of that problem (and its eventual status as a statistic). However, I am not suggesting that the caller's incompetence is producing the outcome. Rather, the suggestion is that citizens use these conversational features as resources to mark events which they themselves may question the police relevance of, offering them to the police operator for an assessment. These calls appear to work equally well in securing a police response. They may even be a way of securing a police response when the problem is not really police-worthy (as in 'they gotta go home and to bed').

Three points about police records and the statistics are raised by this analysis of citizen's calls. First, the fact that all of these calls resulted in a statistic regarding youth gangs cannot be overlooked. Calls such as the 'gang playing tag football under the new lights' are a clear case for arguing that taking the 'outcome' of the call to represent the problem as reported by the caller creates misinterpretations of police problems regarding gangs. Second, a turn-by-turn analysis of calls reveals the various practices of the police and the caller which provide a richer and more detailed understanding of how problems are constituted as 'gang' problems in the interaction. Third, this interactional achievement of the police and the caller in the call is a critical and consequential step in generating the record and statistic about 'gangs' and projects a particular organizational career for the incident at the patrol level.

The response by patrol

The patrol response, and the records generated therein, constitute further categorizations, negotiations and interpretations of a 'gang' incident. How this response can be analysed using interactional and record data is the focus of this section.

Patrol officers often encounter considerable ambiguity in determining the nature of the problem they are dispatched to handle. The citizen's description of the problem, which is encoded into some organizationally actionable, yet cryptic category by the operator (e.g. 'gang'), requires officers to interpret what that category 'means' in the context of the actual police response. The police task when responding to a call such as a 'gang' or group disturbing the neighbourhood is: (1) if possible, approach the area without being seen to 'find' and 'see for oneself' the reported problem; (2) determine if the behaviour constitutes a problem that requires police action; and (3) take some action. Officers then report to dispatch a 'code' that either confirms or disconfirms the original 'gang' categorization. They then record this disposition in their patrol logs. Each step entails important interpretative work by the police, as the next two examples illustrate.

Over this three-month period, the gang car made only one arrest and brought three drunks to the station house for protective custody. While the gang car was generating substantial statistics on gang activities, in most cases, the police were doing nothing more than 'brooming', a police term which means moving a group. Usually, a brooming results in the group moving to another corner, which the police consider a legitimate, if only a temporary, solution, hoping the next corner chosen by the group will not house a citizen who calls in a complaint. The problem is that standing on the corner is *not* illegal and while citizens frequently call to complain about it, there is little the police can do. Yet, if the calls continue, they create problems for the officer (Meehan 1992).

The following example illustrates the problem of evaluating 'what the citizen has called about' and deciding what the police can, or should, do about it. The caller reported there was a 'noisy gang playing a radio on top of the car which woke me up'. The officers approached the scene of the call unobtrusively and upon arrival could *not* 'hear' *loud* music. Three people (between 18 and 20 years old) were sitting on the hood of a car with a portable radio on top of it. The radio was playing, but not loudly. The officers had a brief discussion and then spoke to the group:

```
(11)    [Field Tape Number One]
Off 1:    Should I broom them or just let them
Off 2:    I don't know what do you think you wanna do anything?
Off 1:    They're not doing anything
          (3.0)
Off 2:    They're not doing anything ((we drive the car over to the group))
Off 2:    Somebody just called I don't know who it was but if we have to–if they call again, we'll
          have to make you move all right?
Cit:      okay
```

This example highlights a major problem for the police. As long as there are calls about a group, the police have to take some action, even if the police can see there is no problem. A key consideration is that the police can exert some control over the group, but not over the caller's behaviour.

In this example, the police don't hold the group accountable or responsible for the problem, but rather, it is the caller's problem. The officer's disposition, reported to the dispatcher and in his logs, was 'Seven Paul (7-p)' which indicates *for the record*, there was a 'gathering causing annoyance (outside)' and a 'service was rendered'. This disposition confirms the dispatcher's original categorization as a 'gang' call. The gang designation is interesting in light of the officers' judgement that the caller, not the group, is the problem. Was there a 'gathering causing annoyance?' Not really. The officers could have reported the disposition under one of the 'Adam' codes, which would have indicated the call was 'not a bona fide incident'. Given the comparison between the caller's report of a gang playing loud music, and the police assessment of the situation at the scene, the 'Adam' code would seem to have been appropriate in this case. However, by using the Seven Paul code and reporting services rendered, and not using the Adam code, the police contribute to the statistical database representing 'gang' problems that do not, in their own assessment, exist in this case.

By contrast, even when there were problems (e.g. loud, disturbing behaviour) caused by groups involved in illegal activities (such as drinking and/or smoking pot), the police would still 'broom' the group in an effort to displace the problem. For example, two calls to a public housing project within 20 minutes, resulted in 'brooming' a group the officers knew were responsible for making noise and drinking. In the first call, the caller reported a 'noisy gang on the roof drinking with a loud radio'. When we arrived, a group of five teenagers (ages 15–17) in the courtyard area had a radio playing loudly. One officer went up to the roof, the other instructed the kids to turn off the radio and to keep it off because it was bothering people in the apartments. When we returned the second time the caller reported that the 'gang' was still playing the radio, but when we arrived the radio had been turned off and the youths were milling about the courtyard. The following encounter ensued:

(12) [Field Tape Number One]
Off 2:   Hey, somebody keeps-somebody's calling on you guys what's the story
Kid 1:   HUH?
Off 2:   Somebody's calling. Were you making a lot of noise here or what?
Kid 1:   Nope!
Off 2:   Why don't you guys move okay so we don't have to come back here again all right?
Kid 2:   Yeah
Off 2:   Go around to the other corner ((kids begin to leave))
Off 2:   They must be smoking ((dope)), there's no bottles around
Off I :   They had some beer earlier I broke some upstairs
Off 2:   Was there?
Off 1:   I broke some on the roof-they had some Michelob -Lowenbrau, looked like I'm not sure maybe a six pack.

The disposition of this call was also Seven Paul. One methodological point of comparison about the officer's record work is relevant here. On the other 34 gang car shifts, Seven Paul was the disposition code in 75 per cent (n = 77) of the calls. The

Adam code, was only used once over the whole three-month period of the gang car programme. Thus, officers' general tendencies were to confirm 'gang' calls dispatched to them as 'gang' calls (see Meehan 2000 for further analysis).

Conclusion

The police are responsive to the political and organizational contexts which selected 'gangs' as a problem for the community. Certainly, the people of Corktown, as well as Bigcity, had their share of problems with young people who hang out on corners, make noise, drink and harass neighbours and engage in some criminal activity. 'Gangs' are real and not themselves an artifact of organizational recordkeeping practices. On the other hand, activities by groups that the police considered were 'real gangs' did not constitute a significant proportion of the incidents handled by the gang car but resulted nonetheless in official 'gang' statistics. Treating these gang statistics as reflecting actual gang activity reifies gangs to the point where a fiction *is* created: that 'gangs' and their activities are the primary source of trouble for the community the political organization can 'solve'. Indeed, it is *this* fiction that the recordkeeping practices can effectively create and manage. In this sense, the popularized conception of the gang problem is a complex artifact: the consequence of increasing police attention to the activities of young people in the community and of shifting definitions and perceptions of gangs in the community. As such, the 'gang' problem can only be examined through the various interactional and record-keeping practices that create this version of reality.

The recordkeeping practices of the police easily accommodate and manage the various political and organizational pressures brought to bear upon police officers. The management of documentary reality is an important competency and resource for any individual who is accountable to a bureaucracy. Social scientists tend to ignore this process and often approach the matter of their use of official statistics and police records with a *caveat emptor*, warning readers that a certain amount of 'measurement error' is attributable to organizational processes. But this is not enough. It is not solely an issue of measurement error, but rather that organizational features of policing, and other organizations, which can change from year to year, determine the incident count and records from which those statistics are derived. Social science research can fruitfully study those interactional and recordkeeping processes that constitute the careers of organizational statistics rather than treating statistics as standing in a correspondent relationship to the incidents they purport to represent.

Notes

1. In Bigcity, the 911 emergency number handles between 500,000 and 600,000 calls per year; an average of about 1,600 calls on any given day (24-hour period). The 911

emergency number receives calls from all parts of the city. Thus, there is no special operator for a particular section(s) of the city (including Corktown). Each call is automatically routed into a queuing system and the call is handled on a 'first come-first served' basis by the next available operator. The police telephone operators in Bigcity are trained civilians, whereas the dispatchers are sworn officers. All transcription symbols are taken from the transcription system developed by Gail Jefferson (see Schenkein 1978). All references to persons and places have been changed to preserve the anonymity of speakers.

2. I also rode with the gang car on eight other evenings and in terms of types of call and police response, the evening analysed in this chapter was representative of these other gang car shifts I observed. The Corktown gang car was fielded three evenings (Thursday–Saturday) per week in two, four-hour shifts with two patrol logs generated each evening. In patrol logs, officers record all calls for service assigned by dispatch in addition to other activities officers undertake on a given evening (e.g. routine patrol of parks, field interrogations).

········ References

Agar, Michael (1973) *Ripping and Running*. New York: Seminar Press.

Agar, M. and MacDonald, J. (1995) 'Focus groups and ethnography', *Human Organization*, 54(1): 78–86.

Alba, Richard D. and Reid, M. Golden (1986) 'Patterns of ethnic marriage in the United States', *Social Forces*, 65: 202–23.

Allen, Theodore (1997) *The Invention of the White Race*. Vol. 2: *The Origin of Racial Oppression in Anglo America*. London and New York: Verso.

Allistone, Simon (2002) 'A conversation analytic study of parents' evenings'. PhD dissertation, University of London, Goldsmiths' College.

Aptheker, Herbert (1992) *Anti-Racism in US History: The First Two Hundred Years*. New Hampshire: Greenwood.

Arminen, I. (1998) *Therapeutic Interaction: A Study of Mutual Help in the Meetings of Alcoholics Anonymous*. Helsinki: The Finnish Foundation of Alcohol Studies (Volume 45).

Arminen, I. and Leppo, A. (2000) 'The dilemma of two cultures in twelve-step treatment: professionals' responses to clients who act against their best interests', in M. Selzer et al. (eds), *Listening to the Welfare State*. Aldershot: Ashgate. pp. 183–212.

Armitage, L.K. (2001) 'Truth, falsity, and schemas of presentation: a textual analysis of Harold Garfinkel's story of Agnes', *Electronic Journal of Human Sexuality*, 4 (www.ejhs.org).

Asad, Talal (ed.) (1973) *Anthropology and the Colonial Encounter*. New York: Humanities Press.

Atkinson, J. Maxwell (1978) *Discovering Suicide: Studies in the Social Organization of Sudden Death*. London: Macmillan.

Atkinson, J. Maxwell (1982) 'Understanding formality: notes on the categorisation and production of "formal" interaction', *British Journal of Sociology*, 33: 86–117.

Atkinson, J. Maxwell (1984) *Our Masters' Voices*. London and New York: Methuen.

Atkinson, J. Maxwell and Drew, Paul (1979) *Order in Court: The Organization of Verbal Interaction in Judicial Settings*. London: Macmillan.

Atkinson, J. Maxwell and Heritage, John (eds) (1984) *Structures of Social Action: Studies in Conversation Analysis*. Cambridge: Cambridge University Press.

Atkinson, Paul (1990) *The Ethnographic Imagination: Textual Constructions of Reality*. London: Routledge.

Atkinson, Paul and Coffey, Amanda (1997) 'Analysing documentary realities', in D. Silverman (ed.), *Qualitative Research: Theory, Method and Practice*. London: Sage. pp. 45–62.

Atkinson, Paul, Coffey, Amanda, Delamont, Sara, Lofland, John and Lofland, Lyn (eds) (2001) *Handbook of Ethnography*. London: Sage.

Barbour, R. and Kitzinger, J. (eds) (1999) *Developing Focus Group Research: Politics, Theory and Practice*. London: Sage.

Barnes, Barry (1977) *Interests and the Growth of Knowledge*. London: Routledge and Kegan Paul.

Barron, Milton (1946) *People Who Intermarry*. New York: Syracuse University Press.

Beach, Wayne A. (1993) 'Transitional regulators for "casual" "okay" usages', *Journal of Pragmatics*, 19: 325–52.

Bell, Allan (1991) *The Language of News Media*. Oxford: Blackwell.

Bettelheim, Bruno (1977) *The Uses of Enchantment*. New York: Vintage Books.

Bhimji, Fazila (2001) 'Retrieving talk from the simple past and the present progressive on alternative radio', *Journal of Pragmatics*, 33: 545–69.

Biemer, P.P., Groves, R.M., Lyberg, L.E., Mathiowetz, N.A. and Sudman, S. (eds) (1991) *Measurement Errors in Surveys*. New York: John Wiley & Sons.

Bingham, W. and Moore, B. (1925) *How to Interview*. New York: Harper & Row.

Blaxter, M. (1983) 'The causes of disease: women talking', *Social Science and Medicine*, 17: 59–69.

Bloor, M., Frankland, J., Robson, K. and Thomas, M. (2001) *Focus Groups in Social Research*. London: Sage.

Blumer, Herbert (1969) *Symbolic Interactionism*. Englewood Cliffs, NJ: Prentice-Hall.

Boden, Dierdre and Zimmerman, Don H. (eds) (1991) *Talk and Social Structure: Studies in Ethnomethodology and Conversation Analysis*. Cambridge: Polity Press.

Bourdieu, Pierre (1990) *The Logic of Practice*. Stanford, CA: Stanford University Press.

Bourdieu, Pierre (1996) 'Understanding', *Theory, Culture & Society*, 13(2): 17–37.

Bourdieu, Pierre and Wacquant, Loic J.D. (1992) *An Invitation to Reflexive Sociology*. Chicago: University of Chicago Press.

Bowditch, Christine (1993) 'Getting rid of troublemakers: high school disciplinary procedures and the production of dropouts', *Social Problems*, 40(4): 493–509.

Boyd, Elizabeth (1998) 'Bureaucratic authority in the "company of equals": the interactional management of medical peer review', *American Sociological Review*, 63: 200–24.

Boyd, Elizabeth and Heritage, John (forthcoming) 'Taking the patient's personal history: questioning during verbal examination', in J. Heritage and D.W. Maynard (eds), *Communication in Medical Care: Interaction Between Physicians and Patients*. Cambridge: Cambridge University Press. Chapter 6.

Braun, V. (2000) 'Heterosexism in focus group research: collusion and challenge', *Feminism & Psychology*, 10(1): 133–40.

Braun, V. and Kitzinger, C. (2001a) 'Telling it straight? Dictionary definitions of women's genitals, 1989–1998', *Journal of Sociolinguistics*, 5(2): 214–32.

Braun, V. and Kitzinger, C. (2001b) 'The perfectible vagina: size matters', *Culture, Health and Sexuality*, 3(3): 263–77.

Braun, V. and Kitzinger, C. (2001c) '"Snatch", "hole" or "honeypot"? Semantic categories and the problem of non-specificity in female genital slang', *Journal of Sex Research*, 38(2): 146–58.

Briggs, Charles L. (1986) *Learning How to Ask: A Sociolinguistic Appraisal of the Role of the Interview in Social Science Research*. Cambridge: Cambridge University Press.

Bulmer, Martin (1984) *The Chicago School of Sociology: Institutionalisation, Diversity and the Rise of Sociological Research*. Chicago: University of Chicago Press.

Button, G. (1987) 'Answers as interactional products: two sequential practices used in interviews', *Social Psychology Quarterly*, 50: 160–71.

Cameron, D. (1997) 'Performing gender identity: young men's talk and the construction of heterosexual masculinity', in S. Johnson and U.H. Meinhof (eds), *Language and Masculinity*. Oxford: Blackwell. pp. 47–64.

Camic, Charles (1989) 'Structure after 50 years: the anatomy of a charter', *American Journal of Sociology*, 95(1): 38–107.

Camic, Charles (1995) 'Three departments in search of a discipline: localism and interdisciplinary interaction in American sociology, 1890–1940', *Social Research*, 62(4): 1003–33.

Cannell, Charles F., Lawson, S.A. and Hausser, D.L. (1975) *A Technique for Evaluating Interviewer Performance*. Ann Arbor, MI: Survey Research Center of the Institute for Social Research, University of Michigan.

Cannell, Charles F., Miller, P.V. and Oksenberg, Lois (1981) 'Research on interviewing techniques', in S. Leinhardt (ed.), *Sociological Methodology*, 12: 389–437.

Carey, M.A. and Smith, M.W. (1994) 'Capturing the group effect in focus groups: a special concern in analysis', *Qualitative Health Research*, 4(1): 123–7.

Chambliss, William J. (1994) 'Policing the ghetto underclass: the politics of law and law enforcement', *Social Problems*, 41(2): 177–95.

Channell, Joanna (1997) '"I just called to say I love you": love and desire on the telephone', in K. Harvey and C. Shalom (eds), *Language and Desire: Encoding Sex, Romance and Intimacy*. London: Routledge. pp. 143–69.

Chapoulie, Jean-Michel (1987) 'Everett C. Hughes and the development of fieldwork in sociology', *Urban Life and Culture*, 15(3/4): 259–98.

Charmaz, K. (2003) 'Grounded theory', in J.A. Smith (ed.), *Qualitative Psychology: A Practical Guide to Research Methods*. London and Thousand Oaks, CA : Sage. pp. 81–110.

Cicourel, Aaron V. (1963) *Method and Measurement in Sociology*. New York: The Free Press.

Cicourel, Aaron V. (1974) *Method and Measurement in a Study of Fertility in Argentina*. New York: John Wiley.

Clark, William A.V. (1996) 'Residential patterns: avoidance, assimilation and succession', in R. Waldinger and M. Bozorgmehr (eds), *Ethnic Los Angeles*. New York: Russell Sage Foundation. pp. 109–38.

Clayman, Steven E. (1988) 'Displaying neutrality in television news interviews', *Social Problems*, 35: 474–92.

Clayman, Steven E. (1992) 'Footing in the achievement of neutrality: the case of news interview discourse', in P. Drew and J. Heritage (eds), *Talk at Work: Interaction in Institutional Settings*. Cambridge: Cambridge University Press. pp. 163–98.

Clayman, Steven E. (1993) 'Booing: the anatomy of a disaffiliative response', *American Sociological Review*, 58: 110–30.

Clayman, Steven E. (2004) 'Arenas of interaction in the mediated public sphere', *Poetics*, 32: 29–49.

Clayman, Steven E. and Heritage, John (2002a) *The News Interview: Journalists and Public Figures on the Air*. Cambridge: Cambridge University Press.

Clayman, Steven E. and Heritage, John (2002b) 'Questioning presidents: journalistic deference and adversarialness in the press conferences of US Presidents Eisenhower and Reagan', *Journal of Communication*, 52(4): 749–75.

Clayman, Steven E., Elliott, Marc, Heritage, John and McDonald, Laurie (forthcoming) 'Historical trends in questioning presidents 1953–2000', *Presidential Studies Quarterly*.

Clifford, James and Marcus, George E. (eds) (1986) *Writing Culture: The Poetics and Politics of Ethnography*. Berkeley: University of California Press.

Cohen, Stan and Taylor, Laurie (1972) *Psychological Survival: The Experience of Long-term Imprisonment*. Harmondsworth: Penguin.

Collins, Harry M. (1985) *Changing Order: Replication and Induction in Scientific Practice*. London: Sage. (2nd edn, 1992, Chicago: University of Chicago Press).

Collins, Harry M. and Yearley, Stephen (1992) 'Epistemological chicken', in Andrew Pickering (ed.), *Science as Practice and Culture*. Chicago: University of Chicago Press. pp. 301–26.

Collins, Randall (1981) 'On the microfoundations of macrosociology', *American Journal of Sociology*, 86(5): 984–1014.

Colmenares, F. (1991) 'Greeting behaviour between male baboons: oestrus females, rivalry, and negotiation', *Animal Behaviour*, 41: 49–60.

Conley, T.D., Devine, P., Rabow, J. and Evett, S. (2002) 'Gay mens' and lesbians' experiences in and expectations for interactions with heterosexuals', *Journal of Homosexuality*, 44: 83–109.

Corner, John (1991) 'The interview as a social encounter', in Paddy Scannell (ed.), *Broadcast Talk*. London: Sage. pp. 31–47.

Cradock, Robert M., Maynard, Douglas W. and Schaeffer, Nora Cate (1993) 'Re-opening closed questions: elaborations on categorical answers in standardized interviews', Center for Demography and Ecology Working Paper. Madison, WI: University of Wisconsin. pp. 93–124.

Crawford, M. (1995) *Talking Difference: On Gender and Language*. London: Sage.

Crester, Gary A. and Leon, Joseph J. (1982) 'Intermarriage in the US: an overview of theory and research', *Marriage and Family Review*, 5(1): 3–15.

Curry, G. David, Ball, Richard A., Decker, Scott H. (1996) 'Estimating the national scope of gang crime from law enforcement data', in C.R. Huff (ed.), *Gangs in America*. (2nd edn). Thousand Oaks, CA: Sage. pp. 21–38.

Dansiger, Kurt (1990) *Constructing the Subject: Historical Origins of Psychological Research*. Cambridge: Cambridge University Press.

Davidson, Jeanette R. (1991) 'Black–white interracial marriage: a critical look at theories about motivations of the partners', *Journal of Intergroup Relations*, 18(4): 14–19.

de Waal, F. (1996) *Good Natured: The Origins of Right and Wrong in Humans and Other Animals*. Cambridge, MA: Harvard University Press.

Decker, Scott and Kempf-Leonard, Kimberly (1991) 'Constructing gangs: the social definition of youth activities', *Criminal Justice Policy Review*, 5(4): 271–91.

Denzin, Norman K. (1990) 'Harold and Agnes: a feminist narrative undoing', *Sociological Theory*, 8: 198–216.

Denzin, Norman K. (1993) *The Alcoholic Society*. New Brunswick, NJ: Transaction.

Denzin, Norman K. and Lincoln, Yvonne S. (eds) (1994) *Handbook of Qualitative Research*. Thousand Oaks, CA: Sage.

DeVault, Marjorie L. (1999) *Liberating Method: Feminism and Social Research*. Philadelphia: Temple University Press.

Dijkstra, Wil and Ongena, Yfke (2004) 'Question–answer sequences in survey interviews', Unpublished manuscript. Department of Social Research Methodology, Free University, Amsterdam.

Douglas, J. (1967) *The Social Meanings of Suicide*. Princeton, NJ: Princeton University Press.

Drew, Paul (1978) 'Accusations: the use of members' knowledge of "religious geography" in describing events', *Sociology*, 12: 1–22.

Drew, Paul (1984) 'Speakers' reportings in invitation sequences', in J.M. Atkinson and J. Heritage (eds), *Structures of Social Action: Studies in Conversation Analysis*. Cambridge: Cambridge University Press. pp. 152–64.

Drew, Paul (1990) 'Strategies in the contest between lawyers and witnesses in court examinations', in J.N. Levi and A.G. Walker (eds), *Language in the Judicial Process*. New York: Plenum Press. pp. 39–64.

Drew, Paul (1992) 'Contested evidence in courtroom cross-examination: the case of a trial for rape', in P. Drew and J. Heritage (eds), *Talk at Work: Interaction in Institutional Settings*. Cambridge: Cambridge University Press. pp. 470–520.

Drew, Paul (1994) 'Conversation analysis', in R.E. Asher and J.M.Y. Simpson (eds), *The Encyclopaedia of Language and Linguistics* (Vol. 2). Oxford: Pergamon Press. pp. 749–54.

Drew, Paul (2003) 'Conversation analysis', in J.A. Smith (ed.), *Qualitative Psychology: A Practical Guide to Research Methods*. London and Thousand Oaks, CA : Sage. pp. 132–58.

Drew, Paul (forthcoming) 'Mis-alignments in "after-hours" calls to a British GP's practice: a study in telephone medicine', in J. Heritage and D.W. Maynard (eds), *Communication in Medical Care: Interaction Between Physicians and Patients*. Cambridge: Cambridge University Press. Chapter 14.

Drew, Paul and Heritage, John (eds) (1992a) *Talk at Work: Interaction in Institutional Settings*. Cambridge: Cambridge University Press.

Drew, Paul and Heritage, John (1992b) 'Analyzing talk at work: an introduction', in P. Drew and J. Heritage (eds), *Talk at Work: Interaction in Institutional Settings*. Cambridge: Cambridge University Press. pp. 3–65.

Duranti, Alessandro (1992) 'Language and bodies in social space: Samoan ceremonial greetings', *American Anthropologist*, 94: 657–91.

Duranti, Alessandro (1997) *Linguistic Anthropology*. Cambridge: Cambridge University Press.

Durkheim, Emile (1952 [1897]) *Suicide: A Study in Sociology*. London: Routledge and Kegan Paul.

Easterday, L., Papademas, D., Schorr, L. and Valentine, C. (1977) 'The making of a female researcher: role problems in field work', *Urban Life*, 6(3): 333–48.

Edwards, D. (1995) ' Two to tango: script formulations, dispositions and rhetorical symmetry in relationship troubles talk', *Research and Social Interaction*, 28(4):319–50.

Edwards, D. and Potter, J. (1992) *Discursive Psychology*. London: Sage.

Ehrlich, S. (2003) 'Coercing gender: language in sexual assault adjudication processes', in J. Holmes and M. Meyerhoff (eds), *The Handbook of Language and Gender*. Oxford: Blackwell. pp. 645–70.

Ellis, S. and Kitzinger, C. (2002) 'Denying equality: an analysis of arguments against lowering the age of consent for sex between men', *Journal of Community and Social Psychology*, 12: 167–80.

Emerson, Robert M. (1991) 'Case processing and interorganizational knowledge: detecting the "real reasons" for referrals', *Social Problems*, 38(2): 198–212.

Emerson, Robert M. (ed.) (2001) *Contemporary Field Research: Perspectives and Formulations* (2nd edn). Prospect Heights, IL: Waveland Press.

Emerson, Robert M., Fretz, Rachel I. and Shaw, Linda L. (1995) *Writing Ethnographic Fieldnotes*. Chicago: University of Chicago Press.

Espin, O.M. (1995) '"Race", racism and sexuality in the life narratives of immigrant women', *Feminism & Psychology*, 5: 223–38.

Fairclough, Norman (1995) *Media Discourse*. London: Edward Arnold.

Feagin, Joe R. and Vera, Hernan (1995) *White Racism*. New York: Routledge.

Feinberg, P.H. (1990) 'Circular questions: establishing the relational context', *Family Systems Medicine*, 8(3): 273–7.

Fern, E.F. (2001) *Advanced Focus Group Research*. Thousand Oaks, CA: Sage.

Fielding, N. and Thomas, H. (2001) 'Qualitative Interviewing' in G.N. Gilbert (ed.) *Researching Social Life* (2nd edn). London and Thousand Oaks, CA: Sage. pp. 123–44.

Fine, Gary Alan (1991) 'On the macrofoundations of microsociology: constraint and the exterior reality of structure', *Sociological Quarterly*, 32(2): 161–77.

Finestone, Harold (1957) 'Cats, kicks, and color', *Social Problems*, 5(1): 3–13.

Flaskerud, J.H. and Rush, C.E. (1989) 'AIDS and traditional health beliefs and practices of black women', *Nursing Research*, 38(4): 210–15.

Fleuridas, C., Nelson, T.S. and Rosenthal, D.M. (1986) 'The evolution of circular questions: training family therapists', *Journal of Marital and Family Therapy*, 12(2): 113–27.

Fowler, Jr., Roger, Mangione, Floyd J. and Mangione, Thomas W. (1990) *Standardized Survey Interviewing: Minimizing Interviewer-Related Error*. Newbury Park, CA: Sage.

Fowler, Roger, Hodge, Bob, Kress, Gunther and Trew, Tony (1979) *Language and Control*. London: Routledge and Kegan Paul.

Frank, Jerome D. and Frank, Julia B. (1991) *Persuasion and Healing*. Baltimore, MD: Johns Hopkins University Press.

Frankel, Richard (1990) 'Talking in interviews: a dispreference for patient initiated questions in physician–patient encounters', in G. Psathas (ed.), *Interaction Competence*. Lanham, MD: University Press of America. pp. 231–62.

Frankenberg, Ruth (1992) *The Social Construction of Whiteness: White Women, Race Matters*. Minneapolis: University of Minnesota.

Fu, Vincent Kang (2001) 'Racial intermarriage patterns', *Demography*, 38: 147–59.

Gagnon, J. (1977) *Human Sexuality*. New York: Scott, Foresman and Co.

Gamson, J. (1998) *Freaks Talk Back: Tabloid Talk Shows and Sexual Non-conformity*. Chicago: University of Chicago Press.

Gans, Herbert (1979) 'Symbolic ethnicity: the future of ethnic groups and cultures in America', *Ethnic and Racial Studies*, 2: 1–20.

Garfinkel, Harold (1967a) *Studies in Ethnomethodology*. Englewood Cliffs, NJ: Prentice-Hall. (2nd edn, 1984.)

Garfinkel, Harold (1967b) 'Passing and the managed achievement of sexual status in an intersexed person, part 1', in H. Garfinkel, *Studies in Ethnomethodology*. Englewood Cliffs, NJ: Prentice-Hall. pp. 116–85.

Garfinkel, Harold (1988) 'Evidence for locally produced, naturally accountable phenomena of order, logic, reason, meaning, method, etc. in and as of the essential quiddity of immortal ordinary society (I of IV): an announcement of studies', *Sociological Theory*, 6: 103–9.

Garfinkel, Harold (1991) 'Respecification: evidence for locally produced, naturally accountable phenomena of order, logic, reason, meaning, method, etc. in and as of essential haecceity of immortal ordinary society: an announcement of studies', in G. Button (ed.), *Ethnomethodology and the Human Sciences*. Cambridge: Cambridge University Press. pp. 10–19.

Garfinkel, Harold (2002) *Ethnomethodology's Program: Working Out Durkheim's Aphorism*. Lanham, MD: Rowman & Littlefield.

Garfinkel, Harold, Lynch, Michael and Livingston, Eric (1981) 'The work of a discovering science construed with materials from the optically discovered pulsar', *Philosophy of the Social Sciences*, 11: 131–58.

Gavey, N. (1989) 'Feminist poststructuralism and discourse analysis: contributions to feminist psychology', *Psychology Women Quaterly*, 13: 459–75.

Gibson, James J. (1979) *The Ecological Approach to Visual Perception*. Boston: Houghton Mifflin.

Giddens, Anthony (1984) *The Constitution of Society*. Berkeley: University of California Press.

Gilbert, G. Nigel and Mulkay, Michael (1984) *Opening Pandora's Box: A Sociological Analysis of Scientists' Discourse*. Cambridge: Cambridge University Press.

Gill, Virginia and Maynard, Douglas W. (1995) 'On "labeling" in actual interaction: delivering and receiving diagnoses of developmental disabilities', *Social Problems*, 42(1): 11–37.

Glaser, B.G. and Strauss, A.L. (1967) *The Discourse of Grounded Theory*. Chicago: Aldine.

Goffman, Erving (1955) 'On face-work: an analysis of ritual elements in social interaction', *Psychiatry: Journal of Interpersonal Relations*, 18: 213–31.

Goffman, Erving (1967) *Interaction Ritual: Essays in Face to Face Behavior*. Garden City, NY: Doubleday.

Goffman, Erving (1971) *Relations in Public: Microstudies of the Public Order*. New York: Harper & Row.

Goffman, Erving (1979) *Gender Advertisements*. Cambridge, MA: Harvard University Press.

Goffman, Erving (1981a) *Forms of Talk*. Oxford: Basil Blackwell.

Goffman, Erving (1981b) 'Footing', in E. Goffman, *Forms of Talk*. Oxford: Basil Blackwell. pp. 124–59.

Goffman, Erving (1983) 'The interaction order', *American Sociological Review*, 48: 1–17.

Goodwin, Charles (1994) 'Professional vision', *American Anthropologist*, 96: 606–33.

Goodwin, Charles (2000) 'Action and embodiment within situated human interaction', *Journal of Pragmatics*, 32: 1489–522.

Gordon, T., Holland, J. and Lahelma, E. (2000) *Making Spaces: Citizenship and Difference in Schools*. London: Macmillan.

Gossett, Thomas F. (1965) *Race: The History of an Idea in America*. New York: Schoken.

Gough, B. (1998) 'Men and the discursive reproduction of sexism: repertoires of difference and equality', *Feminism & Psychology*, 8(1): 25–50.

Greatbatch, David (1988) 'A turn-taking system for British news interviews', *Language in Society*, 17(3): 401–30.

Greatbatch, David (1992) 'The management of disagreement between news interviewees', in P. Drew and J. Heritage (eds), *Talk at Work: Interaction in Institutional Settings*. Cambridge: Cambridge University Press. pp. 268–301.

Green, G., Barbour, R.S., Barnard, M. and Kitzinger, J. (1993) '"Who wears the trousers?": sexual harassment in research settings', *Women's Studies International Forum*, 16(6): 627–37.

Grindstaff, Laura (2002) *The Money Shot: Trash, Class, and the making of TV Talk Shows*. Chicago: University of Chicago Press.

Groves, Robert M. (1989) *Survey Errors and Survey Costs*. New York: John Wiley.

Gubrium, Jaber F. (1992) *Out of Control*. Newbury Park, CA: Sage.

Gubrium, Jaber F. and Holstein, James A. (1997) *The New Language of Qualitative Method*. New York: Oxford University Press.

Gubrium, Jaber F. and Holstein, James A. (1999) 'At the border of narrative and ethnography', *Journal of Contemporary Ethnography*, 28(5): 561–73.

Gurney, J.N. (1985) 'Not one of the guys: the female researcher in a male-dominated setting', *Qualitative Sociology*, 8(1): 42–62.

Hacking, Ian (1990) *The Taming of Chance*. Cambridge: Cambridge University Press.

Hak, Tony (2002) 'How interviewers make coding decisions', in D. Maynard et al. (eds), *Standardization and Tacit Knowledge: Interaction and Practice in the Survey Interview*. New York: Wiley Interscience. pp. 449–69.

Hallin, Daniel C. and Mancini, Paolo (1984) 'Speaking of the President: political structure and representational form in US and Italian television news', *Theory and Society*, 13: 829–50.

Hammersley, Martyn (1989) *The Dilemma of Qualitative Method: Herbert Blumer and the Chicago Tradition*. London: Routledge.

Hammersley, Martyn and Atkinson, Paul (1983) *Ethnography: Principles in Practice*. London: Tavistock. (2nd edn, 1995, Routledge.)

Hanson, Norwood R. (1958) *Patterns of Discovery*. Cambridge: Cambridge University Press.

Harding, Sandra (1991) *Whose Science? Whose Knowledge?: Thinking from Women's Lives*. Ithaca, NY: Cornell University Press.

Harris, Sandra (1986) 'Interviewers' questions in broadcast interviews', *Belfast Working Papers in Language and Linguistics* (Vol. 8). Edited by John Wilson and Brian Crow. Jordanstown: University of Ulster. pp. 50–85.

Harris, Sandra (1991) 'Evasive action: how politicians respond to questions in political interviews', in P. Scannell (ed.), *Broadcast Talk*. London: Sage. pp. 76–99.

Heath, Christian (1986) *Body Movement and Speech in Medical Interaction*. Cambridge: Cambridge University Press.

Heath, Christian (1992) 'The delivery and reception of diagnosis in the general practice consultation', in P. Drew and J. Heritage (eds), *Talk at Work: Interaction in Institutional Settings*. Cambridge: Cambridge University Press. pp. 235–67.

Heath, Christian and Luff, Paul (2000) *Technology in Action*. Cambridge: Cambridge University Press.

Heritage, John (1984a) 'A change-of-state token and aspects of its sequential placement', in J.M. Atkinson and J. Heritage (eds), *Structures of Social Interaction: Studies in Conversation Analysis*. Cambridge: Cambridge University Press. pp. 299–345.

Heritage, John (1984b) *Garfinkel and Ethnomethodology*. Cambridge: Polity Press.

Heritage, John (1985) 'Analyzing news interviews: aspects of the production of talk for an overhearing audience', in T.A. van Dijk (ed.), *Handbook of Discourse Analysis*, Vol. 3. New York: Academic Press. pp. 95–119.

Heritage, John (1988) 'Explanations as accounts: a conversation analytic perspective', in C. Antaki (ed.), *Analysing Everyday Explanations: A Casebook of Methods*. London: Sage. pp. 127–44.

Heritage, John (1997) 'Conversation analysis and institutional talk: analyzing data', in D. Silverman (ed.), *Qualitative Analysis: Issues of Theory and Method*. London: Sage. pp. 161–82.

Heritage, John (2002a) 'Ad hoc inquiries: two preferences in the design of "routine" questions in an open context', in D. Maynard et al. (eds), *Standardization and Tacit Knowledge: Interaction and Practice in the Survey Interview*. New York: Wiley Interscience. pp. 313–33.

Heritage, John (2002b) 'The limits of questioning: negative interrogatives and hostile question content', *Journal of Pragmatics*, 34: 1427–46.

Heritage, John and Greatbatch, David (1986) 'Generating applause: a study of rhetoric and response at party political conferences', *American Journal of Sociology*, 92: 110–57.

Heritage, John and Greatbatch, David (1991) 'On the institutional character of institutional talk: the case of news interviews', in D. Boden and D.H. Zimmerman (eds), *Talk and Social Structure: Studies in Ethnomethodology and Conversation Analysis*. Cambridge: Polity Press. pp. 93–137.

Heritage, J. and Lindström, A. (1998) 'Motherhood, medicine and morality: scenes from a medical encounter', *Research on Language and Social Interaction*, 31(3/4): 397–438.

Heritage, J. and Maynard, D.W. (eds) (2006) *The Communication in Medical Care: Interaction Between Primary Care Physicians and Patients*. Cambridge: Cambridge University Press.

Heritage, John and Raymond, Geoffrey (forthcoming) 'The terms of agreement: indexing epistemic authority and subordination in assessment sequences', *Social Psychology Quarterly*.

Heritage, John and Roth, Andrew (1995) 'Grammar and institution: questions and questioning in the broadcast news interview', *Research on Language and Social Interaction*, 28(1): 1–60.

Heritage, John and Watson, D. Rod (1979) 'Formulations as conversational objects', in George Psathas (ed.), *Everyday Language: Studies in Ethnomethodology*. New York: Irvington. pp. 123–62.

Herskovitz, Melville (1947) *Man and his Works*. New York: Alfred Knopf.

Hilbert, R.A. (1991) 'Norman and Sigmund: comments on Denzin's "Harold and Agnes"', *Sociological Theory*, 9(2): 264–8.

Hoffman, L. (1981) *Foundations of Family Therapy: A Conceptual Framework for Systems Change*. New York: Basic Books.

Houghton, S., Durkin, K. and Carroll, A. (1995) 'Children's and adolescents' awareness of the physical and mental health risks associated with tattooing: a focus group study', *Adolescence*, 30(120): 971–87.

Houtkoop-Steenstra, Hanneke (2000) *Interaction and the Standardized Survey Interview: The Living Questionnaire*. Cambridge: Cambridge University Press.

Hughes, D. and DuMont, K. (1993) 'Using focus groups to facilitate culturally-anchored research', *American Journal of Community Psychology*, 21(6): 775–806.

Hughes, Everett C. (1971) 'Going concerns: the study of American institutions', in D. Riesman and H. Becker (eds), *The Sociological Eye*. New Chicago: Aldine. pp. 52–64.

Hutchby, Ian (1996) *Confrontation Talk: Arguments, Asymmetries, and Power in Talk Radio*. Mahwah, NJ: Lawrence Erlbaum.

Hutchby, Ian (1999) 'Frame attunement and footing in the organization of talk radio', *Journal of Sociolinguistics*, 3(1): 41–63.

Hutchby, Ian and Wooffitt, Robin (1998) *Conversation Analysis: Principles, Practices and Applications*. Cambridge: Polity Press.

Hyman, H.A., Feldman, J. and Stember, C. (1975 [1954]) *Interviewing in Social Research*. Chicago: University of Chicago Press.

Irvine, J. (1974) 'Strategies of status manipulation in the Wolof greeting', in R. Bauman and J. Sherzer (eds), *Explorations in the Ethnography of Speaking*. Cambridge: Cambridge University Press. pp. 167–91.

Jacobs, Jerry (1967) 'A phenomenological study of suicide notes', *Social Problems*, 15: 60–72.

Jarrett, R.L. (1993) 'Focus group interviewing with low-income minority populations: a research experience', in D.L. Morgan (ed.), *Successful Focus Groups: Advancing the State of the Art*. Newbury Park, CA: Sage. pp. 184–201.

Jefferson, Gail (1973) 'A case of precision timing in ordinary conversation: overlapped tag-positioned address terms in closing sequences', *Semiotica*, 9: 47–96.

Jefferson, Gail (1974) 'Error correction as an interactional resource', *Language in Society*, 2: 181–99.

Jefferson, Gail (1978) 'What's in a "Nyem"?', *Sociology*, 12(1): 135–9.

Jefferson, Gail (1981) 'The abominable "Ne?"': a working paper exploring the phenomenon of post-response pursuit of response', Occasional Paper No. 6, Department of Sociology, University of Manchester, Manchester.

Jefferson, Gail (1990) 'List construction as a task and resource', in G. Psathas (ed.), *Interaction Competence*. Lanham, MD: University Press of America. pp. 63–93.

Jefferson, Gail, Sacks, Harvey and Schegloff, Emanuel A. (1987) 'Notes on laughter in the pursuit of intimacy', in G. Button and J.R.E. Lee (eds), *Talk and Social Organisation*. Clevedon: Multilingual Matters. pp. 152–205.

Johnson, A. (1996) '"It's good to talk": the focus group and the sociological imagination', *The Sociological Review*, 44(3): 517–38.

Jucker, Andreas (1986) *News Interviews: A Pragmalinguistic Analysis*. Amsterdam: John Benjamins.

Jupp, Victor and Norris, Clive (1993) 'Traditions in documentary analysis', in M. Hammersley (ed.), *Social Research: Philosophy, Politics and Practice*. London: Sage. pp. 37–51.

Kahn, Robert L. and Cannell, Charles F. (1957) *The Dynamics of Interviewing: Theory, Technique, and Cases*. New York: Wiley.

Katz, Jack (1988) *Seductions of Crime*. New York: Basic Books.

Katz, Jack (2001) 'From how to why: on luminous description and causal inference in ethnography (Part I)', *Ethnography*, 2(4): 443–73.

Katz, Jack (2002) 'From how to why: on luminous description and causal inference in ethnography (Part 2)', *Ethnography*, 3(1): 63–90.

Kendon, A. (1990) *Conducting Interaction: Patterns of Behavior in Focused Encounters*. Cambridge: Cambridge University Press.

Kernell, Samuel (1986) *Going Public: New Strategies of Presidential Leadership*. Washington: CQ Press.

Kinsey, A.C., Pomeroy, W. and Martin, C. (1948) *Sexual Behavior in the Human Male*. Philadelphia: Saunders.

Kinsey, A.C., Pomeroy, W., Martin, C. and Gebhard (1953) *Sexual Behavior in the Human Female*. Philadelphia: Saunders.

Kissling, E.A. (1996) 'Bleeding out loud: communication about menstruation', *Feminism & Psychology*, 6: 481–504.

Kitzinger, Celia (2000) 'Doing feminist conversation analysis', *Feminism & Psychology*, 10: 163–93.

Kitzinger, Celia (2004) 'Feminist approaches', in C. Seale et al. (eds), *Qualitative Research Practice*. London: Sage. pp. 125–40.

Kitzinger, Celia (2005a) 'Speaking as a heterosexual: (how) does sexuality matter for talk-in-interaction', *Research on Language and Social Interaction*, 38(3).

Kitzinger, Celia (2005b) 'Heteronormativity in action: reproducing the heterosexual nuclear family in after-hours medical calls', *Social Problems*, 52: 477–498.

Kitzinger, Celia and Frith, H. (1999) 'Just say no? The use of conversation analysis in developing a feminist perspective on sexual refusal', *Discourse and Society*, 10(3): 293–316.

Kitzinger, Celia and Peel, E.A. (2005) 'The de-gaying and re-gaying of AIDS: contested homophobias in lesbian and gay awareness training', *Discourse and Society*, 16(2): 173–97.

Kitzinger, J. (1990) 'Audience understanding of AIDS media messages: a discussion of methods', *Sociology of Health and Illness*, 12: 319–55.

Kitzinger, J. (1994) 'The methodology of focus groups: the importance of interaction between research participants', *Sociology of Health and Illness*, 16: 103–21.

Klein, Malcolm (1995) *The American Street Gang*. New York: Oxford University Press.

Klienman, Arthur (1988) *Rethinking Psychiatry*. New York: The Free Press.

Komter, Martha (2003) 'The interactional dynamics of eliciting a confession in a Dutch police interrogation', *Research on Language and Social Interaction*, 36(4): 433–70.

Kozol, Jonathon (1991) *Savage Inequalities: Children in America's Schools*. New York: Harper Collins.

Krueger, R.A. (1994) *Focus Groups: A Practical Guide for Applied Research* (2nd edn). Newbury Park, CA: Sage.

Krueger, R.A. and Casey, M.A. (2000) *Focus Groups: A Practical Guide for Applied Research* (3rd edn). Thousand Oaks, CA: Sage.

Kuhn, Thomas S. (1962) *The Structure of Scientific Revolutions*. Chicago: University of Chicago Press.

Kuklick, Henrietta (1991) *The Savage Within: The Social History of British Anthropology, 1885–1945*. Cambridge: Cambridge University Press.

Labov, William and Fanshel, David (1977) *Therapeutic Discourse*. New York: Academic Press.

Lakoff, G. and Johnson, M. (1980) *Metaphors We Live By*. Chicago: University of Chicago Press.

Land, V. and Kitzinger, C. (2005) 'Speaking as a lesbian: correcting the heterosexist presumption', *Research on Language and Social Interaction*, 38(4): 371–416.

Latour, Bruno and Woolgar, Steve (1979) *Laboratory Life: The Social Construction of Scientific Facts*. London: Sage.

Lave, J. and Wenger, E. (1991) *Situated Learning: Legitimate Peripheral Participation*. Cambridge: Cambridge University Press.

Lavin, Danielle and Maynard, Douglas W. (2001) 'Standardization vs. rapport: respondent laughter and interviewer reaction during telephone surveys', *American Sociological Review*, 66: 453–79.

Lea, S. and Auburn, T. (2001) 'The social construction of rape in the talk of a convicted rapist', *Feminism & Psychology*, 11(1): 11–34.

Lieberson, Stanley (1981) *A Piece of the Pie: Black and White Immigrants since 1880*. Berkeley: University of California Press.

Lucy, John A. (1992) *Language Diversity and Thought*. Cambridge: Cambridge University Press.

Lupton, D. (1998) 'Talking about sex: sexology, sexual difference and confessional talk shows', *Genders*, 20: 45–65.

Lynch, Michael (1991) 'Method: measurement – ordinary and scientific measurement as ethnomethodolgical phenomena', in G. Button (ed.), *Ethnomethodology and the Human Sciences*. Cambridge: Cambridge University Press. pp. 77–108.

Lynch, Michael (1993) *Scientific Practice and Ordinary Action: Ethnomethodology and Social Studies of Science*. Cambridge: Cambridge University Press.

Lynch, Michael (2002) 'The living text: written instructions and situated actions in telephone surveys', in D. Maynard et al. (eds), *Standardization and Tacit Knowledge: Interaction and Practice in the Survey Interview*. New York: Wiley Interscience. pp. 125–50.

Lyons, R.F. and Meade, L.D. (1993) 'The energy crisis: mothers with chronic illness', *Canadian Woman Studies/Les Cahiers de la Femme*, 13(4): 34–7.

Macdonald, Keith (2001) 'Using documents', in N. Gilbert (ed.), *Researching Social Life*. London: Sage. pp. 194–210.

Macfarlane, Robert (2003) *Mountains of the Mind*. London: Granta Books.

Macnaghten, P. and Myers, G. (2004) 'Focus groups', in C. Seale et al. (eds), *Qualitative Research Practice*. London: Sage. pp. 65–79.

Mannheim, Karl (1936) *Ideology and Utopia*. New York: Harvest Books.

Manning, Peter K. (1997) *Police Work: The Social Organization of Policing* (2nd edn). Prospect Heights, IL: Waveland Press.

Margolin, Leslie (1992) 'Deviance on record: techniques for labeling child abusers in official documents', *Social Problems*, 39(1): 58–70.

Marquis, K.H., Cannell, Charles F. and Laurent, A. (1972) 'Reporting health events in household interviews: effects of reinforcement, question length, and reinterviews', in *Vital and Health Statistics: Data Evaluation and Methods Research Series 2, No. 45*. Rockville, MD: US Department of Health and Human Services.

Martinez, Esperanza Rama (2003) *Talk on Television: The Interactional Organization of Three Broadcast Genres*. Vigo: Universidade de Vigo.

Massey, Douglas and Denton, Nancy (1993) *American Apartheid*. Cambridge, MA: Harvard University Press.

Masters, W.H. and Johnson, V.E. (1966) *Human Sexual Response*. Boston: Little, Brown & Co.

Mauksch, L.B. and Roesler, T. (1990) 'Expanding the context of the patient's explanatory model using circular questioning', *Family Systems Medicine*, 8(1): 3–13.

Maynard, Douglas W. (1988a) 'Language, interaction and social problems', *Social Problems*, 35(4): 311–34.

Maynard, Douglas W. (1998b) 'Praising versus blaming the messenger: moral issues in deliveries of good and bad news', *Research on Language and Social Interaction*, 31: 359–95.

Maynard, Douglas W. and Marlaire, Courtney L. (1992) 'Good reasons for bad testing performance: the interactional substrate of educational exams', *Qualitative Sociology*, 15: 177–202.

Maynard, Douglas W. and Schaeffer, Nora Cate (2000) 'Toward a sociology of social scientific knowledge: survey research and ethnomethodology's asymmetric alternates', *Social Studies of Science*, 30: 323–70.

Maynard, Douglas W. and Schaeffer, Nora Cate (2002a) 'Refusal conversion and tailoring', in D. Maynard et al. (eds), *Standardization and Tacit Knowledge: Interaction and Practice in the Survey Interview*. New York: Wiley Interscience. pp. 219–39.

Maynard, Douglas W. and Schaeffer, Nora Cate (2002b) 'Standardization and its discontents', in D. Maynard et al. (eds), *Standardization and Tacit Knowledge: Interaction and Practice in the Survey Interview*. New York: Wiley Interscience. pp. 3–45.

Maynard, Douglas W., Houtkoop-Steenstra, H., Schaeffer, N.C. and Zouwen, J. van der (eds) (2002) *Standardization and Tacit Knowledge: Interaction and Practice in the Survey Interview*. New York: Wiley Interscience.

McCorkle, Richard C. and Miethe, Terance D. (1998) 'The political and organizational response to gangs: an examination of a "moral panic" in Nevada', *Justice Quarterly*, 15(1): 50–64.

Mead, George Herbert (1923) 'Scientific method and the moral sciences', in *International Journal of Ethics*, 23: 229–47.

Meehan, Albert J. (1986) 'Recordkeeping practices in the policing of juveniles', *Urban Life*, 15(1): 70–102.

Meehan, Albert J. (1989) 'Assessing the "policeworthiness" of citizen's complaints to the police: accountability and the negotiation of "facts"', in D.T. Helm et al. (eds), *The International Order: New Directions in the Study of Social Order*. New York: Irvington pp. 116–40.

Meehan, Albert J. (1992) '"I don't prevent crime, I prevent calls": policing as negotiated order', *Symbolic Interaction*, 15(4): 455–80.

Meehan, Albert J. (1993) 'Internal police records and the control of juveniles: politics and policing in a suburban town', *British Journal of Criminology*, 33(4): 504–24.

Meehan, Albert J. (2000) 'The organizational career of gang statistics: the politics of policing gangs', *Sociological Quarterly*, 41(3): 337–70.

Mehan, Hugh (1979) *Learning Lessons*. Cambridge, MA: Harvard University Press.

Mehan, Hugh, Hertweck, Alma and Meihls, J. Lee (1986) *Handicapping the Handicapped: Decision-making in Students' Educational Careers*. Stanford, CA: Stanford University Press.

Merton, Robert K. (1970 [1938]) *Science, Technology and Society in Seventeenth-century England* (2nd edn). New York: Harper & Row.

Merton, Robert K. (1941) 'Intermarriage and social structure: fact and theory', *Psychiatry*, 4: 361–74.

Miller, Gale (1997) *Becoming Miracle Workers*. Hawthorne, NY: Aldine de Gruyter.

Miller, P.V. and Cannell, Charles F. (1982) 'A study of experimental techniques for telephone interviewing', *Public Opinion Quarterly*, 46: 250–69.

Mills, C. Wright (1940) 'Situated action and vocabularies of motive', *American Sociological Review*, 5: 904–13.

Mirowski, Philip (2001) *Machine Dreams Economics Becomes a Cyborg Science*. Cambridge: Cambridge University Press.

Mishler, Elliot G. (1986) *Research Interviewing: Context and Narrative*. Cambridge, MA: Harvard University Press.

Monahan, Thomas P. (1976) 'The occupational class of couples entering into interracial marriages', *Journal of Comparative Family Studies*, 7(2): 175–92.

Montagu, Ashley (1964) *The Concept of Race*. Toronto, ON: Collier.

Moore, Robert J. (2004) 'Managing troubles in answering survey questions: respondents' uses of projective reporting', *Social Psychology Quarterly*, 67: 50–69.

Moore, Robert J. (forthcoming) 'Upshot formulating in standardized interviews and ordinary conversation', *Social Psychology Quarterly*.

Morgan, D.L. (ed.) (1993) *Successful Focus Groups: Advancing the State of the Art*. Newbury Park, CA: Sage.

Morgan, D.L. (1996) 'Focus groups', *Annual Review of Sociology*, 22: 129–52.

Morgan, D.L. (1997) *Focus Groups as Qualitative Research* (2nd edn) Newbury Park, CA: Sage.

Morgan, D.L. and Krueger, R.A. (1998) *The Focus Group Kit* (6 vols). Newbury Park, CA: Sage.

Morgan, D.L. and Spanish, M.T. (1984) 'Focus groups: a new tool for qualitative research', *Qualitative Sociology*, 7(3): 253–70.

Myers, G. (1998) 'Displaying opinions: topics and disagreement in focus groups', *Language in Society*, 27: 85–111.

Myers, G. (2000) 'Entitlement and sincerity in broadcast news interviews about Princess Diana', *Media, Culture, and Society*, 22: 167–85.

Myers, G. and Macnaghten, P. (1999) 'Can focus groups be analysed as talk?', in R.S. Barbour and J. Kitzinger (eds), *Developing Focus Group Research: Politics, Theory and Practice*. London: Sage. pp. 173–85.

Nagel, Thomas (1986) *The View from Nowhere*. New York: Oxford University Press.

Novick, Peter (1988) *That Noble Dream: The 'Objectivity Question' and the American Historical Profession*. Cambridge: Cambridge University Press.

Oliver, Melvin and Shapiro, Thomas (1995) *Black Wealth White Wealth: A New Perspective of Racial Equality*. New York: Routledge.

Ong, Paul and Valenzuela, Abel Jr. (1996) 'The labor market: immigrant effects and racial disparities', in R. Waldinger and M. Bozorgmehr (eds), *Ethnic Los Angeles*. New York: Russell Sage Foundation. pp. 165–91.

Pagden, Anthony (1982) *The Fall of Natural Man: The American Indian and the Origins of Comparative Ethnology*. Cambridge: Cambridge University Press.

Penn, P. (1982) 'Circular questioning', *Family Process*, 21(3): 267–80.

Peräkylä, A. (1995) *AIDS Counselling: Institutional Interaction and Clinical Practice*. Cambridge: Cambridge University Press.

Peräkylä, A. (2004) 'Making links in psychoanalytic interpretations: a conversation analytic view', *Psychotherapy Research*, 14(3): 289–307.

Peräkylä, A. and Vehviläinen, S. (2003) 'Conversation analysis and the professional stocks of interactional knowledge', *Discourse and Society*, 14(6): 727–50.

Platt, Jennifer (1995) *A History of Sociological Research Methods in America, 1920–1960*. Cambridge: Cambridge University Press.

Plummer, Ken (1981) 'Social change, personal change and the life history method: researching the social construction of sexuality', in *An Introduction to Sociology*. Open University Media Booklet No. 1: 15–27.

Plummer, Ken (1990) *Documents of Life: An Introduction to the Problems and Literature of a Humanistic Method*. London: Unwin Hyman.

Polanyi, Michael (1958) *Personal Knowledge: Towards a Post-critical Philosophy*. Chicago: University of Chicago Press.

Pollner, Melvin (1992) 'Left of ethnomethodology: the rise and decline of radical reflexivity', *American Sociological Review*, 56(3): 370–80.

Pollner, Melvin and Emerson, Robert M. (1988) 'The dynamics of inclusion and distance in fieldwork relations', in R.M. Emerson (ed.), *Contemporary Field Research: A Collection of Readings*. Prospect Heights, IL: Waveland Press. pp. 235–52.

Pollner, Melvin and Emerson, Robert M. (2001) 'Ethnmethodology and ethnography', in Paul Atkinson et al. (eds), *Handbook of Ethnography*. London: Sage. pp. 118–35.

Pollner, Melvin and Stein, Jill (1996) 'Narrative mapping of social worlds: the voice of experience in Alcoholics Anonymous', *Symbolic Interaction*, 19(3): 2003–22.

Pomerantz, Anita (1980) 'Telling my side: "limited access" as a "fishing device"', *Sociological Inquiry*, 50: 186–98.

Pomerantz, Anita (1984) 'Agreeing and disagreeing with assessments: some features of preferred/dispreferred turn shapes', in J.M. Atkinson and J. Heritage (eds), *Structures of Social Action: Studies in Conversation Analysis*. Cambridge: Cambridge University Press. pp. 57–101.

Porter, Theodore (1996) *Trust in Numbers*. Princeton, NJ: Princeton University Press.

Potter, J. (1997) 'Discourse analysis as a way of analysing naturally occurring talk', in D. Silverman (ed.), *Qualitative Analysis: Issues of Theory and Method*. London: Sage. pp. 144–60.

Praz, Mario (1970) *The Romantic Agony*. London: Open University Press.

Press, A.L. (1991) 'Working-class women in a middle-class world: the impact of television on modes of reasoning about abortion', *Critical Studies in Mass Communication*, 8: 421–41.

Preves, S.E. (2003) *Intersex and Identity: The Contested Self*. New Brunswick, NJ: Rutgers University Press.

Prosser, J. (1998) *Second Skins: The Body Narratives of Transsexuality*. New York: Columbia University Press.

Puchta, C. and Potter, J. (1999) 'Asking elaborate questions: focus groups and the management of spontaneity', *Journal of Sociolinguistics*, 3: 314–35.

Putnam, Hilary (1987) *The Many Faces of Realism*. La Salle, IL: Open Court.

Quirk, Randolph, Svartvik, Jon, Greenbaum, Sydney and Leech, Geoffrey (1985) *A Grammar of Contemporary English*. London: Longman.

Rawls, Anne Warfield (1987) 'The interaction order *sui generis*: Goffman's contribution to social theory', *Sociological Theory*, 5(2): 136–49.

Raymond, Geoffrey (2000) 'The voice of authority: the local accomplishment of authoritative discourse in live news broadcasts', *Discourse Studies*, 2(3): 354–79.

Raymond, Geoffrey (2003) 'Grammar and social organization: yes/no type interrogatives and the structure of responding', *American Sociological Review*, 68: 939–67.

Robinson, Jeffrey D. (2003) 'An interactional structure of medical activities during acute visits and its implications for patients' participation', *Health Communication*, 15(1): 27–59.

Rogers, M.F. (1992) 'They all were passing: Agnes, Garfinkel and company', *Gender and Society*, 6(2): 169–91.

Rose, Nikolas (1989) *Governing the Soul: The Shaping of the Private Self*. London: Free Association Books.

Ross, Dorothy (1991) *The Origins of American Social Science*. Cambridge: Cambridge University Press.

Roter, Debra and Hall, Judith (1992) *Doctors Talking with Patients/Patients Talking with Doctors*. Westport, CT: Auburn House.

Roth, Andrew (1998) 'Who makes news: descriptions of television news interviewers' public personae', *Media, Culture, and Society*, 20(1): 79–107.

Roth, Andrew (2002) 'Social epistemology in broadcast news interviews', *Language in Society*, 31: 355–81.

Rudy, David R. (1986) *Becoming Alcoholic*. Carbondale, IL: Southern Illinois University Press.

Sacks, Harvey (1967) 'The search for help: no one to turn to', in E.S. Shneidman (ed.), *Essays in Self-Destruction*. New York: Jason Aronson. pp. 203–23.

Sacks, Harvey (1972) 'An initial investigation of the usability of conversational data for doing sociology', in D. Sudnow (ed.), *Studies in Social Interaction*. New York: The Free Press. pp. 31–74.

Sacks, Harvey (1987) 'On the preferences for agreement and contiguity in sequences in conversation', in G. Button and J.R.E. Lee (eds), *Talk and Social Organisation*. Clevedon: Multilingual Matters. pp. 54–69.

Sacks, Harvey (1992) *Lectures on Conversation* (Vols I and II). Edited by G. Jefferson and E.A. Schegloff. Oxford and Cambridge, MA: Basil Blackwell.

Sacks, Harvey, Schegloff, Emanuel A. and Jefferson, Gail (1974) 'A simplest systematics for the organization of turn-taking for conversation', *Language*, 50: 696–735.

Sasson, Theodore (1995) *Crime Talk: How Citizens Construct a Social Problem*. Hawthorne, NY: Aldine de Gruyter.

Schaeffer, Nora Cate (1991) 'Conversation with a purpose – or conversation? Interaction in the standardized survey', in P.P. Biemer et al. (eds), *Measurement Errors in Surveys*. New York: John Wiley & Sons. pp. 367–91.

Schaeffer, Nora C. and Dykema Jennifer (2004) 'A multiple-method approach to improving the clarity of closely related concepts: distinguishing legal and physical custody of children', in Stanley Presser, Jennifer M. Rothgeb, Mick P. Couper, Judith T. Lessler, Elizabeth Martin, Jean Martin and Eleanor Singer (eds), *Methods Testing and Evaluating Survey Questionaires*. New York: Springer-Verlay. pp. 475–502.

Schaeffer, Nora Cate and Dykema, Jennifer L. (forthcoming) 'Improving the clarity of closely related concepts: distinguishing legal and physical custody of children', in S. Presser et al. (eds), *Questionnaire Development*. New York: Wiley Interscience.

Schaeffer, Nora Cate and Maynard, Douglas W. (1996) 'From paradigm to prototype and back again: interactive aspects of 'cognitive processing' in standardized survey interviews', in N. Schwarz and S. Sudman (eds), *Answering Questions: Methodology for Determining Cognitive and Communicating Processes in Survey Research*. San Francisco: Jossey-Bass. pp. 75–88.

Schaeffer, Nora Cate and Maynard, Douglas W. (2002) 'Occasions for intervention: interactional resources for comprehension in standardized survey interviews', in D. Maynard et al. (eds), *Standardization and Tacit Knowledge: Interaction and Practice in the Survey Interview*. New York: Wiley Interscience. pp. 261–80.

Scheff, T. (1990) *Microsociology: Discourse, Emotion and Social Structure*. Chicago and London: University of Chicago Press.

Schegloff, Emanuel A. (1980) 'Preliminaries to preliminaries: "Can I ask you a question?"', *Sociological Inquiry*, 50: 104–52.

Schegloff, Emanuel A. (1982) 'Discourse as an interactional achievement: some uses of 'uh huh' and other things that come between sentences', in D. Tannen (ed.), *Georgetown University Round Table on Languages and Linguistics 1981*. Washington, DC: Georgetown University Press. pp. 71–93.

Schegloff, Emanuel A. (1986) 'The routine as achievement', *Human Studies*, 9: 111–51.

Schegloff, Emanuel A. (1987) 'Between micro and macro: contexts and other connections', in Jeffrey Alexander et al. (eds), *The Micro-Macro Link*. Berkeley: University of California Press. pp. 207–38.

Schegloff, Emanuel A. (1990) 'Discussion of Suchman and Jordan: interactional troubles in face-to-face survey interviews', *Journal of the American Statistical Association*, 85: 248–50.

Schegloff, Emanuel A. (1991) 'Reflections on talk and social structure', in D. Boden and D.H. Zimmerman (eds), *Talk and Social Structures: Studies in Ethnomethodology and Conversation Analysis*. Cambridge: Polity Press. pp. 44–70.

Schegloff, Emanuel A. (1992) 'On talk and its institutional occasions', in P. Drew and J. Heritage (eds), *Talk at Work: Interaction in Institutional Settings*. Cambridge: Cambridge University Press. pp. 101–34.

Schegloff, Emanuel A. (1993) 'Reflections on quantification in the study of conversation', *Research on Language and Social Interaction*, 26: 99–128.

Schegloff, Emanuel A. (1995) 'Sequence organization', Unpublished manuscript, Department of Sociology, University of California, Los Angeles.

Schegloff, Emanuel A. (1997) 'Practices and actions: boundary cases of other-initiated repair', *Discourse Processes*, 23(3): 499–545.

Schegloff, Emanuel A. (2002) 'Survey interviews as talk-in-interaction', in D. Maynard et al. (eds), *Standardization and Tacit Knowledge: Interaction and Practice in the Survey Interview*. New York: Wiley Interscience. pp. 151–57.

Schegloff, Emanuel A. (forthcoming) *A Primer of Conversation Analysis: Sequence Organization*. Cambridge: Cambridge University Press.

Schegloff, Emanuel A. and Sacks, H. (1973) 'Opening up closing', *Semiotica*, 8(4): 289–327.

Schenkein, James (1978) *Studies in the Organization of Conversational Interaction*. New York: Academic Press.

Schudson, Michael (1982) 'The politics of narrative form: the emergence of news conventions in print and television', *Daedalus*, 111: 97–113.

Schuman, Howard (1982) 'Artifacts are in the mind of the beholder', *The American Sociologist*, 17: 21–28.

Schuman, Howard and Presser, Stanley (1981) *Questions and Answers in Attitude Surveys*. New York: Academic Press.

Seals, B.F., Sowell, R.L., Demi, A.S., Moneyham, L., Cohen, L. and Guillory, J. (1995) 'Falling through the cracks: social service concerns of women infected with HIV', *Qualitative Health Research*, 5(4): 496–515.

Sedgwick, E.K. (1993) 'Epistemology of the closet', in H. Abelove et al. (eds), *The Lesbian and Gay Studies Reader*. London: Routledge. pp. 45–61.

Seidman, Darryl and Couzens, Michael (1973) 'Getting the crime rate down: political pressure and crime reporting', *Law and Society Review*, 8(3): 457–93.

Seidman, S., Meeks, C. and Traschen, F. (2002) 'Beyond the closet? The changing social meaning of homosexuality in the United States', in C.L. Williams and A. Stein (eds), *Sexuality and Gender*. Oxford: Blackwell. pp. 427–47.

Selvini, M. and Selvini Palazzoli, M. (1991) 'Team consultation: an indispensable tool for the progress of knowledge. Ways of fostering and promoting its creative potential', *Journal of Family Therapy*, 13: 31–52.

Shapin, Steven (1994) *A Social History of Truth: Civility and Science in Seventeenth-century England*. Chicago: University of Chicago Press.

Sharrock, W. (1974) 'On owning knowledge', in Turner, R. (ed.), *Ethnomethodology*. Harmondsworth: Penguin. pp. 45–53.

Short, James (1996) 'Preface', in C.R. Huff (ed.), *Gangs in America* (2nd edn). Thousand Oaks, CA: Sage. pp. 21–38.

Silverman, David (1993) *Interpreting Qualitative Data*. London: Sage. (2nd edn, 2001.)

Silverman, David (ed.) (1997) *Qualitative Research: Theory, Method and Practice*. London: Sage.

Silverman, David (1998) *Harvey Sacks: Social Science and Conversation Analysis*. Cambridge: Polity Press.

Silverman, David (2001) *Interpreting Qualitative Data: Methods for Analysing Talk, Text and Interaction* (2nd edn). London: Sage.

Silverman, D. and Gubrium, J. (1994) 'Competing strategies for analyzing the contexts of social interaction', *Sociological Inquiry*, 64(2): 179–98.

Smith, Dorothy (1974) 'The social construction of documentary reality', *Sociological Inquiry*, 44(4): 257–68.

Smith, Dorothy E. (1989) *The Everyday World as Problematic: A Feminist Sociology.* Boston: Northeastern University Press.

Smith, J.A. and Osborn, M. (2003) 'Interpretative phenomenological analysis', in J.A. Smith (ed.), *Qualitative Psychology: A Practical Guide to Research Methods.* London and Thousand Oaks, CA : Sage. pp. 51–80.

Sorjonen, M.-L. (2001) *Responding in Conversation: A Study of Response Particles in Finnish.* Amsterdam: John Benjamins.

Spaights, E. and Dixon, H.E. (1984) 'Socio-psychological dynamics in pathological black–white romantic alliances', *Journal of Instructional Psychology*, 11(3): 132–8.

Speer, S.A. (2001) 'Reconsidering the concept of hegemonic masculinity: discursive psychology, conversation analysis and participants' orientations', *Feminism & Psychology*, 11: 107–35.

Speer, S.A. and Potter, J. (2002) 'Judith Butler, discursive psychology, and the politics of conversation', in P. McIlvenny (ed.), *Talking Gender and Sexuality.* Amsterdam: John Benjamins. pp. 151–80.

Spickard, Paul R. (1989) *Mixed Blood: Intermarriage and Ethnic Identity in Twentieth Century America.* Madison: University of Wisconsin Press.

Stanley, Liz and Wise, Sue (1991) 'Feminist research, feminist consciousness and experiences of sexism', in M.M. Fonow and J.A. Cook (eds), *Beyond Methodology: Feminist Scholarship as Lived Research.* Bloomington: University of Indiana Press. pp. 265–83.

Stephens, Richard C. (1991) *The Street Addict Role.* Albany, NY: SUNY Press.

Stewart, D.W. and Shamdasani, P.N. (1990) *Focus Groups: Theory and Practice.* London: Sage.

Stocking, George W. (1987) *Victorian Anthropology.* New York: The Free Press.

Stocking, George W. (1990) 'Paradigmatic traditions in the history of anthropology', in R.C. Olby et al. (eds), *Companion to the History of Modern Science.* London: Routledge. pp. 712–27.

Stokoe, E.H. (1998) 'Talking about gender: the conversational construction of gender categories in academic discourse', *Discourse and Society*, 9(2): 217–40.

Stokoe, E.H. (1999) 'Mothers, single women and sluts: gender, morality and membership categorization in neighborhood disputes', *Feminism & Psychology*, 13(3): 317–44.

Strauss, A., Fagerhaug, S., Suczeck, B. and Wiener, C. (1985) *Social Organization of Medical Work.* Chicago: University of Chicago Press.

Suchman, Lucy (1987) *Plans and Situated Actions.* Cambridge: Cambridge University Press.

Suchman, Lucy and Jordan, Brigitte (1990) 'Interactional troubles in face-to-face survey interviews', *Journal of the American Statistical Association*, 85: 232–41.

Tainio, L. (2003) '"When shall we go for a ride?" A case of the sexual harassment of a young girl', *Discourse and Society*, 14(2): 173–90.

Takaki, Ronald (1979) *Iron Cages: Race and Culture in 19th Century America.* New York: Knopf.

ten Have, Paul (1999) *Doing Conversation Analysis: A Practical Guide.* London: Sage.

Thomas, W.I. and Znaniecki, F. (1958) *The Polish Peasant in Europe and America.* New York: Dover.

Thornborrow, Joanna (2001a) 'Authenticating talk: building public identities in audience participation broadcasting', *Discourse and Society*, 3(4): 459–79.

Thornborrow, Joanna (2001b) 'Questions, control, and the organization of talk in calls to a radio phone-in', *Discourse Studies*, 3(1): 119–43.

Timmermans, S. (1998) 'Resuscitation technology in the emergency department: towards a dignified death', *Sociology of Health and Illness*, 20: 144–67.

Tolson, Andrew (2001) *Television Talk Shows: Discourse, Performance, Spectacle.* Mahwah, NJ: Lawrence Erlbaum Associates.

Tuchman, Gaye (1972) 'Objectivity as strategic ritual: an examination of newsmen's notions of objectivity', *American Journal of Sociology*, 77: 660–79.

Tuchman, Gaye (1973) 'The technology of objectivity: doing "objective" TV news film', *Urban Life and Culture*, 2(1): 3–26.

Tucker, M. Belinda and Mitchell-Kernan, Claudia (1990) 'New trends in Black American interracial marriage: the social structural context', *Journal of Marriage and the Family,* 52(Feb.): 209–18.

Tudor, S. (1995) 'Tips on controlling focus group crosstalk', in J.M. Bilson (ed.), *Conducting Focus Groups: A Manual for Sociologists on the Use of Focus Groups as a Tool in Social and Market Research.* Washington, DC: American Sociological Association. pp. 105–06.

Turner, Stephen (1994) *The Social Theory of Practices.* Chicago: University of Chicago Press.

Turner, Stephen and Turner, Jonathan (1990) *The Impossible Science: An Institutional Analysis of American Sociology.* Newbury Park, CA: Sage.

van Dijk, Teun A. (1988) *News Analysis: Case Studies of International and National News in the Press.* Mahwah, NJ: Lawrence Erlbaum Associates.

van Dijk, Teun A. (1993) *Elite Discourse and Racism.* Newbury Park, CA: Sage.

van Maanen, John (1988) *Tales of the Field: On Writing Ethnography.* Chicago: University of Chicago Press.

Vehviläinen, S. (1999) *Structures of Counselling Interaction: A Conversation Analytic Study on Counselling in Career Guidance Training.* Department of Education, University of Helsinki, Helsinki.

Vehviläinen, S. (2001) 'Evaluative advice in educational counseling: the use of disagreement in the "stepwise entry" to advice', *Research on Language and Social Interaction,* 34(3): 371–98.

Vehviläinen, S. (2003) 'Preparing and delivering interpretations in psychoanalytic interaction', *Text,* 23(4): 573–606.

Viterna, Jocelyn and Maynard, Douglas W. (2002) 'How uniform is standardization? Variation within and across survey centers regarding protocols for interviewing', in D. Maynard et al. (eds), *Standardization and Tacit Knowledge: Interaction and Practice in the Survey Interview.* New York: Wiley Interscience. pp. 365–97.

Washington, Joseph (1970) *Marriage in Black and White.* Boston: Rowmen and Littlefield.

Waterton, C. and Wynne, B. (1999) 'Can focus groups access community views?', in R.S. Barbour and J. Kitzinger (eds), *Developing Focus Group Research: Politics, Theory and Practice.* London: Sage. pp. 127–43.

Weaver, Paul (1975) 'Newspaper news and television news', in D. Cater and R. Adler (eds), *Television as a Social Force.* New York: Praeger.

Weinberg, Darin (2000) '"Out there": the ecology of addiction in drug abuse treatment discourse', *Social Problems,* 47(4): 606–21.

Weinberg, Darin (ed.) (2002) *Qualitative Research Methods.* Malden, MA: Blackwell.

Wells, W.D. (1974) 'Group interviewing', in R. Ferber (ed.), *Handbook of Marketing Research.* New York: McGraw-Hill. pp. 133–146.

Wetherell, M. and Edley, N. (1999) 'Negotiating hegemonic masculinity', *Feminism & Psychology,* 9(3): 335–56.

Whalen, Marilyn and Zimmerman, Don H. (1987) 'Sequential and institutional contexts in calls for help', *Social Psychology Quarterly,* 50: 172–85.

Whalen, Marilyn and Zimmerman, Don H. (1990) 'Describing trouble: practical epistemology in citizen calls to the police', *Language in Society,* 19: 465–92.

Wheeler, Stanton (1969) *On Record: Files and Dossiers in American Life.* New York: Russell Sage Foundation.

Widdicombe, S. and Wooffitt, R. (1995) *The Language of Youth Subcultures: Social Identity in Action.* Hemel Hempstead: Harvester Wheatsheaf.

Wilkinson, S. (1998a) 'Focus groups in health research: exploring the meanings of health and illness', *Journal of Health Psychology,* 3(3): 329–48.

Wilkinson, S. (1998b) 'Focus group methodology: a review', *International Journal of Social Research Methodology,* 1(3): 181–203.

Wilkinson, S. (1999) 'Focus groups: a feminist method', *Psychology of Women Quarterly,* 23: 221–44.

Wilkinson, S. (2000) 'Women with breast cancer talking causes: comparing content, biographical and discursive analyses', *Feminism & Psychology,* 10(4): 431–60.

Wilkinson, S. (2003a) 'Focus groups', in J.A. Smith (ed.), *Qualitative Psychology: A Practical Guide to Research Methods*. London: Sage. pp. 184–204.

Wilkinson, S. (2003b) 'Focus groups', in G.M. Breakwell (ed.), *Doing Social Psychology*. Oxford: Blackwell. pp. 344–76.

Wilkinson, S. (2005) 'Breast cancer: lived experience and feminist action', in O. Hankivsky et al. (eds), *Women's Health in Canada: Critical Theory, Policy and Practice*. Toronto, ON: University of Toronto Press.

Wilkinson, S. and Kitzinger, C. (2003) 'Constructing identities: a feminist conversation analytic approach to positioning in action', in R. Harré and F. Moghaddam (eds), *The Self and Others: Positioning Individuals and Groups in Personal, Political, and Cultural Contexts*. Westport, CT: Praeger. pp. 157–80.

Wilkinson, S. and Kitzinger, C. (2005) 'Same-sex marriage, equality and psychology', *The Psychologist*, 18(5): 290–93.

Wittgenstein, L. (1953) *Philosophical Investigations*. Edited by G. Anscombe. Oxford: Basil Blackwell.

Wooffitt, R. (1992) *Telling Tales of the Unexpected: The Organization of Factual Discourse*. Hemel Hempstead: Harvester Wheatsheaf.

Woolgar, Steve (ed.) (1988) *Knowledge and Reflexivity: New Frontiers in the Sociology of Knowledge*. London: Sage.

Wootton, Anthony J. (1997) *Interaction and the Development of Mind*. Cambridge: Cambridge University Press.

Wyatt, G., Kurtz, M.E. and Liken, M. (1993) 'Breast cancer survivors: an exploration of quality of life issues', *Cancer Nursing*, 16(6): 440–8.

Zatz, M. (1987) 'Chicago youth gangs and crime: the creation of a moral panic', *Contemporary Crises*, 11: 129–58.

Zelizer, Barbie (1990) 'Where is the author in American TV news?', *Semiotica*, 80: 37–48.

Zimmerman, Don H. (1970) 'The practicalities of rule use', in J. Douglas (ed.), *Understanding Everyday Life*. Chicago: Aldine. pp. 221–38.

Zimmerman, Don H. (1992) 'The interactional organization of calls for emergency assistance', in P. Drew and J. Heritage (eds), *Talk at Work: Interaction in Institutional Settings*. Cambridge: Cambridge University Press. pp. 418–69.

Zimmerman, Don H. and Pollner Melvin 'The everyday world as a phenomenon', in Jack Douglas (ed.), *Understanding Everyday Life*. London: Routledge and Kegan Paul. pp. 80–103.

.... Index

accuracy, documents 64
acknowledgements
  circular questioning 86
  interview responses 15–16, 18–19
action analysis, semi-structured interview
    data 43–7
  see also sequences of actions
adversarial questions 142, 144,
    146–8, 150
advertising slogans 71
agenda statements 86
aggressiveness, interview questions 146–8
Agnes (intersex research subject) 157–60
agreement tokens 17, 202–3
AIDS counselling 82–9
ambiguous responses 11, 24–5
analytic alternation 10
  elaborated answers 20–6
  telephone interviewing 13–14
analytical approach, ethnographic
    research 98
'and' question prefix 202, 204
anomalizing 176, 177–83
answers and responses
  acknowledgements 15–16, 18–19
  ambiguous 11, 24–5
  'don't know' coding category 37, 58–9
  elaborated 20–6, 37–8
  'I dunno' 44–7
  nonconforming 16, 22–4, 36–7,
    120–5, 131–3
  'oh' 18, 123
  oppositional 142
  overlapping 16
  paraphrasing 25, 142
  premature 16, 35–6
  'right' 123
  trivialization by interviewer 42
  type-conforming 119–25
  uncertainty 17

answers and responses cont.
  'well' prefix 17
  see also question and answer sequences
approaches, greetings 92, 93
attitudes
  conceptualisation 103–4
  construction in focus groups 55
audiences, media discourse 144–5
audio recording 28

Bath school 3
belief systems 100–1, 105
'best-case scenario' question orientation
    118, 130
bias
  interview data 155–6, 158–9
  interviewers 11
blame attributions 65–6
Boas, Franz 98–9
body posture
  circular questioning 87
  greetings 93, 94
breast cancer focus group 57–61
bureaucratic opening enquiry 78
Bush, George 139–40, 143, 150

CA see conversation analysis
call-in shows 138, 142
Campanis, Al 151–3
career guidance counselling 88
categorization devices 195, 197–8
CATI see Computer-Aided Telephone
    Interviewing
'cause' opinions 58–61
challenges, focus group participants 54
childhood factors, interracial
    relationships 180–3
circular questioning 83, 84–8
Clayman, Steven E. 146
close salutations 93

co-clients 87
co-construction of talk 150–3
co-topics, emergency service calls 194
coding
    elaborated answers 21–2
    focus group data 52–3
    nonconforming answers 17, 36–7
collegial opening enquiry 78
common-sense knowledge 10
communities, belief systems 100–1
complaint packages 193–4, 201–2
compliments 149–50
Computer-Aided Telephone Interviewing
    (CATI) 13–14
consensus, focus groups 56
constant error, interviewers 11
content analysis 52–3, 58
contextual factors 5–6, 55, 90
controlled feedback 19
controversial remarks 150–3
conversation analysis (CA) 33–4
    focus group data 55–7
    interview data 33–4, 48–9
    media discourse 145–6
    micro-analysis 81
    opinion giving 58–9
    private conversations 163
    relation to practitioners' theories 82
conversational interactions
    access to 163
    characteristics 34–5, 36
    institutional interactions
        contrast 117
    three-part lists 70
Courie, Kate 151
courtroom interactions 115–16, 126–9
CPS see Current Population Survey
cross-examinations 126–9
cultural anthropology 99
cultural beliefs, sex 158
cultures
    as research objects 103
    worldviews 100
Current Population Survey (CPS) 9, 20

data collection
    racial phenomena 171–2
    sex and gender issues 155–6
detail levels, comparison of analysis
    methods 94–7
dialogue, social scientific community
    102, 104
Diana, Princess of Wales 44–5
disagreement tokens 202–3

dispute domains, ethnographic
    research 102–3
distance salutations 92
distancing, opinion giving 59–61
doctor–doctor interactions 77–8
doctor–patient interactions
    conversational structure 118
    sex and gender issues 165–6
    turn-taking 33
    yes/no questions 116, 124–5, 129–30
documents 63–80
    interactive role 74–8
    interpretative analysis 66–7
    newspaper reports 64–6
    perceptions of reality 66–7
    professional texts 82
    suicide notes 67–74
    telephone interactions 75–6
    see also recordwork
Dole, Bob 149, 150–1
'don't know' response category 37, 58–9
Douglas, Jack 66–7
drug users 105–9

Edinburgh school 2
educational testing interviews 19
Eisenhower, Dwight 146–8
elaborated answers
    interviews 37–8
    surveys 20–6
emergency service calls 190–210
    complaint packages 193–4, 201–2
    conversational features 195–8
    maximization of police-worthiness 204–6
    operator formulations 194–201
    patrol responses 206–9
    sequences of actions 118
    yes/no questions 115, 202
emotional accounts
    paradoxes 73–4
    spatial metaphors 72–3
error, interviewers 11
ethnographic research 97–112
    greetings 90–1
    language and social action 104–9
    objectivity 97–104
experience, ownership 86

Family Systems Theory 83
feedback 18–19
first speaker position 58–9
focus groups 50–62
    attitude construction 55
    benefits 32

focus groups *cont.*
  consensus reaching 56
  conversation analysis 55–7
  data coding 52–3
  interactional basis 52–5
  procedures 50–1
  sex and gender issues 161–3
folk knowledge citations 59
foreign affairs, interview questions 148
'forms of life' (media discourse) 135–7

gang policing 190–210
Gans, Herbert 172–3
Garfinkel, Harold 157–60
gaze orientation
  circular questioning 87
  greetings 92, 93, 94
gender *see* sex and gender
gender differences, greetings 94, 95
Goffman, Erving 91
grammatical construction, yes/no questions
    119, 121, 124
greetings 89–95
  comparison of analysis methods 93–5
  ethnographic observation 90–1
  video micro-analysis 91–3

head positioning, greetings 92, 93, 95
health visitors 120–1, 164
Heritage, John 146
heterosexism 161–3, 164–6
'how' questions 88
Hypergamy theory 174

'I dunno' response 44–7
identities 116–17, 128–9
implicit communications 69
institutional interactions
  conversational interactions contrast 117
  recordkeeping 192
  sequences of actions 117–18
  turn-taking 193
  yes/no questions 116–18, 125–33
institutional racism 172
interpretative analysis, documents 66–7
Interpretative Phenomenological Analysis
    (IPA) 39–43
interracial relationships 173–89
  anomalizing 176, 177–83
  reasons for entering 173–4, 177–8
  strategic ambiguity 176, 183–7
interruption
  focus group discussions 51
  interview questions 16

interviewers
  analytic alternation 10
  co-implication 153
  selective topic development 41–3
  sources of variability 10–11
  trivialization of responses 42
  see also journalists
interviews 28–49
  action analysis 43–7
  applications 28–32
  bias issues 11, 155–6, 158–9
  conversation analysis 33–4, 48–9
  interactional basis 38–43
  media discourse 138–53
  normative expectation breaches 34–8
  sex and gender issues 156, 160–1
  structured 29, 34–8
  thematic analysis 43–7
  types 29–32
  unstructured 31–2
  see also news interviews;
      survey interviews
IPA *see* Interpretative
    Phenomenological Analysis

Jacobs, Jerry 67–8
journalists 115, 139, 143–4, 146–8
  see also interviewers

Katz, Jack 67, 68
Kendon, A. 91–5
Kinsey, Alfred 155
knowledge, tacit and common-sense
    10, 13–14
Koppel, Ted 151–2

language
  importance to social sciences 1–2, 4–5
  interactional basis 100–1
  as social action 33–4, 104–9
  worldview creation 100
laughter
  focus group interactions 59
  survey interviews 20–1
lawyers 115–16
lesbians 166–9
Letters and Science Survey Center (LSSC) 20
lexical choice 118
line supervision 83
lists, use in interactions 70–2
LSSC *see* Letters and Science Survey Center

macro-sociology 2
masculinity 164–5

'master identity' 172–3
media discourse 135–54
    audiences 144–5
    compliments 149–50
    controversial remarks 150–3
    conversation analysis 145–6
    ground rules 137–40
    interviews 138–53
    presidential news conferences 146–8
    question design 141–8
    specific media messages 148–53
    tasks, norms and constraints 143–5
    see also news interviews
metaphors, emotional accounts 72–3
micro-analytic techniques 3, 81, 89
moderators, focus groups 50–1
mountaineering 73
murder explanations 67

natural sciences 3
negative polarity items 143, 152
negative questions 141–2, 143
neutral questions 143–4
news conferences 138–9, 146–8
news interviews
    audience acknowledgement 145
    selective topic development 41–2
    turn taking 33–4, 138–40
    see also media discourse
newspaper sources 64–6
nonconforming responses
    coding 36–7
    elaborations 22–4
    surveys 131–3
    uncertainty 16
    yes/no questions 120–5
normative standards
    breaches in interviews 34–8
    journalists 117, 143–4
    suicide note content 68–70

objectivity, ethnographic research 97–104
observation, sex and gender research 156
official statistics 192–3, 206
'oh' response 18, 123
opening enquiries 78
operator formulations, emergency service
        calls 194–204
opinion statements
    first speaker position 58–9
    quoting and paraphrasing 142
oppositional responses 142
optimization principle 130
organizational career constructions 190–1

orientational metaphors 72–3
Osborn, M. 39–43
overlapping responses 16
ownership
    emergency service calls 205
    experience 86

paradoxes, emotional accounts 73–4
paraphrasing
    ambiguous responses 25
    oppositional responses 142
parent–teacher meetings 76–7
participants
    counselling interactions 84
    focus groups 51
peer reviews 77–8
physical appearance, interracial
        relationships 178–80
police interrogations 115
policing 190–210
political speeches 71
preferences
    doctor–patient interactions 130
    surveys 131
    yes/no questions 141–2, 143, 152
premature responses 16, 35–6
presidential news conferences 146–8
presuppositions
    doctor–patient interactions 130
    surveys 131
    yes/no questions 141–2, 143, 152
primordial tasks 84, 88
probes
    interviewer bias 11
    nonconforming answers 17
    paraphrasing 25
'problem' creation 195
professional action 82–9
    circular questioning 84–7
    practitioners' theories 82, 87–9
professional norms, journalists 117, 143–4

qualitative research 28
quantitative research 28–9, 146–8
question and answer sequences
    circular questioning 84–6
    news interviews 139–40
    survey interviews 16–19
questions
    adversarial 142, 144, 146–8, 150
    aggressiveness 146–8
    'and' prefix 202, 204
    'best-case scenario' orientation 118, 130
    circular 83, 84–8

questions *cont.*
  design 143–4
  'how' questions 88
  interruption 16
  media discourse 141–8
  negative 141–2, 143
  neutral 143–4
  reformulating 59
  'what' questions 88
  wording 30–1
  see also yes/no questions

racial phenomena 171–89
  anomalizing 176, 177–83
  data collection 171–2
  interracial relationships 173–87
  physical appearance 178–80
  socialization 180–3
  strategic ambiguity 176, 183–7
racism 99, 172, 183–7
rapport
  doctor–patient interactions 129–30
  survey interviews 20–1
Rather, Dan 139–40, 143, 150
rationalization 74
Reagan, Ronald 146–8
recipient design principle 130
recordings
  audio 28
  video 81–96, 191
recordwork, gang policing 190–210
reflexive approach, ethnographic research
    98, 102–4
reflexivity 4
reformulating questions 59
reification 97–8
relativism 103
responses *see* answers and responses
'right' response 123
risk assessment discussions, focus
    groups 56–7
ritual behaviour, greetings 89
role-based identities 116–17, 128–9
routinization, media discourse 138

salutations 92, 93
  see also greetings
Sapir, Edward 99–100
scientific method 2
second-hand data 155–6
selectivity, semi-structured interview
    questions 41–3
self-identification 45–7
self-implicative accounts 107–9

semi-structured interviews 29–31, 39–48
sense-making 74
sequences of actions
  greetings 90–3
  institutional interactions 117–18
  yes/no questions 118–25
  see also question and answer sequences
seriousness, emergency service
    calls 201–2
sex and gender issues 155–70
  'Agnes' case study 157–60
  data collection 155–6
  heterosexism 161–3, 164–6
  lesbians 166–9
  non-research settings 163–9
  research settings 157–63
shared experiences 53–4, 56
silences, focus group interactions 61
Smith, J.A. 39–43
social constructions
  gangs 192
  gender 157–8
social processes, reification 97–8
social sciences
  heterogeneity of research community 102
  role of language 1–6
social structures 69–70
socialization, interracial relationships 180–3
spatial metaphors 72–3
standardization
  concerns 11–13
  interviews 34
  purpose 10–11
  surveys 10–13
strategic ambiguity 176, 183–7
street life
  drug culture 105–9
  gangs 190–210
structured interviews 29, 34–8
studio audiences 145
suicide 66–7
suicide notes 67–74
survey interviews 9–27
  analytic alternation 13–14
  elaborated answers 20–6
  interviewing sequence 14–19
  nonconforming responses 131–3
  preferences and presuppositions 131
  rapport 20–1
  standardization 10–13
  trajectory changes 23–4
  validity 12
  yes/no questions 130–3
systemic nature of problems 83

tacit knowledge 5, 10, 13–14
talk shows 138
telephone interactions
  role of documents 75–6
  survey interviews 9–27
texts *see* documents
thematic analysis
  focus group data 52–3
  semi-structured interview
    data 39–43
therapeutic communities 104–9
third-turn acknowledgements
    15–16, 18–19
three-part interviewing sequence 14–15
three-part lists 70–2
trajectory changes, survey interviews 23–4
trivialization by interviewer 42
the Troubles 64–6
'turn distance' 204
turn-taking
  doctor–patient interactions 33
  emergency service calls 193
  institutional interactions 193
  media discourse 138–40
two-part interviewing sequence 15
type-conforming responses 119–25

uncertain responses 17
unstructured interviews 31–2

validity, standardized survey
    interviews 12
values and attitudes, construction in
    focus groups 55

verification
  nonconforming elaborated
    answers 23
  premature responses 16
video recordings 81–96
  greetings 89–95
  police cars 191
  professional action 82–9

'well' response prefix 17
'what' questions 88
White House journalists 146–8
Whorf, Benjamin Lee 100
witness testimony 126–9
word choice 118
wording of questions 30–1
work contexts *see* institutional interactions
worldviews 100

'yes but' phenomenon 37–8
yes/no questions 115–34
  doctor–patient interactions 116,
    124–5, 129–30
  emergency service calls 115, 202
  grammatical construction 119,
    121, 124
  institutional interactions 116–18, 125–33
  media discourse 141–2, 143
  nonconforming responses 120–5
  preferences and presuppositions
    141–2, 143, 152
  sequences of actions 118–25
  survey interviews 130–3
  type-conforming responses 124–5